COMMEMORATING TRAUMA

COMMEMORATING TRAUMA

The Paris Commune and Its Cultural Aftermath

Peter Starr

Fordham University Press

New York 2006

Library of Congress Cataloging-in-Publication Data

Starr, Peter, 1956–
    Commemorating trauma : the Paris commune and its cultural
aftermath / Peter Starr—1st ed.
      p. cm.
    Includes bibliographical references and index.
    ISBN-13: 978-0-8232-2603-0 (hardcover : alk. paper)
    ISBN-10: 0-8232-2603-4 (hardcover : alk. paper)
    1. Starr, Peter, 1956– 2. Paris (France)—History—Commune, 1871.
3. France—Politics and government—1870–1940. 4. France—
History—Third Republic, 1870–1940. I. Title.
    DC316.S73   2006
    944.081′2—dc 22

                                2006000687o

Printed in the United States of America
07 06   5 4 3 2 1
First edition

For Liza and Julia

Contents

Acknowledgments

Although written largely over the past several years, this book has its roots in my graduate work at Johns Hopkins's Humanities Center. Of all the extraordinary scholars with whom I had the pleasure of studying at Hopkins, several had an important role in helping me to conceptualize the unpublished dissertation from which this study evolved. Special thanks to Michael Fried, Neil Hertz, Ruth Leys, and Richard Macksey as well as to a remarkable cadre of fellow Hopkins students, whose work over the past two decades has done so much to shape how we look at the French nineteenth century. They include David Bell, Suzanne Guerlac, Lawrence Schehr, and Beryl Schlossman.

At various stages in the genesis of this project, I have been blessed with the support and good counsel of Frank Paul Bowman, Ross Chambers, Lawrence Kritzman, Dominick LaCapra, Juliet Flower MacCannell, and Albert Sonnenfeld. Peggy Kamuf, Karen Pinkus, Hilary Schor, Nancy Vickers, and Margaret Waller have been the best of colleagues—and the best of friends. The support of USC's College of Letters, Arts and Sciences has been unwavering throughout. Special thanks to Deans Joseph Aoun, Marshall Cohen, and Beth Meyerowitz.

Once again, I am indebted to Helen Tartar for her professionalism, her good humor, and her truly uncanny knack for book titles. Beth Wilson did an extraordinary job in copyediting this manuscript. Many thanks to Jean Skipp for her help in preparing the index.

To my wife, Alice, and my daughters, Liza and Julia, I owe a debt that no acknowledgment or dedication can hope to express. So too my debt to "the mothers": Martha Starr and Elizabeth Hill. Much love to you all.

A portion of chapter 1 appeared in *Contemporary French Civilization* 29, 1 (2004). Earlier versions of chapters 4 and 5 appeared in *MLN* 99, 5 (1984) and *Nineteenth-Century French Studies* 18, 1/2 (1989/90) respectively. Thanks to the editors and publishers of those journals for permission to use this material here.

Note on Translations

Throughout this volume, quotations from published translations of French texts give the page reference for the French edition, followed in italics by the corresponding page(s) of the English translation (for example: Sartre, *Idiot*, 3:447/*5:413*). In many cases I have modified the published translation to better reflect textual features of the original French. Responsibility for such modifications, as well as for the translation into English of all hitherto untranslated French texts, is my own.

COMMEMORATING TRAUMA

Introduction
The Commune and the Right to Confusion

> Perhaps it would be worth dwelling on this realm of confusion—
> which is simply that in which the whole human *opera buffa* is played
> out—to understand the pathways by which analysis proceeds, not
> only to restore order here but also to establish the conditions of
> possibility of its restoration.
>
> —Jacques Lacan, "L'Instance de la lettre dans l'inconscient"
>   (The Instance of the Letter in the Unconscious)

> This century is meant to confuse everything. We are marching
> toward chaos.
>
> —Stendhal, *Le Rouge et le noir* (The Red and the Black)

In the opening chapter of his *Mimesis*, Erich Auerbach draws a famously sharp distinction between legend and history. In legend, he writes, thinking of Homer: "All cross-currents, all friction, all that is casual, secondary to the main events and themes, everything unresolved, truncated, and uncertain, which confuses the clear progress of the action and the simple orientation of the actors, has disappeared" (19). Legend thus "detaches [its material] from its contemporary historical context, so that the latter will not confuse it" (19). To legend's essential simplification, Auerbach opposes the complex richness of historical narrative, approximated by the stories of the Old Testament but fully realized only in the course of the nineteenth century. Whether we witness the historical event directly or learn of it from others, Auerbach writes, that event

> runs much more variously, contradictorily, and confusedly; not until it has
> produced results in a definite domain are we able, with their help, to classify
> it to a certain extent; and how often the order to which we think we have
> attained becomes doubtful again, how often we ask ourselves if the data

before us have not led us to a far too simple classification of the original events! (19)

If we reread the two epigraphs above in light of Auerbach's distinction, we see that it is not enough simply to assume, with Lacan, that the "whole human *opera buffa*" plays itself out under the sign of confusion, though in the way that Lacan means this—as a necessary function of the self's radical heteronomy—it certainly does.[1] Nor is it sufficient to follow the Marquis de la Môle in speaking of the French nineteenth century as "meant to confuse everything" (though the breakdown of class distinction to which the marquis's conception of "chaos" alludes is likewise indisputable). Rather, the confusions specific to, say, the revolutionary dynamics of late nineteenth-century France themselves need to be read through that complex, and properly endless, negotiation with confusion that is historical analysis in Auerbach's terms.

The principal aim of this book is to examine the function of confusion in a body of French fiction defined by that historical moment which includes the Franco–Prussian War, the Paris Commune, and the first decade of the Third Republic. How, the book asks, does the literary and/or philosophical representation of confusion both reflect and inflect the confusions inherent in an ongoing process of social upheaval evident in late nineteenth-century France—a process whose benchmarks include democratization and the blurring of social classes, a persistent and evolving revolutionism, radical reconfigurations of the city as lived environment, and the development of specifically capitalist logics of commerce, with their corollary conception of desire as properly endless? More specifically, how might such representations of confusion be read as effects of, or responses to, the historical traumas occasioned by the events of the so-called Terrible Year (*année terrible*), from the French army's defeat at Sedan (September 1870), through the Prussian occupation and first siege of Paris, to the Paris Commune (March–May 1871) and the bloody reprisals that attended its demise? By titling this study *Commemorating Trauma,* I mean to underscore confusion's literary inscription, in and around the Terrible Year, in a process of endlessly repeated commemoration that served a clear foundational role for the early Third Republic.

You may have noted a significant shift in the meaning of the term "confusion" in the course of my last paragraph. When one evokes the confusions that resulted from such massive tectonic shifts as the breakdown of an inherited class structure or the development, under the twin pressures of capitalism and revolutionary experience, of a functionally modern conception of the crowd, one intends a state of phenomena whose elements "are mixed to such an extent that it is impossible to distinguish among them" (*confus*, def. 2, *Petit Robert*). The cognates of "confusion" in this sense, which the *Petit Robert* dates back to 1370, include several of the most privileged terms in the lexicon of French realist fiction: *désordre*, *trouble*, *chaos*, *anarchie*, *mélange*, and *pêle-mêle*. It is not just that late nineteenth-century French authors inherited a world given to what they perceived as social, political, even sexual anarchy; nor that the political and military battles which defined the age—the uprising of March 18, 1871, for example, or the fighting at Sedan—were of a complexity that precluded comprehension from all but the most panoptic of vantages. Realist fiction not only dealt with confusion, chaos, fragmentation, or anarchy; it actually *required* them, on both ideological and aesthetic grounds. As Leo Bersani has written, thinking mainly of Balzac:

> The realistic novel gives us an image of social fragmentation contained within the order of significant form—and it thereby suggests that the chaotic fragments are somehow socially viable and morally redeemable. The novel makes esthetic sense out of social anarchy. And the society being judged subtly profits from this novelistic order, even though the order includes a great deal of social criticism. (60)

How late realist and naturalist novels might equally profit from a confusion or chaos that *resists* the (always tenuous) subsumption to order that Auerbach finds in historical narrative and Bersani finds in realist fiction is a question to which I will repeatedly return as my argument unfolds.

If "confusion" in this first sense signifies a lack of perceivable patterning in the phenomenal world, the term's second meaning is more squarely focused on the individual as cognitive agent. To suggest that "confusion" both contributed to and resulted from the historical traumas of the Terrible Year is to deploy the term in what is arguably its dominant modern sense, as denoting a lack of clarity or order in cognitive functions. Lest we assume that the age of positivism represented a pinnacle in France's self-described proclivity to "clear and distinct" ideas, it is worth recalling not only how mythic that supposed penchant ultimately is,[2] but also how the writers of the French nineteenth century, in the words of Alain Corbin,

> were less on their guard than we are about being confused. To be sure they had their forms of lucidity, their tools of analysis, their modes of implication unlike ours. Still, they had not learned, as we have, to hunt down illusions,

to unmask attitudes, to reveal the ambivalence of commitments, to look for hidden compartments. Their forms of expression were thus clearer. (154)

The specific conjunction of discursive confusion with an ambivalence frankly tolerated, even cultivated, will prove a nodal point in the analyses that follow.[3]

In the annals of modern revolutionism, few events have been met with a wave of vitriolic condemnation comparable with that visited upon the Paris Commune. Much scholarly work over the past several decades has gone into showing how the Commune was vilified (by journalists, writers, and men of science alike) as a hotbed of madness, disorder, anarchy, or orgiastic dissolution, and the Communards themselves dismissed as barbarians, monsters, animals, bandits, alcoholics, hysterics, or perverts.[4] Given this litany of abuse, both overtly polemical and cloaked in the garb of disinterested science, the anti-Communard critique of a certain confusion endemic to the Commune's ideology is easy to miss. Alongside Maxime du Camp's reduction of the Commune to a "fit of raging jealousy and social epilepsy," for example, the London *Times*'s characterization of the Commune's only manifesto as a "confused medley of contradictory and ill-conceived ideas, of absurdities, of arrogant pretensions, and of lies" cannot help but appear of minor interest (quoted in Lidsky, 47, and in Christianson, 321; cf. Lefebvre, 375–76).

By titling this introduction "The Commune and the Right to Confusion," I have engaged in a bit of punning provocation. It is not so much that one would have difficulty justifying a "right to confusion," since the very concept of an inalienable "right" by no means precludes, and may arguably be founded upon, the possibility of an individual's acting against his or her self-interest (if that is in fact what we do when we are confused). The provocation lies, rather, in the yoking of the terms "right" and "confusion," such that the latter quite markedly deflates the former's high-mindedness. We may enjoy a right to confusion, as a corollary to the more generally accepted right to freedom of thought and judgment, yet most of us would be loath to claim it.

But there is a second, more interesting way in which this title is provocative. To link the Paris Commune of 1871 to a "right to confusion" through the copulative conjunction "and" is to imply that it was the Communards themselves who claimed such a right. At the very least, this implication flies in the face of a long-standing tendency within French revolutionary rhetoric to conceive of morality, logical deduction, principled judgment, and luminous certainty not only as coextensive but also as patently favorable to the revolutionary cause. Consider how these qualities get yoked to an "exact sense of the right" in the following passage from the second, Commune–era iteration of *Le Père Duchêne*:

> The Revolution has its morals,
> Because the Revolution is nothing more than an act produced by logical
>   deduction from the demands of the proletariat.
> What gives revolutionaries their force,
> Their faith, their tranquillity, their certainty, their serenity in life and
>   impassibility in the face of death,
> Is logic,
> An exact sense of the right,
> A correctness of judgment. . . .
> The *Père Duchêne* said as much eighty years ago:
> "Once we have seen the light, they can blind us all they want; we will keep
>   the memory of the sun eternally alive."
> Logic,
> That's the main thing. (No. 58, quoted in Bellet, 114)

Elsewhere in this same number of *Le Père Duchêne*, one finds the injunction, "So be logical, you patriots, / And you, above all, citizen members of the Commune! / Be logical" (no. 58, quoted in Bellet, 114).

The ultimate irony is not that the Communards may have failed to live up to their rhetorical ideals, as the anxious insistence here clearly intimates, but rather that it was those elements of French society who were most inclined to dismiss the Commune's ideology as hopelessly confused who tended to arrogate *to themselves* an implicit "right to confusion." Such is the point I will be making in the analysis of several literary texts of the post–Commune era—of Flaubert's *La Tentation de saint Antoine* (*The Temptation of Saint Anthony*) and *Bouvard et Pécuchet*, first and foremost, but also of Zola's *La Débâcle* (*The Debacle*) and *Au Bonheur des dames* (*The Ladies' Delight*).[5] If Bersani is right in suggesting that realist and naturalist fiction staked its claim on the promise of order regained, if the realist writer was the de facto partisan of a specifically literary "party of Order," then the task of a project such as this is to examine how realist fiction comes to hijack the power of an ambient confusion, how it turns that power to its own ends, often at the expense of its aesthetic and ideological goals.[6]

❧

Although six of this book's seven chapters explicitly focus on one (or at most two) literary or filmic text(s), its method is as much theoretical and intellectual historical as it is strictly literary. My readings of literary texts by Victor Hugo, Gustave Flaubert, and Émile Zola; of historical accounts by Prosper-Olivier Lissagaray, Karl Marx, and Henri Lefebvre; and of films by Grigory Kozintsev and Leonid Trauberg and by Peter Watkins, consistently resonate with arguments from a wide range of intellectual disciplines—from nineteenth-century natural history, psychology, political economy, moral philosophy, and history, to twentieth- and twenty-first century psychoanalysis, existential philosophy, Marxist historiography, queer theory, and trauma theory (by Étienne Geoffroy Saint-Hilaire, Ernest Renan, Sigmund Freud, Melanie Klein, Jean-Paul Sartre, Claude Lefort, Slavoj Žižek, Judith Butler, Dominick LaCapra, and many others). I dare say a few readers will find this catholicity of reference troubling. (A reviewer of my *Logics of Failed Revolt* once complained bitterly of my having discussed Lacan's work on the death drive and French university enrollments in the mid-1960s within the same ten-page span.) Of such readers, happily now a distinct minority, I would ask why we should expect cultural phenomena, such as the dynamics of confusion at issue here, to respect a typology of intellectual language games that is as fundamentally contingent and conventional as it is ever-shifting.

The first three chapters of this study examine a complex dance with confusion on the part of works by Karl Marx, Henri Lefebvre, Émile Zola, and Victor Hugo—works that address the Commune directly or, in the case of Hugo's *Quatre-vingt-treize* (*Ninety-three*), with an obvious indirection.

In the course of a brief survey of events leading up to, and resulting from, the Paris Commune, chapter 1 examines the multiple grounds on which the Commune has been perceived as confounding, not only by participants and contemporary commentators (such as Lissagaray, Edmond Lepelletier, and Georges Clemenceau), but also more recently in Henri Lefebvre's important *La Proclamation de la Commune* (*The Proclamation of the Commune*, 1965). After outlining three such grounds—the ineluctable "fog of revolution," the fluidity of the Commune's ideology, and its idealistic disembodiment of political power—the chapter turns to Lefebvre's take on the positive *uses* of revolutionary confusion. By associating confusion with festivity and the lived experience of revolutionary passion, by insisting on the power of confused yet profound images, and by foregrounding confusion's link to a necessary futurity, the chapter argues, Lefebvre effectively critiques a traditional

Marxist perception of the Commune's ideological confusion as a product of theoretical underdevelopment, the overcoming of which is implicitly exemplified by Marxist analysis itself.

No work in the French literary tradition explores the sources of confusion in the events of the Terrible Year as fully and as insightfully as the penultimate volume in Zola's *Rougon-Macquart* series, *La Débâcle*. Chapter 2 focuses on the enactment and disavowal of confusion in the plotting of Zola's novel, with special attention to the melancholic confusion of Zola's emblematic Communard, Maurice Levasseur. Ambivalence plays a key role in the argument of this chapter, which moves from the ideological ambivalence inherent in Zola's "theoretical" republicanism to the more melancholic ambivalence of a character—Maurice—caught between melancholic self-violence and paranoid suspiciousness. Essential to the representation of Maurice, I argue, is a structure of disavowal much like that which Daniel Pick has shown to be inherent in degeneration theory: Maurice is both "us" (as figure for a degeneration of the "French race") and irretrievably "other."

Victor Hugo's *L'Année terrible* and his subsequent *Quatre-vingt-treize* subsume revolutionary violence and terror to a cycling of history's melancholic spiral. Reading Hugo's twin accounts of the Paris Commune and the Terror, chapter 3 interrogates the poet's vision of "triumphant mourning" as a condition of human progress. A reading of the symbolically rich *massacre de Saint Barthélémy* sequence from *Quatre-vingt-treize* shows how Hugo's recourse to a conscience-driven sentimentalism effectively precludes any overcoming of confusion in his work. The chapter concludes by arguing that Hugo parries the traumatic effects of the *année terrible* by assuming history's melancholic ambivalence into that single transhistorical image that closes *Quatre-vingt-treize*'s portrait of the historical Terror.

None of the works analyzed in the following three chapters—Flaubert's *La Tentation de saint Antoine*, his *Bouvard et Pécuchet*, and Zola's *Au Bonheur des Dames*—directly and sustainedly thematizes revolutionary violence. Yet all three, I argue, engage the problems of confusion, melancholy, and trauma in ways that help open up the specific dilemmas of post–Commune France.

Flaubert's letters during and after the Terrible Year are filled with complaints against a present time of decaying values and boorishness—among the French, surely, but also among the ostensibly more scientific Prussians. It is in this light that chapter 4 scrutinizes the final, 1874 version of Flaubert's *Tentation* to show how it reflects both an attraction to science as an institution of power and a penchant for confusion as the negation of science and its ruses. The deep melancholy that plagued Flaubert in the wake of 1870–71 plainly colors the work's vitalism. But this vitalism is also marked by the reemergence of a "desire that makes one live" on the far side of what Sartre saw as Flaubert's "historical death."

Chapter 5 reads Flaubert's posthumous *Bouvard et Pécuchet* as an extension—albeit a tonally complex one—of the novelist's epistolary rants against bourgeois conformism, egalitarian ideology, and a growing democratization of knowledge and power. The two former copy clerks of the novel's title incarnate the specifically liberal values of critical vigilance and judgment. But the sporadic nature of their judging faculties—and the novel's related fostering of a readerly confusion—mean that they (and we) can find meaning only in a melancholic desire for judgment, and in an ironic textuality miming that desire. The chapter concludes by juxtaposing *Bouvard* with Ernest Renan's *La Réforme intellectuelle et morale* (*Intellectual and Moral Reform,* 1871) as instances of post-traumatic working through.

Zola's *Au Bonheur des dames* links the confusions, perversions, entropic levelings, and disintegrative effects unleashed by modern capitalism to an originary trauma—the decapitation of ladies—that it couches in quasi-revolutionary terms. Yet the *Bonheur* disavows its best insights into such confusions by positing an expressly patriarchal (and undeniably creaky) "happy" ending. Where the analysis of previous chapters privileges the articulation of confusion with melancholic ambivalence, chapter 6 shows Zola's *Bonheur* as transmuting such a melancholy into the moral masochism of protagonist Denise Baudu. Denise's nature as a symbolic, disembodied masochist—analogous, in this respect, to the all-suffering Marianne of Republican ideology—effectively anticipates, the chapter argues, a critical rebirth of Republican faith.

In its own way, each of this study's first six chapters addresses the complex relation between the confusions and melancholies attendant to the collectively traumatic experience of the Terrible Year, and the transcendence of that trauma through the positing of an essential futurity. Chapter 7 explores the twentieth-century afterlife of this trauma/futurity nexus through a reading of what are arguably the two most important films yet made on the Paris Commune—Grigory Kozintsev and Leonid Trauberg's *New Babylon* (1929) and Peter Watkins's *La Commune (Paris, 1871)* (2000). Whereas *New Babylon* attempts to overcome a melancholy clinging to the memory of the Commune through enactment of a specifically aesthetic revolution, *La Commune* (and Watkins's contemporaneous writings) look to an ideal of filmmaking as democratic process to forestall a melancholy that arises, for Watkins, from the capitalist co-optation of that revolution.

In a rightly celebrated piece on the value of "thick description" for the anthropological study of culture, In *Interpretation of Cultures*, Clifford Geertz notes that "Cultural analysis is intrinsically incomplete. And, worse than that, the more deeply it goes the less complete it is" ("Thick Description," 29). In thinking through the place of confusion within a cultural force field largely defined by the traumas of the Terrible Year, I have sought to situate my work at what for Geertz would be a moderate degree of cultural depth, at precisely that point where Auerbach sees historical analysis as pivoting between classificatory gain and the reemergence of doubt. As the summaries above suggest, my analysis in the chapters that follow is not a linear one. Rather, it is marked by the repeated returns and inflections of a cluster of central problematics, definable around such concepts as

- melancholy, mourning, and masochism;
- trauma (both collective and individual);
- ambivalence, disavowal, and degeneration;
- republicanism, liberalism, democracy, and the (dis)embodiment of political power;
- futurity and revolution (political or aesthetic);
- desire, and of course . . .;
- confusion (in its multiple senses).

To conclude this introduction, I should like briefly to evoke four of the (clearly interrelated) argumentative trajectories allowed by such a descriptively "thick" presentational approach.

Melancholy and Trauma. Much has been written over the past several decades on the medicalization of the psyche and the social bond in early Third Republic France.[7] In examining the traumas of the *année terrible* and their role in shaping fundamentally melancholic forms of desire, I aim to complement a body of excellent work on what Janet Beizer has called the "hystericization of culture" (8). Given that Charcot and others explained the "hysterical shattering of the personality" as the consequence of an experience of extreme terror or fright, what is at stake in the shift from hysteria to melancholy as the product of specifically traumatic experience (Leys, 4)?[8] How might the representation of melancholic confusion (that of Zola's

Maurice, for example) differ from the enactment of melancholic ambiva-lence (in the endings of *La Débâcle* and *Quatre-vingt-treize* or in the structure of *Bouvard et Pécuchet*) as a modality of working through the traumas of the Terrible Year? How and why, as in Flaubert, might melancholy get grafted onto a specifically vitalist model of desire? How (in the cases of Hugo, Zola's Denise, and Lefebvre's tragic Communards) does a certain emblem-atic suffering intervene in the field of social and political trauma? How might the melancholy (and related cognitive confusion) that followed upon the Terrible Year be ultimately worked through—or not—by the positing of a necessary futurity? These are among the principal questions that cluster in these pages around the problem of melancholy.

The Uses of Confusion. In a highly suggestive piece on the value of confu-sion and obscurity in aesthetic thought of the German Enlightenment, Jef-frey Barnouw has shown how A. G. Baumgarten developed Leibniz's insights into the intrinsic confusion of sensation and sensuous cognition in order to ground the new science and art of aesthetics (29). If sensation is understood, with Leibniz, as an " 'assemblage confus' [confused assem-blage], emerging into consciousness," then it follows, as Baumgarten sug-gests, that an idea is "lively, rich, and fruitful in proportion to its confusion" (33, 35).

This linking of confusion with aesthetic power was by no means peculiar to the Germans. In his *L'Avenir de la science* (*The Future of Science*), composed after the events of 1848 but not published until 1890, the young Ernest Renan develops an expressly dialectical model for the coming into being of a new "scientific philosophy": "a science which would no longer be dry, barren, and excluding, but which, in becoming complete, would become religious and poetical" (968/*282*). Prior to the contemporary age of arid analysis and rampant individualism—the antithetical moment in his dialec-tic—Renan sees a first, syncretic age of the human spirit, "that of complex-ity and confusion," an essentially religious and philosophical premodernity, marked by rich organic communities in which "all the elements of human-ity" coexist "in a confused but beautiful unity" (968–69/*283–84*).

As Renan's language here implies, the recuperation of phenomenal con-fusion for aesthetic effect commonly entails a political dimension. In the first three chapters of this study, I will frequently have occasion to examine the aesthetic–political fruitfulness of particular confoundings—from the theo-retically confused symbols and images that Lefebvre finds at the origin of the Commune's power, to the levelings inherent in Zola's chaotic crowds, and the conjuncturally defined efficacy of Hugo's sublime catalogs. From chapter 4 on, however, our attention will shift to confusion's stake in the elaboration and progressive solidification of a specifically modern concept of desire *as such*, understood—obliquely in *Bouvard*, then directly in the *Bonheur*—as a corollary to the rise of our modern consumer societies.[9]

Democratization. As my epigraph from Stendhal clearly suggests, the rhetoric of social confusion in nineteenth-century France frequently served as a response to mounting democratization, and this in two senses. In the expressly political sense of that term, one finds a clear but halting progress toward democratic modalities of government: from the institution of universal suffrage with the Constitution of 1848; through what Marx called the "mock democratism" of the Second Empire's plebiscites, which turned popular sovereignty into an alibi for imperial power (*Commune*, 38); to the municipal elections of March 26, 1871, in the early days of the Commune. Here is Louis Barron, writing in his 1889 account of the Commune, *Sous le Drapeau rouge* (*Beneath the Red Flag*):

> O illusion! Not to see that the insurgents are already logically organized
> and that we would change nothing about that organization, even if it is
> found derisive and called disorder and confusion, for disorder and confusion
> are of the very essence of voluntary troops under leaders who are freely
> elected—that is to say, subordinated to their subordinates. (Quoted in Ross,
> *Emergence*, 131)

But "democratization" also names a more general—and, for many French literati of the period, more fundamentally traumatic—breakdown of class barriers. Before and (especially) after the Terrible Year, writers such as Renan and Flaubert (discussed in chapters 4 and 5) sought to stem the mounting tide of an egalitarian ideology, ostensibly fed by rampant egotism and base jealousy, by calling for a society based on supposedly natural differences of talents and gifts, a natural aristocracy.

In many respects, this breakdown was overstated. As Stewart Edwards has argued, the Haussmannization of Paris (discussed in chapter 1) actually accelerated the division of the city into class districts, replacing an earlier "vertical" division of the population on the floors of given buildings (from the bourgeois on the first and second floors to the servants in the garret) (8). Likewise, the explicitly racialist reinscription of class division in anti–Communard writing signaled both the perceived threat of an entropic social leveling and the extent to which such leveling was by no means realized. But the entropic threat would distinctly shape French literary, philosophical, and medical writing well into the early years of the twentieth century. Discussing Gustave Le Bon's 1895 *Psychologie des foules* (*Psychology of the Crowd*), for example, Daniel Pick writes: "'Democracy' in any form . . . tended to pull civilization towards the primitive 'homogeneity' from which, like an organism, it had slowly differentiated itself" (93).

If democratization was thus commonly read as a catalyst of cultural degeneration, several of the works I shall be analyzing here do reflect, albeit obliquely, on the possible conditions of a positive democracy. Chief among these is the stipulation (most closely identified with the work of Claude Lefort) that the space of power in a democratic frame remain a properly empty one, occupiable only by symbolic figures or temporary squatters. I examine the pertinence of this stipulation in my reading of Lefebvre in chapter 1, then again in the analysis of *Au Bonheur des dames* in chapter 6.

Ambivalence. Despite (or rather because of) the power of the confusion diagnosis as a form of stigmatization, its literary enactment after 1870–1871 frequently gives rise to a complex tension between inclusion and exclusion, between that gesture which constitutes an "us" (rational, logical, not confused) and that which designates an "other" (confused, hysterical, degenerate). Although clearly related to a structure of disavowal implicit in late nineteenth-century theories of degeneration, this tension is best understood, I argue, as a form of melancholic ambivalence, variously exemplified by the pivoting between melancholia and paranoia in *La Débâcle* (chapter 2) and by that realization inherent in *Bouvard* that even the raging *bourgeoisophobe* is essentially bourgeois (chapter 5). If the pursuit of melancholic ambivalence thus implies a certain ethic whereby fundamental social anxieties are assumed to oneself without *simply* being projected onto others, that ethic issues (as I argue in chapter 5) from a specifically liberal tension between the quest for individual distinction and a tolerance of difference (or punishment, in what *Bouvard* calls the mode of "silly gentleness"). Whereas liberal ideology is by and large predicated on the conceptual mastery of cognitive confusion, its ethic implies an entropic blurring of difference, whose function in the long and halting process of building republican consensus in the wake of the traumatic divisions of the Terrible Year can hardly be overestimated. In this respect, as so often in what follows, the rites of confusion function as both the signs of profoundly felt collective traumas and the means of their overcoming, as both symptoms and (often curiously mimetic) attempts at a cure.

I   *Why Confusion? Why the Commune?*

Confusion, I have suggested, is both this study's principal subject *and* its historiographical limit. How and why, we will be asking, were the events most central to the history of the Paris Commune of 1871 perceived as confounding by contemporary participants and commentators? How did these forms of confusion differ from those felt to be endemic to French society under the Second Empire or, later, the Third Republic? How did the confusion diagnosis as applied to the Commune come to serve a progressivist vision of history? What were the *uses* of confusion, from a revolutionary point of view or from the point of view of a revolutionary aesthetic? How did the strategic appropriation of a revolutionary confusion to which they themselves were generally hostile help certain highly visible French authors work through the confounding events of 1870–1871? As my quotations from Auerbach and Geertz have suggested, moreover, confusion will also function here as a necessary methodological risk. In addressing the questions above, I aim to trace a historical trajectory that avoids both the Scylla of mimicked confusion and the Charybdis of overly simple (Auerbach would say "legendary") classification.

In order to give some sense of the rich historical context within and against which the literary and filmic texts I will be analyzing in chapters 2 through 7 actively negotiate with confusion, this opening chapter contains a brief overview of French political history from the beginnings of the Second Empire through the first two decades of the Third Republic. In the course of this survey, whose limitations are as obvious as they are inevitable, I will lay out some of the grounds on which those who lived through the events of this period would have had reason to find them confounding. This line of inquiry leads me to examine, in a crucial middle section, the function of the confusion diagnosis in two key texts of Marxist literature on the Commune: Karl Marx's "The Civil War in France" of 1871 and Henri Lefebvre's 1965 study, *La Proclamation de la Commune*.

From Empire to Commune

In December 1848, just half a year after the "June Days" had put a bloody end to the so-called February Revolution, a newly enfranchised French electorate overwhelmingly elected Louis-Napoléon, nephew of Napoléon Bonaparte, president of the republic. "In the oddest election of the nineteenth century," Roger Williams writes of the elections of December 10, "the Radicals had supported Louis-Napoléon, thinking him a Socialist; the Moderate Republicans, thinking him a Jacobin; the Orleanists, supposing him a Liberal; the Catholics, confident he would defend the Faith against radical onslaught" (51). "Just because he was nothing," Marx quipped, Louis-Napoléon "could signify everything save himself" (*Class Struggles,* 72).

On December 2, 1851, in the face of a constitution that limited him to a single four-year term, Louis-Napoléon dissolved the Legislative Assembly, laying the groundwork for a restoration of empire the following month. From its establishment in January 1852 to its demise in September 1870, the Second Empire was marked by extraordinary economic growth, in whose benefits the lower classes largely failed to share.[1] Rapid construction of the nation's railways; the establishment of great credit institutions, beginning with the Crédit Foncier de France and the Crédit Mobilier in 1852; industrialization of the French north; and an increasing concentration of capital and the means of production in the hands of a privileged few—these are but some of the developments that would lead Friedrich Engels to find in the Second Empire "the exploitation of France by a gang of political and financial adventurers, but at the same time an industrial development as had never been possible under the narrow-minded and timorous system of Louis-Philippe" (introduction, 24).

No initiative better symbolizes the empire of Napoléon III—its expansionist spirit as well as its speculative corruption—than the so-called Haussmannization of Paris. From 1853 to the regime's end, Baron Georges-Eugène Haussmann led a massive effort to revolutionize the city's urban landscape. In laying out the great boulevards that characterize Paris as we know it today, Haussmann sought to replace the city's "warren of dangerous slums with public monuments and commercial development attractive to a new class of clean-living, high-spending, Empire-supporting bourgeois" (Christianson, 95). In the process, he managed to displace the Parisian working class from the city's center to its newly incorporated peripheral quarters; to facilitate the movement of troops and artillery in the event of a popular uprising; to rationalize and sanitize a city made safe for bourgeois commerce; and, not incidentally, to make those who speculated on expropriated land exceptionally rich.

Compounding the disruptive effect of the Second Empire's transformation of Paris as lived environment was the extraordinary pace of technological innovation in that period. As Rupert Christianson notes, the Second Empire saw "advances in the science of everything from aluminum to margarine, the dry-cell battery to the compressed-air drill, Pasteurization to electroplating, and prototypes of the colour photograph, the gas engine and refrigerator"—not to mention the *vélocipède*, an ancestor of the modern bicycle (114). The spectacle of these "enormous material changes," when coupled with the equally momentous explosion of wealth,

> bred an excitement that was often exhilarating. But it also drove the city's top note to the pitch of hysteria—a sound of emptiness, insecurity, anxiety, symptomatic of lives without purpose or direction, poisoned by the virus of boredom. (114)

As the empire declined, the Parisian craving for amusement became ever more frantic, leading a columnist from *La Vie parisienne*, looking back on the year 1869, to find "chaos, chaos everywhere" (quoted in Christianson, 73). One product of this craving for amusement was a much-noted breakdown of class distinction. When Maxime du Camp, for example, complains that "one does not know nowadays if it's honest women who are dressed like whores or whores who are dressed like honest women," he points to an amusement-driven confusion of social classes, much like that of which Zola would make so much in his novels of the Second Empire, *Nana* especially (quoted in Christianson, 83).

The regime of Napoléon III was born in the wake of the Revolution of 1848, out of the belief—most closely associated with the peasant classes—that only a return to Bonapartism could spare France yet another episode of revolutionary anarchy. But as memories of the February Revolution dimmed, the empire found its influence likewise on the wane (Plessis, 202). A new generation steeped in positivist ideology saw the empire as profoundly tainted by its perceived alliance with the Catholic Church. Catholics, for their part, took umbrage at the emperor's intervention in the struggle for Italian unity (Plessis, 203). A deterioration of imperial power that Alain Plessis has argued was already in place in 1858 accelerated markedly with the economic crisis of 1866–1867. Working-class political activity surged, culminating in the strikes of 1869–1870 among the miners of Carmaux, the silk workers of Lyon, the weavers of Rouen, and many others

(Lefebvre, 77–78). Neither the laws of May and June 1868, granting new freedoms of the press and new rights of assembly, nor a last-minute attempt by Émile Ollivier to construct a more liberal empire, sufficed to stem a growing dissatisfaction with the regime, even among its bourgeois supporters. As a character from Zola's *La Débâcle* would put it, "The Empire grown old . . . turned back to liberalism too late, thereby hastening its own undoing" (413/*34–35*).

Even in the heyday of the empire, Napoléon III was never a strong and steady leader. "At once headstrong and a dreamer," one early historian writes, "he was full of rash plans, but irresolute in carrying them out" (Wiraith, 869–70). Nor has history been kind to the fundamental paradoxes of his doctrine, such as his furthering of bourgeois commercial interests in the guise of populism, his reliance on simple plebiscites in the name of universal suffrage, or his pursuit of colonial power under the rubric of peace. In "The Eighteenth Brumaire of Louis Bonaparte," Marx speaks of the emperor's "confused groping hither and thither," as he "seeks now to win, now to humiliate first one class and then another," as ultimately arraying "all [classes] uniformly against him" (615). Such a pattern of contradiction Marx ascribes to the emperor's need to satisfy various masters: a growing middle class, the buttress to a civil order it was his mission to safeguard; the "people in general," whom he wanted to make "happy within the frame of bourgeois society"; and the *Lumpenproletariat*, from whose ranks he and his entourage are notoriously said to have sprung (615). But by early 1870—with the emperor suffering from the stone that would kill him three years later, the economy in recession, and the court split between the partisans of Empress Eugénie (eager to establish a line of imperial succession) and the backers of Ollivier—the emperor had been reduced to a shadow of his former (flighty and demagogic) self.

Historians have generally seen the French declaration of war against Prussia on July 19, 1870, as doubly determined. By reporting conversations between King Wilhelm of Prussia and the French ambassador, Benedetti, on the question of Spanish succession so as to suggest that France had been slighted, Prussian Chancellor Otto von Bismarck all but forced the French to initiate a war that he rightly expected would further the cause of German unity. On the French side, the empress and her faction looked to armed conflict as a means of restoring the prestige of both France and its emperor, thus silencing a mounting opposition. The initial war wariness of that opposition—from Adolphe Thiers and Jules Favre in the center to Louis Blanc and Félix Pyat on the left—was quickly drowned in nationalist fervor, as large crowds took to the streets of Paris, ardently shouting "To Berlin! To Berlin!"

By early August, however, news from the front had become increasingly dire, prompting Napoléon III to join General MacMahon's army at Châlons. Over the next several weeks, leaders of the bourgeois Republican opposition engaged in a delicate balancing act, trying to fill that void in the space of power left by the emperor's de facto abdication, without thereby ceding power to the forces of revolution. As Marx would write of the period immediately following the empire's fall: "That Republic has not subverted the throne, but has only taken its place become vacant" ("Civil War," 46).

On September 3, news reached Paris of MacMahon's defeat at Sedan, of the capture of 100,000 French troops, and of the emperor's surrender. The following day, huge crowds took to the streets of Paris in what was widely felt to be an unprecedented display of nonviolent, Republican festivity. During a special session of the Assembly in the Palais-Bourbon, Jules Favre and Léon Gambetta persuaded a crowd that had occupied the building to march to the Hôtel de Ville, where the republic was to be proclaimed. At the very moment at which Henri Rochefort, supported by the radical Blanquists, was to have read the list of a truly revolutionary government, Favre managed to substitute a list of his own, composed principally of bourgeois Republican deputies. Thus was born the Government of National Defense, satirized by Marx as the "Government of National Defection" and by Henri Lefebvre as the *gouvernement des Jules* (Jules Simon, Jules Favre, and Jules Ferry) ("Civil War," 49, 112).[2] In thus co-opting popular enthusiasm in order to forestall establishment of a more revolutionary republic, the bourgeois deputies stamped September 4 with what Henri Lefebvre has called "the double sign of spontaneity and intrigue, of feverish improvisation and slow-ripened skill, of dramatic ambiguity and swindling pure and simple" (112). But it may well have been, as Lefebvre goes on to suggest, that the Parisian crowd which took to the streets on September 4 was not yet ready for radical change; "their gripe was with the Empire, not with capitalism" (115).

From September 18 on into the cold Parisian winter, the city lay besieged by the Prussian army. Isolated from the world outside, with which it communicated principally by means of carrier pigeons and perilous manned balloon flights, Paris came to know hunger, disease, and massive unemployment. "The emergence of horse, dog, cat and rat as part of the Parisian diet became a staple of conversation" (Christianson, 210). Breakdowns in the city's sanitation system caused mortality rates to triple. Only a rapid expansion in the ranks of the National Guard stemmed the tide of unemployment, but many guardsmen passed their days and nights in an alcoholic stupor.

In the face of such a collapse of the very structure of Parisian society, Lefebvre has found a countervailing reconstruction, "a new restructuring, from the bottom up" (179). With the proliferation of revolutionary clubs and the establishment of a loosely organized web of popular political organizations, political power became increasingly diffuse. The battalions of the National Guard, an organization once dominated by the foes of revolution, grew ever less inclined to enforce the government's will against the people. One finds embryonic attempts to form mutual aid societies and to secularize education. In short, much of the initiative we have come to associate with the Commune—including that decentralization which was both the Commune's glory and its downfall—was well in process in the fall and early winter of 1870.

From its inception, the Government of National Defense took as its primary objective the establishment of peace with Prussia; in this it was faithful to the will of both the peasantry and the provincial ruling class. But when Parisians learned on October 31 that Thiers was on the verge of signing an armistice with Prussia, large numbers took to the streets. The day saw repeated confrontations between disorderly but determined crowds calling for the formation of a commune, government officials eager to calm the mounting storm, and battalions of the National Guard intervening on both sides of the battle.

In trying to convey some sense of the radical uncertainty that participants in the events of October 31 would have felt as to who held power at any given moment, Henri Lefebvre repeatedly evokes states of chaos and confusion. Thus, of the moment around 1:15 P.M. when the president of the Government of National Defense, General Jules Trochu, addressed the crowd in front of the Hôtel de Ville, Lefebvre writes: "It was the height of confusion" (213). Some four hours later, after a group of National Guardsman under Gustave Flourens had taken members of the government prisoner, and Flourens himself had announced the formation of a Committee of Public Safety, "confusion once again reached its highest pitch" (214). Lefebvre then speaks of a "new confusion" when, around 8 P.M., "good" battalions loyal to the government used a tunnel to retake the Hôtel de Ville and free the captive Jules Favre and Jules Simon. (I will return to the grounds for

Lefebvre's particular investment in the trope of confusion later in this chapter.)

The uprising of October 31 ended with the insurgents ceding power back to the Government of National Defense, in exchange for promises (both subsequently broken) to conduct full municipal elections and to hold harmless the uprising's leadership. The government went on to win a vote of confidence in a plebiscite on November 3, but the issuing of arrest warrants for the leaders of October 31 (Blanqui, Flourens, Lefrançais, Vallès, et al.) served to sour public opinion (Edwards, 85). As Lefebvre would put it, the central government's victory was a "façade," but one that was slowly "cracking" to pieces: "It is henceforth in the newly-autonomous neighborhoods and arrondissements of besieged Paris that important decisions are made, that social life is reorganized or maintained" (176).

What would prove to be the first of two sieges that Paris would undergo during *l'année terrible* ended through an armistice with Prussia, negotiated by Favre on January 26, 1871, and ratified by the Assembly on March 1. In that agreement, France ceded to the new German state nearly all of Alsace and a large part of Lorraine, while agreeing to pay an indemnity of 5 billion gold francs (subsequently reduced by the value of lost railway concessions) and granting the Prussian army a triumphal entrance into Paris. Wildly popular among the high bourgeoisie, the armistice was initially met with "stunned silence" by the hitherto intensely nationalistic people of Paris (Edwards, 115).

The dissolution of the Government of National Defense in the wake of the armistice agreement triggered a round of national elections on February 8, as a result of which power was vested in a National Assembly housed in Bordeaux and led by Adolphe Thiers—historian of the Revolution, onetime minister under Louis-Philippe, and leader of the centrist *tiers parti*. Setting a trend that would continue well into the Third Republic, the majority of those who were elected to the Assembly were in fact Monarchists. (Victor Hugo and Louis Blanc—both delegates from Paris—were notable exceptions.) Only a long-standing rift between supporters of the Royalist Comte de Chambord and those of the Orleanist claimant, the Comte de Paris (the grandsons of Charles X and Louis-Philippe, respectively) precluded what many republicans feared would be an inevitable move toward restoration.

Paris, in the meantime, was becoming increasingly radicalized. During the night of February 26 and 27, some 50,000 armed members of the National Guard—Lefebvre calls them "the future troops of the Commune"—

gathered on the Champs-Élysées in response to rumors of the imminent arrival of the Prussian army (24). A crowd seized the Guard's cannons—dispersed throughout those quarters in the west of Paris which the Prussians were to enter by agreement on March 1—and dragged them off to the safety of the popular quarters in the north and northeast.

The weeks following the Prussian army's forty-eight-hour occupation of Paris (March 1–3) saw a "complete breakdown of all forms of official government" in the city—a breakdown that was, as Stewart Edwards notes, "partly festive, partly violent" (123). Relations between the National Assembly and working-class Paris deteriorated with the Assembly's suppression of radical newspapers, its sentencing of Auguste Blanqui and Gustave Flourens to death for their role in the events of October 31, and its lifting of the wartime moratorium on rent and the collection of debts. But no move infuriated Republican Paris more than the Assembly's decision not to return from Bordeaux to that city, but rather to go to Versailles, the seat of French monarchy, "a disgraced town in the eyes of patriots, an accursed city" (Lefebvre, 223).

In the early morning of March 18, 1871, French army troops entered Paris in an attempt to make off with the cannons of the National Guard, many of which had been dragged to the heights of Montmartre and Buttes-Chaumont by the crowd of February 26. Execution of this mission was, as the Commune's greatest chronicler, Prosper-Olivier Lissagaray, puts it, "as foolish as the conception"—in part because its planners had failed to provide sufficient horses to remove the cannons once they had been seized, in part because army troops generally refused to fire on the crowds that had come out in defense of the cannons (111/78). The scenes of joyful fraternization between army troops and the Parisian populace on the morning of March 18 helped to establish a widespread image of the Commune as festival—in Lenin's phrase, as a "festival of the oppressed"—to which I will return in a moment (quoted in Edwards, 277).[3]

But March 18 was not without its causalities. A midmorning clash on the Place Pigalle resulted in the death of an army captain, three gunners, and five horses, one of which was cut up for meat by the famished crowd. That afternoon, two army generals were executed in the garden of the National Guard headquarters on the rue des Rosiers—Claude Lecomte for having ordered his troops to fire on the crowd at Montmartre during the events of the morning (they refused), and Clément Thomas for his repressive role in the June Days of 1848. Although many of the bullets discovered in the bodies of Lecomte and Thomas were found to have come from the *chassepots* of army deserters and not from the National Guard, their deaths would stand as crucial evidence of supposed Communard barbarism in the months and years to come.

Looking back on the events of March 18, participants and spectators would repeatedly insist on the confusion endemic to the actions of the revolutionary crowd. Thus Georges Clemenceau, then deputy for Paris, would report of the scene on Montmartre: "Armed guards were running about in all directions and in the greatest confusion. . . . they called out, they were shouting; it was all a perfect bedlam" (quoted in Gullickson, 30). Likewise, Edmond Lepelletier described the exuberant crowd accompanying General Lecomte and his captors to the National Guard post at the base of Montmartre in these terms:

> Men, women, children, soldiers, and national guards surrounded the general and descended the rue Muller, in noisy confusion. People cried, jeered, sang the Marseillaise, cheered the Line, and booed Vinoy. All was a disorderly jostling, pierced by the strident sounds of a bugle. (Quoted in Gullickson, 31)

Perhaps the most interesting account of the morning on Montmartre, however, is the following passage from the anonymous *La Vérité sur la Commune*:

> The confused din of vague rumors filled the streets, muffled rumble of the popular storm. . . . Suddenly, a bugle sounded, casting its strident notes to the wind. Ten, twenty, a hundred bugles answered; furious drums beat out the ominous call to arms. Montmartre, yanked from its sleep, stirred to its depths, spread out through its streets, and massed in its squares. All of this spontaneously, catching fire like a train of gunpowder, exploding like a mine. The storm was unleashed. (Quoted in Lefebvre, 244)

Steeped in an idiom that asserts itself with a vengeance in Hugo's own writings on the Commune, this passage shows how the confusion diagnosis can serve, as it does in Hugo, as the rhetorical prelude to claims of a newfound unity of purpose (note the striking personification of Montmartre) on the part of the tempestuous mass. Or, as Lissagaray writes in his *Histoire de la Commune de 1871*,

> A single cry answered, echoing with the life in two hundred thousand breasts: "Long live the Commune." . . . The quick reports of the cannons, the bands, the bugles, the drums, blended into a formidable communion. . . . A single flame warmed these souls, reuniting the petite bourgeoisie and the

proletariat, touching the middle bourgeoisie. At such moments a people can be recast. (153–54/*129–30*; cf. 199)

In the early afternoon of March 18, an increasingly panicked Thiers ordered the national government and what was left of its army to evacuate Paris and retreat to Versailles. By evening, despite a last-ditch effort by Jules Ferry to hold on to the Hôtel de Ville, Paris belonged to the insurgents. Although the Paris Commune would be officially proclaimed only on March 28, following municipal elections on March 26, the consensus among historians is that the Commune effectively began with the events of March 18.

The Commune and the "Dust of Confusion"

The Paris Commune lasted little more than two months. For much of that time, Paris was under siege, subject to near daily bombardment by the forces of Versailles, who (like the Prussians before them) aimed to starve the city into submission. Internally, the Commune was plagued by deep uncertainties as to where power effectively lay, with the Central Committee of the National Guard, the mayors of the twenty arrondissements, the Commune itself, and (later) the Committee of Public Safety all staking their claims. Despite these impediments, the Commune managed to implement, albeit sketchily, a series of social reforms whose more complete implementation would be left to the Third Republic or to later socialist movements: the establishment of workers' cooperatives and special workshops for the employment of women, the secularization of education, nationalization of church property, and the separation of church and state.

But when Rupert Christianson asks, "What exactly was it, this Commune?," in his 1994 book, *Paris Babylon*, he notes that "the dust of confusion is still not settled, even after so many of the issues it raised are dead ones" (296). Despite (and, in some obvious measure, because of) a massive corpus of memoirs and historical studies—Robert Le Quillec's 1997 critical bibliography of the Commune runs to some 426 pages—we are far from closing the book on the uprising.

Why, to borrow Christianson's metaphor, are we still blinded by the "dust of confusion"? I see three, closely interrelated reasons. First, as the accounts of October 31 and March 18 quoted above clearly attest, revolutionary events and revolutionary times tend to be perceived as confusing by those who participate in them; there is a "fog of revolution" every bit as thick as Clausewitz's "fog of war." Second, the Commune's ideology was intensely fluid, if not contradictory or outright confused—and only appears more so when one reads the Commune against a specific vision of history (such as the Marxist dialectic) or in light of future revolutionary moments (such as the October Revolution or May 1968).[4] Third, the very uncertainties as to who was in charge that triggered a generalized sense of confusion on October 31 and March 18 were largely replicated in fundamental Communard principles on the ideal nature of political power. In the paragraphs that follow, I expand upon the second and third of these points.

In seeking to understand the Paris Commune, to find a certain measure of order in the events, historians have usefully pointed to a series of specific tensions at the heart of Communard ideology and practice. Stewart Edwards, for example, signals an apparent disjunction between the Commune's rhetoric and its actions: "The legalistic scruples of the Central Committee following 18 March, the monetary orthodoxy of the Financial Commission, the constitutional emphasis on municipal rights of many of the 'minority,' the hope of a peaceful communal revolution, were far from the intemperate revolutionary feeling of the popular *Hébertisme* of the *enragés* expressed by the popular organs of opinion" (293). Henri Lefebvre refines this point by noting that certain of the essentially loose revolutionary groupings that went into the Commune's revolutionary mix, such as the Blanquists and the Jacobins, were not motivated by ideology or doctrinal passion so much as by an attitude of revolutionary action (394).

Above all, however, commentators have been struck by a tension implicit in the Edwards quote above, that between the Commune as a part of a larger federative structure and the Commune as the epitome of a unified republic. One the one hand, the Commune was clearly the outgrowth of a movement toward greater municipal self-governance already well in place at the end of the Second Empire. In the federative view, Paris's Commune was exemplary not because Paris was the revolution incarnate, but simply because it had outlasted parallel communes in other French cities (including Lyon, Marseilles, Toulouse, Saint-Étienne, and Creusot). As a communiqué from the Central Committee of the National Guard put it, "Paris aspires to no dictatorship other than that of example" (quoted in Lissagaray, 143). This view stressed the inalienable importance of democratic principles—those same principles which the Central Committee had so plainly in mind when, in the wake of March 18, they conceived their most pressing duty as calling for citywide elections.[5]

On the other hand, the Commune's practical need to hold Paris up as an anti–Versailles found powerful reinforcement in the historical Jacobin conception of the republic as one and indivisible (Lefebvre, 312). As Versailles tightened its military noose around the city, the Commune found itself increasingly drawn to "the Jacobin ideal of a strong directing executive, culminating in the formation of a five-man Committee of Public Safety at the beginning of May" (Edwards, 219).

In order to examine how this tension between federative plurality and republican unity plays itself out in a specific instance of the confusion diagnosis, I turn to the following passage, in which Lefebvre sets forth the grounds for his characterizing Communard ideology as "a very confused ideologico-political complex, within which different, even contradictory aspects converge and intermingle" (136):

> For the Proudhonists, the Commune and federalism involve decentralization. For the Blanquists, it's the revolutionary Commune of 1792 and 1793, animating spirit of the Republic one and indivisible, centralizing and dictatorial. For the last Fourrierists, it's the realization of the phalanstery, alveole of a new society. For those in the International, it's a bit of all this, plus something more: for some, Proudhonists by inspiration, it's confusedly understood as a generalized self-management [*autogestion*]; for others, it's already the fairly summary communism of which they dream; for still others, it's the dictatorship of the proletariat, confusedly understood. For all, except for the neo–Jacobins and the Blanquists—and here we touch on the essential point—it's the destruction of the current centralized state and the constitution of a new state, already in the process of withering away.
>
> The ideological unity of these tendencies will never get further than an unstable and endlessly questioned state of compromise, which will be shattered as soon as the Commune takes power. (137–38)

In other contexts, Lefebvre speaks of Proudhonian doctrine as mixing reformist and revolutionary principles "in an inextricable state of confusion and conflict" or evokes a "great confusion of revolutionary measures" within the International's Commune-era program, split as it was between demands for "a fundamental reconstruction of society, . . . reformist measures acceptable within the frame of advanced democracy, and liberal measures at home in a formal democracy . . ." (394, 356). But the function of the confusion diagnosis is markedly different here, where it applies to those elements of the International who "confusedly" understand the Commune as representative of either a generalized self-management or the dictatorship of the proletariat. In this context, the adverb "confusedly" signals the Communards' imperfect grasp of principles that would be more perfectly articulated later—by Marx, Engels, and Lenin reflecting on the Commune, in the case of the dictatorship of the proletariat, or by worker's self-management movements in Tito's Yugoslavia, or in France, as Lefebvre writes.

To put this use of the confusion diagnosis in some perspective, consider the function of confusion in and around Marx's best-known text on the Commune, "The Civil War in France"—composed in April and May 1871 and delivered to the General Council of the First International on May 30 of that year. Here, as elsewhere, it is Marx's position that capitalist production is doomed to "constant anarchy and periodic convulsions" until such time as the means of national production fall under the control of a system of "united co-operative societies" (76). To borrow a phrase from the first outline of Marx's text, the Commune thus afforded a "rational medium" through which a class struggle necessarily shaped by the convulsions of the capitalist order could "run through its different phases in the most rational and humane way" (156). Whatever confusions the Commune itself may have been subject to are attributed to the relative underdevelopment of the current socialist movement, from which Marx's analysis then takes a certain distance by stressing its clarity of insight into the laws of historical causality, its sharp sense for the ironies of history, and its ability to distinguish essential from accidental phenomena or "completely new historical creations" from "older and even defunct forms of social life" (73).

This yoking of a diagnosis of confusion through underdevelopment to a claimed clarity of historical insight is much in evidence in Engels's 1891 introduction to the "Civil War," where he writes that the demands of the French proletariat over the years leading up to the Commune were "more or less clear and even confused, corresponding to the state of development reached by the workers of Paris at the particular period, but in the last resort [note the reductionist translation] they all amounted to the abolition of the class antagonism between capitalists and workers" (23).

In classical Marxism, in other words, specific confusions tend to be seen as the product of a theoretical underdevelopment whose overcoming is largely exemplified by the analysis itself. But might there not be a sense in which confusion has a positive function, and might not the Commune be precisely the place to look for it? I will address these questions by first examining certain Communard presuppositions about the nature of political

power and then by turning to Henri Lefebvre on the specific *uses* of revolutionary confusion.

Of the many truisms that recur in accounts of the Commune, perhaps
none is more insistent than the claim that the Commune lacked a clear,
identifiable leader. When it comes to giving that lack a face, the consensus
choice is Auguste Blanqui, imprisoned in Toulon on March 17 for his role
in the events of the previous October. In the account of a meeting at the
Hôtel de Ville during the night of March 18, at which (we are told) "a
sparsely attended meeting of the Central Committee spins in circles, in a
confused dialogue," Lefebvre speaks of the missing Blanqui as the only revolutionary capable of conceiving the specific situation of March 18 "in its
totality" (281).

Was Thiers's imprisonment of Blanqui thus the masterstroke that assured
the Commune's eventual demise? Would a single charismatic leader have
served to tame the organizational anarchy that arose through the proliferation of committees, many lacking a strong unity of purpose, in what the
Commune's own delegate for war, Louis Rossel, would call "this incoher-
ent revolution" (quoted in Edwards, 226)?[6] To argue in the affirmative
would be to miss the extent to which the Commune fully exemplified what
Claude Lefort has more recently argued is a fundamental precept of true
democracy: the fact that, in democracy, "the *place of* power is . . . tacitly
recognized as an empty place, unoccupiable by definition—a symbolic
place, not a real one" (126).[7]

In one respect, Marx's reading of the Commune is fully compatible with
Lefort's analysis. By insisting that all governmental officials be elected by
universal suffrage, by making them permanently subject to recall, and by
paying them no more than a worker's wage, the Commune is said to have
effected a "shattering [*Sprengung*]" of the Bonapartist state, with its twenty-
year track record of repression and corruption, and to have replaced it with
a "new and truly democratic" state power (Engels, introduction, 33).[8] And
yet, from the perspective of the late twentieth or early twenty-first century,
Marx's analysis fails sufficiently to account for the specifically *symbolic* nature
of that empty place which is the space of power in a democratic frame, the
fact that any figure of democratic power is never more than a placeholder.

It is into this breach that Henri Lefebvre steps with his 1965 study, *La
Proclamation de la Commune*. Composed concurrently with the second volume of his *Critique de la vie quotidienne*, in what Lefebvre himself has called
a "state of confusion" brought on by his quitting the Communist Party
amid the turmoil of the Algerian War, *La Proclamation* is best known for

having precipitated Lefebvre's final break with Guy Debord and, more substantively, for the way it highlighted questions of revolutionary festivity and symbolic action in the historical run-up to the events of May 1968 (Ross, "Lefebvre," 71f.).[9]

As one might expect of a text that antedates both the French intelligentsia's turn from communism (1976–77) and the fall of the Soviet Union (1991), Lefebvre's book gives much time to a series of debates that no longer resonate with their original force.[10] The book remains vital, however, and is especially interesting in the way it uses analysis of the Commune as lived experience so as actively to inflect the Marxist take on revolutionary confusion.

Near the end of *La Proclamation*, Lefebvre chides "the Stalinists, avowed or shamefaced," for their ritual critique of the Commune's "incoherencies" and their bemoaning "the manifest lack of a political 'apparatus,'" adding:

> It is thus time no longer to see the Commune as the typical example of a
> revolutionary primitivism whose errors have been overcome, but rather as
> an immense experiment, both negative and positive in its implications,
> whose truth we have not yet recovered and fulfilled. (392)

Adopting this approach, Lefebvre insists elsewhere, does not mean eschewing "the demands of analysis and historical exposition" (22). A historical narrative, like Lefebvre's own reconstruction of March 18, must indeed account for both "the confusion and disorder of the facts" *and* "the order that they divulge," such as the strategies of Thiers's forces or the embryonic structures of the nascent Commune (233). In order to unpack such an order, however, one must focus specifically on the manner in which "Paris lived its revolutionary passion," thus coming to terms with an essential confusion to which the strictly analytical approach remains blind (22).

What I take to be the heart of Lefebvre's argument begins with his differentiating the latent spirit of nineteenth-century French political and social life from its German counterpart. If the German spirit was theoretical and epic in character, he suggests, its French counterpart was fundamentally dramatic and grounded in praxis, such that "in France, needs and actions are directly theoretical" (20). This spirit, Lefebvre notes, "is not incumbent upon individuals and indeed is only incompletely reflected in the consciousness, ideology or work of individuals. It falls rather to the people and to the nation, as the confused and powerful unity of the various social strata and classes that make up the people" (20).

Drawing heavily upon an unpublished diary he had found in the holdings of the Feltrinelli Foundation in Milan, Lefebvre stresses how the events of March 18 evolved "in an atmosphere of popular festival" (Ross, "Lefebvre," 78).[11] Compare Lefebvre's account of the March 18 fraternization—

> The immense crowd surrounds the soldiers and paralyses the movement of cannons. Groups form. Money is raised to offer bread and wine to the famished and parched soldiers (who had not brought along their rucksacks). People chat. They cry, "Long live the army!" Cafés and cabarets are opened. Housewives go home to fetch their humble provisions, which they spread out on tables. The crowd fêtes and regales the soldiers. Several go so far as to exchange their rifles for a glass of wine. The seething mass becomes a community, becomes a communion. (*Proclamation*, 245)

—with the following, more programmatic passage:

> The Paris Commune? It was above all an immense and grandiose fête, a fête that the people of Paris, essence and symbol of the French people and people in general, offered to itself and to the world. A festival of spring in the City, of the disinherited and the working class; a revolutionary fête and fête of the Revolution; a total festival, the greatest of modern times, unfolding from the beginning in magnificence and joy. (20–21)

In an idiom that reminds us how tightly Lefebvre's thought of the early 1960s was interwoven with that of Guy Debord, Lefebvre acknowledges that the "spectacle" which the people staged for itself in moments of Communard festivity "diverts it [*le détourne*] from itself," thus assuring the Commune's transformation into a form of "absolute tragedy, a Promethean drama played without a trace of frivolity" (22).[12] In nearly the same breath, however, Lefebvre suggests a more necessary link between festivity and tragedy:

> But from the outset, the Fête contained within itself drama in its primordial sense: a collective and real festivity, lived by the people and for the people, a colossal festivity attended by the voluntary sacrifice of the principal actor in the throes of his failure—tragedy. (22)

Inasmuch as Lefebvre appears to need the willing self-sacrifice of the Commune's principal actor (the people) in order to explain how "the scattered and divided city becomes a community of actions, and how, in the course of the Fête, the community becomes communion"—inasmuch, in other words, as tragedy "clears the way for a fundamental spontaneity"—it is by no means self-evident that one can still speak of the fall into tragedy as a hijacking, a *détournement* (22, 409).[13]

What is the ideological usefulness of Lefebvre's conception of festivity? At times, it effects a reversal of values, allowing Lefebvre to speak of those who possess nothing, and who use the fête to overcome a dearth of time and space in their everyday lives, as the "truly rich" (124). At others, it initiates a dialectical movement, whereby Lefebvre looks beyond an apparent decline of drama and festivity in the contemporary world to the dialectical over-coming of that decline in a "metamorphosis of (everyday) life into an end-less fête"—a transformation whose means, he suggests, "are here, at our disposal, in techniques and machines, in electronics and cybernetics" (39–40).[14] In both instances, festivity appears closely linked to what is arguably the master concept of Lefebvre's work, that of "everyday life."[15]

For my purposes, however, what is crucial about Lefebvre's festivity is the way it foregrounds significant confoundings, significant breakdowns of habitual distinction. At the heart of what Lefebvre variously calls the "seeth-ing" or "fused" mass, the barriers or dams separating public life from private life, the street from the house, political life from everyday life are, as he puts it, "blown up" (245, 181).[16] In the Commune, Lefebvre writes,

> social practice . . . transforms itself immediately into community, into communion, within which work, joy, leisure, the satisfaction of needs—and above all, social needs and the need for sociability—can no longer be severed one from the other. (389)

No confounding is more fundamental to Lefebvre's argument, however, than the overcoming of class divisions through the festive constitution of "the people" In *La Proclamation*, "the people" is variously an inclusive and an exclusive designation, pointing at times to a "confused and powerful unity of the various social strata and classes," at others to the "disinherited," the "proletarians" (20–21). Lefebvre plainly knows how to finesse this ten-sion, as when he writes that the Commune was "brought about by the peo-ple of the capital in their entirety (excepting only the elements of black reaction), animated by the proletarian core" (33). Yet read against the back-drop of Marxist theory, and especially of the debate over the dictatorship of the proletariat, Lefebvre's argument comes down squarely on the side of a spontaneous revolutionary festivity emblematized by the events of March 18—a festivity that manifests "a fundamental will to change the world, life, and things such as they are, a spontaneity pregnant with the highest form of thought, a total revolutionary project" (23).

If the revolutionary fête is thus coextensive with the constitution of the "people" as a "confused and powerful unity," the catalyst of that unity is a still more fundamental confusion. In the crucial third part of his book, titled "The Ideologies and Prestige of the Commune," Lefebvre argues that the success of the Paris Commune depended upon the power of certain confused yet profound images, images that operate not on the level of fully elaborated ideology but, rather, "on that of a social consciousness inserted directly into praxis" (126).

Consider, for example, the image of Paris. One should, and Lefebvre does, ask how the Commune was shaped by such geographic and demographic trends as the gentrification and emptying out of Paris's center, and the corresponding proletarianization of the peripheral quarters (131ff.). But such analysis suffices only if it helps account for that naïve, but politically powerful, image of Paris inviolate that arises in reaction to the trauma that was the city's violation:

> the image of Paris, that which the Parisian people have of their city—a powerful image, figure of a city holy and inviolable, both a cradle of liberty and liberty's preferred home. We shall see that it is impossible, without this image underlying ideologies, compared to which it is more confused and more profound, to understand the Commune's prestige and to explain its political existence. (120–121)

Several pages later, Lefebvre returns to the power of confusion in an analysis of Manichaean representation, said to have reigned in the mid-to-late nineteenth century "in all its freshness and spontaneity" (122). Implicitly enrolling Marx himself in the critique of those, such as Althusser,[17] whose fetishizing of theoretical rigor causes them to miss the practical *effect* of certain so-called errors, Lefebvre writes:

> Marx's analysis leads us to think that Manichaean dualism, repudiated by scientific consciousness, nonetheless constitutes a naïve but strong form of class consciousness. Despite their confusion and their obscurity, *or perhaps on account of their confusion and their obscurity*, the images of poverty and of wealth align the people and proletariat on one side, the bourgeoisie, aristocracy, and dominant classes on the other. . . . Representations from this period were thus given to misunderstandings and illusions, even to egregious errors with respect to scientific concepts. And yet never perhaps will class consciousness prove to have been so quick, so lively and complex, so charged with affect, so animated and efficient, so tied up with a consciousness of history. (125, 127; emphasis added)

Rather than dismiss revolutionary slogans and myths as vague, obscure, or confused, far better to ask how they accomplish a "unity in action," how they exemplify "social consciousness inserted directly into praxis"—indeed, how they "enter into" life itself (140, 126, 390). Arguing against those who would clamor for "a political party that is centralized and monolithic, armed with an ideology and a rigorously coherent theory," Lefebvre goes so far as to suggest that the unity of action so characteristic of the Commune would have been irreparably harmed by "premature ideological clarification" (140). Without the confusions and vagaries of decidedly unscientific binaries, utopias, myths, and slogans, Lefebvre argues against his rigorist counterparts, there quite literally would have been no Commune.[18]

The crucial terms behind Lefebvre's thus linking the confusion and the Commune are *spontanéité,* on the one hand, and *le vécu* on the other. Of the "experience of 1871"—note the focus on *le vécu*—he writes, "This experience [or experiment, *expérience*] was realized in a great confusion, that inherent to spontaneous and creative life" (140).[19] Throughout *La Proclamation,* Lefebvre sees the Commune's unarguable weakness as clearing the ground for an essential spontaneity. Thus, in the wake of his calling Communard ideology "a very confused ideologico-political complex," Lefebvre writes:

> The junction and imbrication of these disparate elements [the Commune's myths, utopias, and ideologies] constitutes a political and ideological "complex" of a prodigious power, since it unites affect and volition, dream and thought, past and future. This ideological power—a truly explosive mixture, destined to clear the way for the most spontaneous of forces—contains within itself the seeds of its loss. In the trial by practice, the mixture cannot help but explode into heterogeneous fragments. (136, 138)

This passage is interesting on several levels. Lefebvre's analysis gives pride of place to the way certain naïvetés enter into revolutionary practice, thus opening the way for spontaneous creation. But in the case of the Commune—as indeed in the case of May 1968, three years later—the ideological mix that was the source of the uprising's spontaneity appears to have contained within itself the seeds of its demise, and this precisely to the extent that this ideological mix underwent a "trial by practice."[20] Curiously, an analysis that seeks to counter theoreticist rigor with an awareness of how specific naïvetés, confusions, and the like effectively enter into revolutionary practice, helping to constitute the people as a "confused and powerful unity," thus ends with the dispersal of that unity "in heterogeneous fragments." Indeed, the most tangible gain therefrom may well be theoretical, since "in the seething confusion, Marx perceived and cast his lot with a force projecting itself toward the future"—namely, his theory of the withering away of the state (390).

One final remark on the ramifications of this projection. In several of the literary texts I will be reading in subsequent chapters, including Zola's *Débâcle* and the two late works by Flaubert, the enactment of confusion grows out of a specifically bourgeois melancholy attributable to the Commune as traumatic event. The textualization of confusion originates, in other words, in what Dominick LaCapra has called a "compulsive repetition of traumatic scenes—scenes in which the past returns and the future is blocked or fatalistically caught up in a melancholic feedback loop" (21).

Lefebvre's account is by no means blind to trauma. The failure of the Commune, in his reading, announces a "long crisis" of European revolutionism that culminates in the traumatic experiences of Stalinism and fascism. Still, Lefebvre's analysis is resolute in its linking of confusion to an essential futurity, where the anticipation of what might be implicitly forestalls the fall back into melancholy. Thus he writes, of the Parisian masses:

> Their disorder contains within itself a new virtual order. . . . The Commune anticipated, through action, both the possible and the impossible. As a result, even unfeasible projects and decisions, like the federative project, which never went beyond the status of political intentions, retain a profound meaning. (390)

One might tax this position as naïve, but is it not precisely Lefebvre's contention that such naïvetés can and do have a profound political effect?[21]

Beyond the Commune

After this brief (and I hope focusing) survey of the various grounds on which the Commune has been deemed confused, let us pick up our brief history of the period where it left off.

The Damoclean sword hanging over the head of the Commune for nearly all of its two-month existence was the army of Versailles. During the night of May 21 and 22, that army entered Paris through the city's largely unguarded western gates, thus initiating what would come to be called *la semaine sanglante* (the bloody week) (May 22–28).

Why did the Commune fall?[22] Versailles's strengthening of its army's resolve through a propaganda campaign designed to highlight Communard "atrocities" (many of them fictional) surely helped the government avoid a repeat of the fraternization of March 18. Equally significant was the fact that the Prussian army allowed the troops of Versailles to enter neutral territory in order to take the 17th and 18th arrondissements, including the Butte de Montmartre, from the north. But the principal military responsibility for the Commune's fall lies with the Parisians themselves. The lack of any centrally planned strategy for the city's defense, coupled with the Communards' quasi-mythic reverence for the barricade, suggest that they valued a spontaneous, fraternal defense of individual working-class quarters over a more unified strategy. From a military perspective, the Commune's commitment to the building of decentralized revolutionary communities was very much its undoing.

Zola's *Débâcle* includes a marvelously apocalyptic scene in which Jean Macquart, in the uniform of the French army, rows his wounded Communard friend, Maurice Levasseur, across the Seine as Paris burns: "The boat seemed to be floating on a river of fire. In the dancing reflections of these huge conflagrations the Seine appeared to be bearing along blazing coals" (893/491). No image from the *semaine sanglante* has proven as tenacious and as powerful as that of Paris aflame. Although many of the most notable fires (such as those at the Palais Royal, the Louvre, the Tuileries Palace, and the Hôtel de Ville) were set by retreating Communards, others (including fires at the Ministry of Finance and at numerous private residences) were started by incendiary shells launched by Versailles.

In the immediate aftermath of the *semaine sanglante*, rumors abounded that the fires were the work of a group of savage, debauched, unkempt, and unsexed incendiary she-devils, collectively known as *les pétroleuses*. In her *Unruly Women of Paris,* Gay Gullickson shows that the figure of the *pétroleuse* is

> the product of two cultural phenomena: a long-standing Western iconographic tradition that made allegorical figures female, and dichotomous cultural conceptualizations of female nature which made it possible for them to represent both good and evil, the natural and the unnatural. (219–21)

Abundantly referenced in caricatures and eyewitness accounts of the Commune, the largely mythic figure of the *pétroleuse* served to shift public attention away from the atrocities committed by the government in the wake of the Commune, and thus helped assure that the Commune would lose what Gullickson calls the "war of representation" (218).

To gauge the full extent of that loss, consider the actual casualty figures on both sides of the battle. Over the course of the *semaine sanglante*, the Commune and its supporters killed approximately seventy hostages, including the archbishop of Paris. By contrast, the days and weeks that followed the Commune's fall saw upwards of 25,000 Parisians killed, some for the most spurious of reasons (as when the Marquis de Gallifet ordered 111 white-haired prisoners shot, on the grounds that they were old enough to have fought on the barricades in 1848) (Edwards, 344). Of the nearly 50,000 Communards arrested, approximately 4,500 would be incarcerated in France, and an equal number deported to the brutally inhospitable camps of New Caledonia. As early as May 29, just one day after Marshal MacMahon assured upper-class Parisians of a return to "order, work and security," *The Times* of London—no great admirer of the Commune—would tell its readers that "the wholesale executions inflicted by the Versailles soldiery, the triumph, the glee, the ribaldry of the 'party of Order,' sicken the soul" (quoted in Lefebvre, 388; Edwards, 345). And yet, thanks to countless references to the death of the archbishop and repeated representations of the notorious *pétroleuses*, it was the image of specifically Communard barbarities that would haunt France's collective imagination in the decades to come.

However anarchic the purgations and repressions that followed upon the Commune may have been, the events played a crucial unifying function—in one instance immediately, in the other at a temporal remove. For much of the half-century leading up to the Commune, the French bourgeoisie had been split into multiple factions; Legitimists (supporters of the older branch of the Bourbon dynasty) had been at odds with their Orleanist counterparts, Bonapartists with Republicans, and so on. But the very threat of a working-class regime effectively closed these divides. As Stewart Edwards writes, "This temporary junction lasted sufficiently to give birth to the Third Republic and to the establishment of parliamentary democracy in France" (363).

On the side of the working class, this unifying effect was more belated. Thanks to the Commune's defeat and to the execution, detention, deportation, or exile of so many of its leaders, French working-class political organizations remained severely weakened for the better part of a decade. As Dominique Lejeune has noted, socialism resurfaced in France only in the 1880s, triggered by economic depression, the deleterious effects of industrialization, mounting popular dissatisfaction with the moderate republican regime, and the passage of a general amnesty for Communards in July 1880 (53). For its unity of purpose, this renascent working-class movement would need to look no farther than to the Commune and its brutal repression. Indeed, the execution of captured Communards at the Père-Lachaise cemetery on May 27, at what would come to be called the *mur des fédérés* (wall of the federals), has served as one of the "founding traumas" of the modern French Left—"founding" in the sense that it became "the valorized or intensely cathected basis of identity for an individual or a group rather than [posing] the problematic question of identity" (LaCapra, 23).

The Third Republic

Each of the literary texts I analyze in subsequent chapters addresses the Paris Commune—directly or indirectly—through a negotiation with confusion. But the confusions seemingly endemic to the Commune are only part of the story here. Nearly as significant, although surely less traumatic, were the confusions inherent in French political and cultural life in the early years of the Third Republic, at the time these texts were in fact written.

Where Henri Lefebvre has served as our modern-day Virgil to the particular muddle that was the Commune, Theodore Zeldin can fill that same role for the Third Republic. In the *Politics and Anger* volume of his magisterial *France 1848–1945*, Zeldin repeats and refines the historical commonplace that sees the Third Republic as "one of the most confusing and paradoxical of political regimes": "It was supposed to mark the advent of democracy, but it produced disconcertingly little fundamental change in the structure of the state, which remained monarchical, or even *ancien régime*, in many ways" (206). Ostensibly a "free, egalitarian and fraternal society" predicated on the value of consensus, the Third Republic was in fact run by "an oligarchy of discredited professional politicians," who catered to the interests of influential constituents while choosing to ignore widespread corruption (206). In France's first durable republican regime, Zeldin finds "an extraordinary gap between the principles which were proclaimed as guiding the politicians and the legislation actually passed": "Confused and inconsistent programmes were advocated in the name of logic and rationality. . . . It does not help matters that the right-wing parties call themselves left wing, and that the radicals turn out to be conservatives" (206).[23]

As to why this "apparently chaotic system" was "tolerated, even popular," Zeldin argues that it prospered because it "protected values which were deeply cherished, even if they were not popularly admitted" (207). Just what were those closely held, if unspoken, values? And how did they help secure the republic's improbable survival?

In an essay on the hysteria diagnosis in Third Republic France, Jan Goldstein eloquently states a paradox to which nearly all who write on the early republic subscribe: "In its opening years, the Third Republic was painfully unsure of its political identity—republican largely as an accident of history, controlled in fact by monarchists and anti–Communard, proclerical upholders of what was called 'the moral order'" ("Diagnosis," 228). Only a series of missteps by the various Monarchist factions—most notably, the Comte de Chambord's refusal to accept the tricolor as the national flag of France, opening the way for MacMahon's presidency in 1873—forestalled a seemingly inevitable restoration.

What this argument tends to obscure is the fact that, in the wake of the Commune, Monarchists and Republicans reached a relative consensus around the values of "peace," "order," and "work"—thus concealing, at least for a time, a fundamental fault line separating partisans of a secular, liberal state and those who saw religion as the prime guarantor of social order (Mayeur, 10–11). Likewise, the argument ignores the speed with which supposed Monarchists made their peace with the new Republican order. As Dominique Lejeune notes, Adolphe Thiers (the former Orleanist minister who served as first president of the Third Republic) moved quickly, if at first tacitly, into the ranks of committed Republicans—a move that culminated in his full profession of Republican faith in an address to the Assembly on November 13, 1872 (29). In the final analysis, the Third Republic survived in part because its partisans spoke forcefully to the social and economic aspirations of that *couche sociale nouvelle* (Gambetta's phrase for the petite and middle bourgeoisie) whose importance had been significantly strengthened by the Second Empire, in part because they knew how to enlist the rural electorate by projecting "the image of a wise, fraternal Marianne, of a Republic both conservative and egalitarian" (Mayeur, 51–52).

In January 1875, the Third Republic was formally established with the passage of a new constitution. Ironically, the specific impetus for this document, which split legislative powers between the Senate and Chamber of Deputies (the latter elected by direct manhood suffrage) and fixed the president's term of office at seven years, came from the Orleanists. Finding themselves unable to effect an immediate restoration, supporters of the Comte de Paris sought to establish "institutions that were sufficiently supple as to favor such a restoration in the future" (Lejeune, 37). Composed of but three laws and lacking any explicit proclamation of fundamental principles, the Constitution of 1875 was in essence a compromise between Monarchist and Republican factions and lacked "the qualities which most theorists had recommended and generations of statesmen had striven for: logic, clarity, order, and completeness" (Zeldin, 207). But, like the republic whose foundation it was, the Constitution of 1875 survived because its very inefficiency "allowed unprecedented free play to . . . prejudices, private interests and local customs," because it "based itself on *débrouillage*, the art of getting by somehow" (Zeldin, 208).

The years immediately following passage of the constitution were marked by bitter conflicts between Legitimists and Orleanists, strong Republican control of the Chamber of Deputies, and the failed clericalist coup d'état of May 16, 1877, the effect of which was to "prove again to the country the incompetency of the monarchists" (Bodley, 877). But it was only with the election of Jules Grévy as president in January 1879, which assured Republican control of both the presidency and the legislature, that the so-called *république des ducs* (republic of dukes) gave way to a republic of Republicans. The debacle of the *seize mai* and this subsequent consolidation of Republican control opened the way to a campaign for free, compulsory, secular education, led by the republic's minister of education, Jules Ferry. Through laws such as those laicizing French universities (February 27, 1880) and promoting secondary education for girls (December 21, 1880), Ferry and his allies aimed to solidify the republic while promoting equality of opportunity and favoring "a unitary vision of the national community" (Lejeune, 60; Mayeur, 113 ff.).

Consolidation of the republican system also triggered a reprise of colonial expansionism, largely stalled since the fall of the Second Empire. Designed to buttress that nationalist sentiment so sorely tried by the Second Empire's humiliating withdrawal from Mexico in 1867, under pressure from the United States, and by defeat at the hands of the Prussians in 1870, the colonialist wave of the early 1880s saw the annexation of Tahiti (1880) and the establishment of French protectorates in Tunisia (1881), Tonkin and Annam (1885), and Madagascar (1885) (Lejeune, 144 ff.).

Interrogating the Sphinx

For the purposes of this study, however, the most significant cultural development in early Third Republic France was doubtless the widespread attempt—by scientists, doctors, and laypersons alike—to pathologize social revolt. Either directly or indirectly, arguments around the concepts of "degeneration," "moral contagion," "hysteria," and "alcoholism" became ways of interrogating the Commune—in Marx's memorable phrase, "that sphinx so tantalizing to the bourgeois mind" ("Civil War," 68).

On March 24, 1871, with the Commune in its infancy, historian Hippolyte Taine wrote in a letter to his wife that "never was the decomposition of society more evident" (quoted in Edwards, 175). Published over the course of two decades, Taine's massive history of revolutionary and imperial France, *Les Origines de la France contemporaine* (1876–94), argues that a process of decomposition originating in the French Revolution culminated in the events of the *année terrible*, most notably, the Franco–Prussian War and Paris Commune. In the process, Taine suggests that social revolt itself can "gravely disturb the body and mind, and indeed set off an epidemic of insanity" (Pick, 69).

In one sense, this argument was not particularly new. Immediately following the February Revolution of 1848, Brierre de Boismont had suggested that French society contained a "considerable floating mass" of potential madmen, the signs of whose future madness included "general irritability, flightiness, loosely knit logic, and . . . extreme impressionability" (Goldstein, "Contagion," 210). Yet, as Daniel Pick has shown, late nineteenth-century France saw a marked displacement of the

> dominant scene of degeneration . . . from the individual (specific cretins, criminals, the insane and so on) and even the family (whose neuropathic strains were explored by Féré and Magnan) to society itself—crowds, masses, cities, modernity. (4; cf. 222)

"It took national defeat by Prussia and the Paris Commune," Pick writes, "to seal the importance of this word [*dégénérescence*] in historiography, social diagnosis, cultural critique" (50).[24]

In the months and years that followed the Commune, one finds a more or less rationalist reduction of the uprising to a "normal," even "foreseeable" manifestation of psychological truisms masquerading as social laws. To the extent that this reduction entailed what Jan Goldstein sees as a progressive "confusion and conflation of the medical and political spheres," it is at least partly attributable to what Goldstein calls "the consistent tendency of the French psychiatric profession . . . to gravitate towards an alliance with the French state" ("Contagion," 191; "Diagnosis," 221).

The act of marshaling medical and psychiatric categories in the diagnosis of revolutionary events reached what is arguably its most hysterical pitch in the writings of Maxime du Camp, for whom the Commune variously evinced a bad case of delirium tremens, a "furious and epidemic pyromania," or an "attack of raging envy and social epilepsy" (quoted in Glazer 64, 69; and in Lidsky, 47). In *Les Convulsions de Paris*, Du Camp's metaphoric zeal leads him to attribute the Commune to a national form of "hydrocephalus," as the scum of the provinces is suctioned into the "enlarged head" that is Paris, to ferment therein (quoted in Lidsky, 57–58).

More interesting in this regard, because it emanates from two men of science, is Vigouroux and Juqelier's designation of alcoholics, hysterics, and degenerates as *contagionnables*, responsible for setting off a series of events that would in turn help spread the contagion of madness (Glazer, 67). As Jan Goldstein has shown, the concept of "moral contagion" enjoyed a significant vogue in post–Commune France, lending a certain scientific credibility to those who opposed the growing trend toward political democratization and, in the process, helping to found the new sciences of crowd psychology, criminology, and sociology ("Contagion," 182). Even the usually level-headed Freud was swept up in the vogue. On arriving in Paris to work with Charcot in 1885, Freud would write to Minna Bernays that the Parisians are "of a different species from ourselves," a "people given to psychical epidemics, historical mass convulsions" (*Letters,* 187–88).

As Paul Lidsky meticulously demonstrated in his 1969 study, *Les Écrivains contre la Commune*, the vast majority of French literati shared in, and served as mouthpieces for, a generalized sense of bourgeois panic in the face of supposed Communard barbarism. At times, as in Du Camp, this involved seeing the Commune as the manifestation of a psychosocial pathology. Thus Edmond de Goncourt sees abject drunkenness in the faces of the National Guard on March 19 and Flaubert, writing to George Sand on April 30, speaks of Paris as "completely epileptic" as a result of the Versaillais siege (*Journal,* 2:397; *Correspondance,* 4:315). At other times, that generalized sense of panic helps fill the anti–Communard bestiary, as when Théophile Gautier evokes "the hyenas of 93 and the gorillas of the Commune" or when Flaubert speaks of the Communards as "rabid dogs" (quoted in Lidsky, 46, 77).[25] At still other times, the Commune is seen as the result of an international conspiracy masterminded by foreigners who carry "the revolutionary virus" (Lidsky, 67).

But the best gauge of how deeply traumatic the events of the Commune were for bourgeois literati was the extent to which these pathologizing rhetorics were adopted by writers nominally on the left. As we shall see in the following chapter, Lidsky's tone is only slightly hyperbolic when he writes of Zola's depiction of the Commune: "Fever of the besieged, madness of the leaders, bestiality, and demented nightmare are henceforth the only possible explanations for the Commune" (51). Likewise, despite his republicanism, Anatole France characterizes the Commune itself as a "committee of assassins," a band of "rascals," a "government of crime and dementia" (quoted in Lidsky, 54). Even George Sand describes the events as "the Saturnalia of madness" (quoted in Lidsky, 52). In a letter to Flaubert from June 1871, a deeply melancholic Sand writes:

> I, who have such patience with my species and have looked so long on the bright side, now see nothing but darkness. . . . I imagined that all the world could become enlightened, could correct itself, or restrain itself; that the years I had passed with my fellows could not be lost to reason and experience. And now I wake from a dream to find a generation divided between idiocy and delirium tremens. (in Flaubert, *Correspondance,* 4:335/ *2:178*)

As Lidsky well observes, the cumulative effect of these various rhetorical strategies—the pathologization of social action, the depiction of Communards as bandits or beasts, the apocalyptic sense of a fall into darkness—was to deny the Commune any specifically *political* import, in favor of a more mythic or melodramatic vision of it as "an apocalypse, a catastrophe of Biblical nature" (46). Just how these representations might have grown out of, and fed, a widespread sense of melancholy is a question to be addressed in the following chapter.

2   *The Time of Our Melancholy: Zola's* Débâcle

If there is anything on which contemporary readers of Zola's *La Débâcle* have tended to agree, it is that the novel evinces an ideological complexity which belies the relative simplicity of its characterization. Lucienne Frappier-Mazur, for example, shows how competing conceptions of national identity in Zola's 1892 novel on the Franco–Prussian war and subsequent Paris Commune reemerge as an "oscillation" between a pacifistic acceptance of the other and a call for purificatory retribution ("Guerre," 180). Sandy Petrey speaks of *La Débâcle* as imprisoned in an interstice insofar as it chooses both nature *and* artifice, nature *and* history (94, 88). Or, closer to the specific dynamic I want to examine here, Charles Stivale argues that the novel's "moralizing dénouement" reproduces a "tendentious ambivalence" characteristic of Zola's political writing on the Commune (151).

The aim of this chapter is to use the concept of "confusion" in the wide range of its manifestations in *La Débâcle*—military, historical, ideological, sexual, and so on—to unpack the several forms of ideological ambivalence at the heart of Zola's novel. No other text of Zola's uses the term "confusion" as often or to such patently critical effect, yet that critical thrust is curiously undercut by the novel's deployment of confusion to specific aesthetic ends. In the first section of this chapter, I explore the tension between Zola's critique of confusion and his recourse thereto in terms of a larger pattern of disavowal typical of Zola's plotting. This focus on disavowal leads, in the chapter's middle section, to an analysis of the melancholic ambivalence inherent in Zola's take on Republican ideology. Drawing upon the work of Daniel Pick, I show how the melancholy of Zola's narrator and his contemporaries—the "our melancholy" of this chapter's title—is resonant with a form of disavowal implicit in late nineteenth-century theories of racial degeneration. In the third and final section, I focus on the ways in which the novel's representation of the Paris Commune entails a play of melancholic self-violence and paranoid suspiciousness that, in the wake of

Freud and Melanie Klein, I see as melancholic or depressive in its very ambivalence. Crucial to the first section, and again to the third, is the question
of how Zola's novel, written over two decades after the events of *l'année
terrible*, was shaped by a continuing need to work through the anxieties and
traumas occasioned by those events. More overtly than in any of the other
literary texts that are the subject of this study, the textualization of confusion
in *La Débâcle* is thus a first step toward confusion's (always provisional)
overcoming.

Confusion, Anxiety, Disavowal

> Never had there been a greater muddle, nor more anxiety.
> —Emile Zola, *La Débâcle*

> In practice, in 1870, the most unimaginable confusion reigns;
> contradictory rules and orders follow one upn the other. Plans to
> mobilize, transport and equip French troops are executed badly, or
> not at all.
> —Henri Lefebvre, *La Proclamation de la Commune*

Some 200 pages into *La Débâcle*, we find its protagonist, Maurice Levasseur, lying with his regiment in a cabbage field during the opening hours of
the battle of Sedan. Having overheard a report that Marshal MacMahon had
been wounded and that the French army was in retreat to the north, Maurice reflects upon "the confusion and final chaos into which the army was
falling, with no chief, no plan, pulled in every direction, while the Germans
were making straight for their goal with their clear judgment and machinelike precision" (600 f./*213*).

I think it fair to say that no reader of *La Débâcle* has ever been surprised
by these thoughts. In the pages leading up to this moment, Zola meticulously details the disarray of a French army led by the mere "shadow emperor," engaged in a series of futile marches and countermarches, and ill-
provisioned to the point of lacking even a map of France (444/*64*, 472/*90*).[1]
In a crucial passage juxtaposing the sources of Prussian strength with those
of French weakness, the Alsatian Weiss—husband of Maurice's sister, Henriette—speaks of the empire as having weakened allegiance to the French
fatherland by compromising individual liberty, and of the French army itself
as weighed down by the laurels of its victories in the Crimea and Italy, cor-
rupted by a system of hired replacement soldiers, too certain of victory to

modernize its forces, and led by a pack of mostly mediocre, rival generals (413/34–35).[2]

Above all, however, Zola's novel attributes the disarray of the French army leading up to Sedan to the contagious effect of an inaction at the very top of the chain of command—"a slow paralysis, starting at the top from the Emperor, a sick man incapable of any quick decision, which was beginning to creep through the entire army and disorganize it, reduce it to nothing" (410/31). As an effect of what the novel calls the "complete effacing of the emperor," in other words, the reader is invited to feel an "infinite dismay and indecision, contrary plans fighting one another and replacing each other from hour to hour" (443/63). The very insistence with which first Maurice (in I, iii), then Delaherche (in II, vi), seek to lay eyes on the deathly figure of Napoléon III—their tormented need "to see and know"—is symptomatic of that erasure (495/111). But this effacing of the emperor also anticipates the novel's oft-remarked effacing of the Commune's historical leaders (see Stivale, 149; Petrey, "République," 88). In *La Débâcle,* the existence of such a void in the space of power, legitimate or otherwise, is not meant to allow for the advent of true democracy (as we saw that it does for Lefort) or for a spontaneous popular revolutionism (as Lefebvre argues in his reading of the Commune). Rather, it is the effect of a pathology, both medical and sociopolitical, a pathology underscored by the novel's insistence on the manipulative machinations of the Spanish-born Empress Eugénie, marching the emperor off to a certain death "with all her obstinate determination" (443/63).[3]

In Zola's representation, the confusion pursuant to this lack of political and military leadership afflicting France at the fall of the Second Empire is compounded by the jingoistic victory fantasies of the Parisian press, the inevitable deflation of which leads to a crisis of faith in the very idea of the French nation:

> The final effect of these continuous lies in the papers was disastrous. The men had lost all confidence and no longer believed anything. The imaginings of these overgrown children, at first so fertile in wild hopes, were now collapsing into wild nightmares. (587/*199–200*)

> And then again more confusion and the most contradictory theories about plans the generals might have. As though he had been cut off from the world, Maurice only learned then what had happened in Paris: the stupefying shock of defeat on a whole people certain of victory, the terrible

outburst of emotion in the streets, the recall of both Chambers, the fall of the liberal administration that had organized the plebiscite, the Emperor deprived of the title of Commander-in-Chief and forced to hand over the supreme command to Marshal Bazaine. (442–443/*62*)

In whipping up a hysterical rhythm of hope and despair, the press plays into a propensity that Zola's narrator sees as inscribed in the very "temperament" of the French "race":

The whole temperament of the race showed itself in this sublime confidence suddenly crashing down with the first reversal of fortune into a despair that galloped away with these lost soldiers, defeated and scattered before ever striking a blow. (426/*47*)

What this constant disillusionment of hope is said to effectively kill is the great legend of the Napoleonic army, in which

periods ran into one another [*se confondaient*], and it all seemed to be independent of history in a terrible collision of all nations. English, Austrians, Prussians, Russians passed by in turn and together, in passing alliances, and it was not always possible to know why some were beaten rather than others. But in the end they all were beaten, beaten inevitably in advance, in a surge of heroism and genius that swept armies away like straw. (447/*67*)

As Maurice's reflections in the cabbage field clearly suggest, Zola's remedies to the confusions that beset the French army and the society of which it is a reflection include logic, mathematical calculation, machinelike rectitude, dispassionate method, and the sense of overarching fatality that follows therefrom (453/*72–73*). Although Maurice is granted insight into the power of these traits and habits of mind, the novel clearly situates them on the side of the Prussians, with a partial and significant exception made for the Alsatian Weiss.

In one significant respect, however, Zola's remedy appears to partake of the original poison. That sense of fatality by which the novel's more insightful characters—and, by extension, the text as a whole—attempt to rise above the ambient confusion suggests a certain investment, both aesthetic and ideological, in legendary mythification. For if, in the epic tales of Maurice's grandfather, those nations which dare to take on the Napoleonic military machine are "beaten inevitably in advance," so too, quite obviously, are the French in Zola's novel. Much of the aesthetic effect of *La Débâcle*'s brilliant opening chapter depends upon its fostering in the reader an anxious waiting for that death and disaster which Zola's characters, though deprived of the insight embedded in the novel's title, plainly know to be coming. I would argue that the function of the at first sight surprising "but" in the following extract ("But a great shiver of excitement had run through . . .") is precisely to divert our attention away from the ways in which the novel's sense of overarching fatality ("the inexorable law") serves mythically to disavow the fundamental complexity of historical phenomena, suggested here by the phrase "so that now nobody really knew which side the provocation had come from":[4]

> People argued about this candidature of a German prince for the throne of Spain, and in the confusion that had gradually developed everybody seemed in the wrong, so that now nobody really knew which side the provocation had come from, and the one inevitable thing had remained unaltered, the inexorable law which at a given moment throws one nation against another. But a great shiver of excitement had run through Paris, and he could still see that burning evening, with crowds surging along the boulevards, bands waving torches and shouting, "To Berlin! To Berlin." (408/30)

Zola's text knows full well, in other words, that the question of who touched off the Franco–Prussian War is a highly vexed one. Yet it silences that question by positing a transcendent law whereby peoples, like animals in the wild, are fated to struggle for their survival. A confusion native to the question of political motives, and by extension to the very writing of history, is thus effectively erased by the novel's recourse to the confusion of the hysterical crowd.

It is certainly no surprise that Zola, the novelist of the hereditary flaw, would so patently espouse a fatality inscribed in the reader's foreknowledge of the historical events his novel tracks. What is surprising, however, is that this master of the rhythms of rising dramatic tension would have devoted the entirety of *La Débâcle*'s first part—over 160 pages in the Pléiade edition—to a seemingly endless succession of scenes marked by nothing so much as confusion, inaction, and anxious waiting.

The fundamentally traumatic nature of the events of *l'année terrible* provides an answer to this conundrum. For Freud, as Eric Santner notes, trauma does not arise from the experience of loss per se; rather, it is "the absence of appropriate affect—anxiety—[that] leads to traumatization" (25). Writing along similar lines, but with a Heideggerian twist, Dominick LaCapra characterizes "traumatic *Dasein*" as the experience of

> being back there, anxiously reliving in its immediacy something that was a
> shattering experience for which one was not prepared—for which one did
> not have, in Freud's term, *Angstbereitschaft* (the readiness to feel anxiety).
> (89–90)

In other words, the event from which trauma proceeds is not just, in Cathy Caruth's words, "an event that . . . is experienced too soon, too unexpectedly, to be fully known," Freud's paradigm for such an event being of course the primal scene (*Unclaimed*, 7). It is just as crucially an event for which *one did not know to be anxious*.

But if anxiety for Freud is what "plunges [the ego] into disarray owing to a breaching of [its] protective shield," it also serves as "the ego's guard against future shocks." Anxiety, Ruth Leys writes, "is both *cure* and *cause* of psychic trauma" (28). Might we not interpret the mise-en-scène of anxiety and the fear of death in the seemingly interminable first part of Zola's *Débâcle* as a means of retroactively rectifying a past lack of *Angstbereitschaft*, most tellingly emblematized by the crowds on Parisian streets jubilantly shouting "To Berlin!"? Might not the essentially formalist complaint that the novel's eight opening chapters represent a breach of narrative economy thus miss the essential motive for its enactment of anxiety—a will to work through the traumas of 1870–1871, even at the remove of some twenty years?

This is not to suggest, of course, that Zola's novel does not pursue a definite aesthetic agenda. Although the representation of confusion can at times be linked to a reenactment of anxiety for collective therapeutic effect, at others it sets the stage for aesthetic recuperation. Zola's aesthetic investment in confusion is never more clear than in his representation of crowds at moments of high historical drama. The stunning set piece that is the battle at Bazailles, for example, culminates in Henriette Weiss's becoming "an object, a piece of flotsam washed along in a swirling stream of people [*piétinement confus de foule*] flowing along the road" (642/252). At moments of panic or in the heat of battle, Zola's crowds become little more than a torrent of clothes without the bodies they clothe and separable body parts: "a flood in which could be glimpsed a woman's skirt, a man's jacket, a mane of white hair . . ." (633/243–44). Here, as in *Au Bonheur des dames*, the function of the torrential crowd or mass is to set up a movement of aesthetic recuperation, most strikingly emblematized in *La Débâcle* by that scene in which

King Wilhelm of Prussia surveys the battlefield around Sedan such as to transpose it into a gigantic but "delicate" Impressionist tableau.[5]

> The atrocious, bloody battle itself, seen from such a height in the setting sun, was like a delicate painting: dead horsemen and disemboweled horses flecked the plateau of Floing with gay splashes of color; further to the right, towards Givonne, the final scramble of the retreat made an interesting picture with whirling of black dots running about and falling over themselves; and again on the Iges peninsula to the left a Bavarian battery with its guns the size of matches looked like a piece of nicely adjusted mechanism, for the eye could follow its regular, clockwork movements. It was unhoped-for, overwhelming victory, and the King had no remorse, faced as he was with these tiny corpses, these thousands of men less than the dust on the roads, the great vale in which the fires of Bazailles, the slaughter of Illy, the anguish of Sedan, could not prevent unfeeling nature from being beautiful at this serene end of a perfect day. (687/295)

In this little bit of texual machinery—the literary equivalent of the Bavarian battery as "a piece of nicely adjusted mechanism"—Zola embeds a disavowal of confusion for aesthetic gain in the gaze of the Prussian king.

In my Introduction, I referenced a series of thinkers—from Leibniz and Baumgarten to Ernest Renan—for whom aesthetic experience was integrally dependent upon a certain confusion. Zola's work clearly exemplifies Leibniz's account of sensuous cognition as the coming into consciousness of the confused assembly of "colors, odors, . . . and other particular objects of the senses" (quoted in Barnouw, 30). And, like Renan, he dreams of synthetic scenarios—such as the battlefield gaze of King Wilhelm—where aesthetic appreciation is fully compatible with, indeed partially dependent upon, a certain analytic acumen. But what is arguably most characteristic of Zola's novelistic use of confusion is his inscription of confusion within a scenario of disavowal. We know very well, his texts seem to say, that the experiences of war or revolution (and their echoes in the domains of shopping, theatrical performance, and urban life) derive aesthetic richness from an inherent confusion. Still, that confusion can and must be mastered by a panoptic gaze that is at once analytical, attuned to the fatal laws of history and science, *and* aesthetically sensitive.

Ambivalence

This conclusion is arguably perilous in two respects. It risks overstating the ease with which analytic acumen and aesthetic sensibility can be united in a single agent—a risk that Zola's choice of King Wilhelm, of whom readers otherwise know little, obliquely acknowledges. But it also tends to flatten out the ambivalence of Zola's text in those cases where aesthetic gain comes to undermine ideological critique. Witness, on this point, the telling conjunction of adjectives when the novel's narrator evokes "the *grandiose and monstrous* conception of the destruction of old society . . . so that the idyll of a new golden age might spring to life," or when, in an article for *Le Figaro* defending his novel, Zola writes of the "*beautiful and abominable* legend [of 'our French soldier']" as the real cause of "our frightful disasters" (911/508, 1459; emphasis added).

In order to address the ambivalence of Zola's novel from a specifically ideological point of view, I would like to turn to a passage where this "beautiful and abominable legend" is shown to have its ideological uses. On the eve of October 31, when large numbers of Parisians took to the streets to protest the Government of National Defense's armistice talks with Prussia, we find Maurice back in Paris, figuratively bleeding from the wound of Sedan and infected by a generalized "malady of distrust and daydreaming":

> This was the final stage of the evolution in him which ever since the first battle lost had been destroying the Napoleonic legend and the sentimental Bonapartism he derived from the epic narratives of his grandfather. He had even already left behind theoretical moderate republicanism [*il n'en était plus à la république théorique et sage*] and was tending towards revolutionary violence, believing in the necessity of terror to sweep away the incompetent and the traitors who were busy murdering the fatherland. (860/459)

The crucial word here is "theoretical". When Zola writes in *Le Figaro*, circa 1880, "I am theoretically for the Republic," the word "theoretically" signals the gap between Zola's faith in what Daniel Delas has called "the dynamic of a positive, social Republic," whose advent Zola saw as inevitable, and his profound exasperation with the parliamentary mores of an Assembly he saw as hopelessly mediocre (quoted in Delas, 34 and 31). There is thus a marked confluence of aesthetic and ideological value in Zola's description of the republic as "this overflowing river whose course impotent hands always attempt to stop with pebbles and sand" (quoted in Delas, 30). Inasmuch as Zola's impatience with those who governed in Third Republic France would be repeated in Maurice's ill opinion of the Commune's leaders (in a passage quoted below), we can also read the relentless futurity of this image as countertraumatic, as a means of having done with the Commune's traumatic return as past event within the present dynamics of Third Republic France.

This theoretical Republican is nonetheless prone to condemning his character Chouteau as a "public-bar theorist who spoiled the few good ideas he picked up here and there in the most appalling mess-up of rubbish and lies" (586/*199*). Not only does this characterization expressly revisit a commonplace bourgeois conception of the cabaret as a site of chaos and protorevolutionary confusion, it also stigmatizes the supposed bric-a-brac of contemporary revolutionary discourse.[6]

> He was the corrupter, the bad workman from Montmartre, the housepainter who strolled the streets and went on binges, who half digested bits of speeches heard at public meetings and mixed up a lot of asinine rubbish with the great principles of equality and liberty. . . . Chouteau triumphantly trotted out his theories, a muddied stream in which floated the Republic, the Rights of Man, the rot of an Empire that had to be overthrown, the treasons of the leaders who commanded them, each one of whom had sold himself for a million, as had been proven. (437–38/*58*)

These two positions on the question of "theory" come together in the figure of Maurice Levasseur. On the one hand, Maurice clearly acts as an embedded authorial mouthpiece thanks to his allegiance to the "theory" of evolution, his synthetic understanding of that "fate [which] worked against us" and his "only" dreaming of the republic "in a theoretical way" (453/*72*, 440/*60*). Yet, as we have seen, Maurice also falls into revolutionary violence by virtue of his coming to abandon "theoretical moderate republicanism" (860/*459*). The ambivalence of Maurice as a character, in other words, tracks the fundamental ambivalence of "theory" and its derivatives as ideological switch words. Note, in the following passage, how closely Maurice's acknowledgment of the Commune's ideological confusion follows upon the narrator's judgment that, in holding out hope for France's rebirth through purificatory fire, Maurice's thinking is itself muddled:

> The Commune now seemed [to Maurice] to be the avenger of the shameful things they had endured, a kind of liberator bringing the knife to amputate and the fire to purify. None of this was very clear in his mind, and the educated man within him simply called up classical memories of free triumphant city-states or federations of rich provinces imposing their will on the world. If Paris won, he visualized it in glory reconstituting a France of justice and liberty, reorganizing a new society after sweeping away the rotten debris of the old. True, after the elections he had been somewhat surprised by the names of the members of the Commune, with its extraordinary

jumble of moderates, militant revolutionaries and socialists of all colors, to whom the great task was entrusted. He knew some of these men personally, and thought they were a very mediocre lot. Were not the best of them going to clash and destroy each other in the confusion of ideas they represented? (874/472)

In order better to delimit the parameters of Maurice's exemplarity, I turn here to two key passages from Zola's novel. The first finds Maurice a captive of the Prussians on the Iges Peninsula following the army's rout at Sedan. In a state between waking and sleep, Maurice has a vision of the empire being swept away amid universal loathing, of the republic joyfully proclaimed, and of armies of citizens arising to drive the foreigner from French soil. At this point,

> it was all jumbled up [*tout se confondait*] in his poor sick head, the extortions of the conquerors, the bitterness of conquest, the determination of the conquered to fight to their last drop of blood, captivity for the eighty thousand men held there, first on this peninsula and later in German fortresses for weeks, months, possibly years. Everything was breaking up and crashing down for ever in endless woe. (754/359–60)

Maurice's despondent reflections on his exemplarity in the second passage help define the precise scope of this infinite sadness. In a moment of withering self-analysis, during which he falls prey to his "old faculty of tearing himself to pieces," Maurice asks:

> Was he not just the ordinary man, the man in the street of the period, highly educated no doubt, but crassly ignorant of all the things that ought to be known, and moreover conceited to the point of blindness, perverted by the lust for pleasure and the deceptive prosperity of the regime? (715/322)

After Maurice has reviewed a bloodline leading from his grandfather, a "hero" of Napoléon's Grande Armée, to his father the petty bureaucrat, then to himself, "brought up to be a gentleman, a qualified lawyer and capable of the worst sillinesses and greatest enthusiasms, beaten at Sedan in a catastrophe that he knew must be immense and mark the end of the world," Zola's narrator tells us that

> The degeneration of the race, which explained how France, victorious with the grandfathers, could be beaten in the time of the grandsons, weighed down on his heart like a hereditary disease getting steadily worse and leading to inevitable destruction when the appointed hour came. If it had been

victory he would have felt so brave, so triumphant! In defeat he was as weak and nervous as a woman and gave in to one of those fits of despair in which the whole world collapsed. There was nothing left. France was dead. (715/322)

From the evidence of both the novel and Zola's outline, it is very clear that Zola intended Maurice to speak of "us" and for "us." Of Maurice in an earlier incarnation Zola writes: "All of that in the analytical man. In short, the Frenchman, all of us, such as we could have been, reasoning through our malady" (1393).[7] If, as Ruth Leys reminds us, trauma lies neither in the experience of what we persist in calling the "traumatic event," nor in "its delayed revival as a *memory*," but is, rather, constituted "by a dialectic between [these] two events, neither of which was intrinsically traumatic," Zola's *nous* tracks that dialectic precisely (20). The "degeneration of the race" that first manifests itself in the collective as a hysterical rhythm of groundless hope and disillusioned despair, only to be finally embodied as the passive, explicitly feminized melancholy of Maurice Levasseur, thus finds its referent—the French "race" as "us"—inescapably split between the French of 1871 and their counterparts of 1892. Zola's tendency in *La Débâcle* to subsume his otherwise central question of familial degradation ("like a hereditary disease . . .") to that of "our" racial degeneration only serves to underscore how much is at stake here.

In his excellent *Faces of Degeneration*, Daniel Pick has shown how the late nineteenth-century concept of degeneration "involved at once a scenario of racial decline (potentially implicating everyone in the society) and an explanation of 'otherness,' securing the ideology of, variously, the scientist, (white) man, bourgeoisie against superstition, fiction, darkness, femininity, the masses, effete aristocracy" (230). To evoke or encounter "degeneration," in other words, was to participate in a structure of disavowal—to know very well that degeneration was generalized, such that all are "threatened with a world of entropy or some future dissolution of stable positions," but to believe all the same that degeneracy can be localized, that "the degenerate has a definite physiognomy" (231). In Pick's analysis, degeneration likewise becomes a means of disavowing—acknowledging *and* denying—the confusion of "a felt historical and historiographical *powerlessness*":

Degeneration functioned at once as a representation of that crisis, and a means, never wholly successful, of containing, covering over, mastering profound political confusion and historical disorientation. (237)

Between Melancholy and Paranoia

In its insistence on the generalized degeneration of "our" race, coupled with its countervailing will to localize that degeneration (in Chouteau the "bad worker," in Paris as the source of all confusions, etc.), Zola's *Débâcle* plainly conforms to this structure of disavowal.[8] Indeed, the very impetus to write a novel such as *La Débâcle* arises, to my reading, out of a desire to "contain" and "master" the deep-seated (and ultimately unmasterable) "political confusion and historical disorientation" occasioned by the *année terrible*. But this picture is not complete without an account of how the disavowal scenario allows Zola's text to pivot (as it were) between melancholy and paranoia. For if the act of acknowledging one's implication in a collective degeneration implies an infinite melancholy much like that into which Maurice falls as the symbolic embodiment of the French "race" circa 1871, the act of endowing the degenerate with a definite profile, a specifiable otherness, is fundamentally paranoid. That the very pivoting between these two positions inherent in disavowal might *itself* be melancholic is the point toward which I will be working in the remainder of this chapter.

In order to open up this argument, I would like briefly to recall the main lineaments of Freud's account of melancholia—first in his 1917 essay, "Mourning and Melancholia," then in *The Ego and the Id* of 1923. "Mourning and Melancholia" begins with Freud's notoriously vexed attempt to distinguish the two conditions of the essay's title. Mourning, he writes, is "regularly the reaction to the loss of a loved person, or to the loss of some abstraction which has taken the place of one, such as one's country, liberty, an ideal, and so on" (*Standard Edition*, 11:243). Mourning may involve a "clinging to the object through the medium of a hallucinatory wishful psychosis," consistent with the principle that "people never willingly abandon a libidinal position," but eventually, Freud writes, "respect for reality gains the day" (11:244). By contrast,

> the distinguishing mental features of melancholia are a profoundly painful dejection, cessation of interest in the outside world, loss of the capacity to love, inhibition of all activity, and a lowering of the self-regarding feelings to a degree that finds utterance in self-reproaches and self-revilings, and culminates in a delusional expectation of punishment. (11:244)

Freud's further attempts at distinction include the suggestion that melancholia, unlike mourning, involves an object loss that is "withdrawn from consciousness," and the stipulation that "in mourning it is the world which has become poor and empty; in melancholia it is the ego itself" (11:245–46).

Given the explicitness with which *La Débâcle* ties Maurice's infinite sadness to an emptiness in the world occasioned by the consciously understood death of an abstraction—"he gave in to one of those fits of despair in which the whole world collapsed. There was nothing left. France was dead" (715/ *322*)—his would appear to be a case of simple mourning. But it is not, and not just because (as Freud clearly discovered) mourning and melancholia allow for no simple distinction.

In "Mourning and Melancholia," Freud speaks of the melancholic's self-reproaches as "reproaches against a loved object which have been shifted away from [that object] to the patient's own ego"; the melancholic's actions are thus said to "proceed from a mental constellation of revolt, which has then, by a certain process, passed over into the crushed state of melancholia" (11:248). Part of the melancholic's prior erotic cathexis toward that object serves to establish the ego's identification with that object, now abandoned; part is carried back to "the stage of sadism" (Freud could have easily written "masochism"), through a regression that "solves the riddle of the tendency to suicide which makes melancholia so interesting—and so dangerous" (11:249, 11:252). In *The Ego and the Id*, Freud refashions this account by speaking of the identification with the lost object that has been "set up again inside the ego" as the basis of the subject's "character," and by locating sadistic violence within the newly hypothesized superego (19:28). No longer primarily a condition to be resolved through decathexis, melancholia for the later Freud becomes constitutive of the ego inasmuch as "the lost object continues to haunt and inhabit the ego as one of its constitutive identifications" (Butler, *Psychic Life,* 134). Melancholia thus comes to differ from a hypothetical normalcy in degree but not in kind—thanks to the "merciless violence" with which the "excessively strong superego . . . rages against the ego" (19:53).

Countless passages in Zola's novel attest to what a passage quoted earlier called Maurice's "old faculty of tearing himself to pieces" (715/*322*). Given Freud's evocation of a "mental constellation of revolt" as the precondition to a passage into melancholy, one might expect Maurice's melancholia to arise out of his growing disillusionment with the Commune. But such is not the case. The crucial "degeneration of the race" passage cited above,

which instantiates Maurice's analytic self-devouring, conveys Maurice's ru-
minations on the morning of September 2, 1870—half a year prior to the
outbreak of the Commune. Following Freud's contention that the superego
"fulfills the same function of protecting and saving that was fulfilled in earlier days by the father and later by Providence or Destiny," I would argue
that the crucial phrase on which that passage ends—"France was dead"—
suggests that the object of Maurice's melancholic reproaches is something
like the Napoleonic myth of French national destiny, as it is exemplified by
Maurice's paternal forebears.

Perhaps the most telling indication that Maurice's state is one of melancholia, not mourning, involves the question of suicide. As *La Débâcle* unfolds, we witness a growing fraternal feeling between the Parisian Maurice
and his peasant comrade, Jean Macquart. Within the logic of the novel,
however, Maurice's death at the hands of Jean on the barricades of the *semaine sanglante* is more suicide than fratricide, destiny's answer to what
Maurice calls his "desperate impatience" to die (883/481). More precisely,
Maurice's death functions as a compensatory symbolic enactment of the suicide Napoléon III tried to, but could not, attain on the battlefield at Sedan,
in a scene in which (according to Zola) the emperor evinces "a tragic melancholy of infinite grandeur" (1455).[9]

In *The Psychic Life of Power*, Judith Butler draws upon Freud's insight into
the ways in which the identification with lost objects serves to constitute
the ego in arguing that the foreclosure of specifically homosexual desires
"appears to be foundational to a certain heterosexual version of the 'subject'" (23). For Butler, an unfinished (and unfinishable) process of grieving
haunts those "hyperbolic identifications by which mundane heterosexual
masculinity and femininity confirm themselves," while producing "a sociality afflicted by melancholia, a sociality in which loss cannot be grieved because it cannot be recognized as loss" (147, 24). If melancholia is thus
conceived as crucial to "the ontological accomplishment of heterosexual
'being,'" the performance of melancholia in its specific clinical sense—"as
the shameless voicing of self-beratement in front of others"—effects "a de-
tour that rejoins melancholia to its lost or withdrawn sociality" (23, 181). It
is precisely this reprise of a lost sociality that allows Butler to speak of melancholia as initiating "the variable boundary between the psychic and the social" (171).

Whatever qualms one might have about the radically ahistorical nature
of Butler's argument here, its resonances with the melancholy specific to *La
Débâcle* are undeniable. For Maurice's death is not just a fratricide (Jean kills

him) or a suicide (he wants to die). It is also a homicide on the part of the novel's plot, anxious to have done with that homosexually charged confusion (in the etymological sense of "fusion with") characteristic of the "fraternal" coupling of Jean and Maurice:

> Was this not the brotherhood of the earliest days of the world, friendship before there was any culture or class, the friendship of two men united and become as one [*unis et confondus*] in their common need of help in the face of the threat of hostile nature. . . . The one was part of the other, however different they might be, . . . the two of them making a single being in pity and suffering. (521–22/*136–37*)

> They hugged each other in a passionate embrace, made brothers by all they had gone through together, and the kiss they exchanged seemed the gentlest yet the strongest in their lives, a kiss the like of which they would never have from a woman, undying friendship and absolute certainty that their hearts were henceforth one for ever.(785/*389*; cf. *793/396*)

As it unfolds, Zola's plot effects a double disavowal. It cloaks a series of highly sexualized scenes in a legendary rhetoric of archaic fraternity, grounded (at least in Jean's mind) in a paranoid exclusion of women, "those creatures on whose account a man suffers so much" (521/*137*). And it attempts to displace Jean's love for Maurice onto Maurice's sister, Henriette. The foreclosure of homosexuality that Butler sees as constitutive of the heterosexual subject is thus suggested, but it is never fully effected—a point underscored by the fact that Maurice's death ultimately stands in the way of Jean's union with Henriette. Indeed, a generalized melancholy inhabits the novel's final pages, in a way that both points to a necessary sociality and moves us beyond a paranoia ostensibly endemic to the Commune.

Several pages ago, I argued that the exemplary confusion of Zola's Maurice grows out of an infinite sadness that he is said to bear within himself—a melancholy that the novel links to both the degeneration of the French race and the death of the French nation.[10] But of course Maurice is also *La Débâcle*'s most fully realized Communard and, as such, is not immune to an ambient paranoia. Insisting once again on that hysterical rhythm between absolute faith and profound despair that the novel never ceases to evoke and denounce, the following passage shows Maurice in the grips of an epidemic suspiciousness, haunted by a fear of betrayal that marks the spectral return of the historical Terror.

> Shared in common, illusions carried people's souls away and excitement flung them into the dangers of impetuous heroics. Already a crisis of

unhealthy irritability was approaching a sort of epidemic fever, magnifying fear just as much as confidence and letting loose the human herd [*la bête humaine*] to rush off unbridled at the slightest stimulus. . . . Maurice, who had formerly been so fair-minded, also caught this disease of suspicion, with the uprooting of everything he had so far believed in. . . . What however depressed Maurice so much was the great city of Paris, leaping from the heights of self-deception to the depths of discouragement, haunted by the fear of treason in its need for victory. (859/*458*)

Throughout the period leading up to and including the Paris Commune, Maurice will in effect vacillate between this "malady of distrust and daydreaming" and his ability to see how the Commune is vitiated by the "corrosive suspicion in which every one of its members lived" (860/*459*, 876/*474*).

Once again the theory of "degeneration" helps us to frame Maurice's behavior. In work spanning the period between the Commune and the publication of Zola's novel, the French psychiatrist Valentin Magnan wrote of a condition he variously called "chronic delirium" or "the delirium of the degenerates," which he saw as progressing through four phases: a period of incubation, characterized by mild suspicion and unease; a period of hallucinations and persecution mania; a phase of megalomania and disordered ambition; then madness proper. As Theodore Zeldin has noted, Magnan's model of the fall into madness served as a crucial forebear for Emil Kraepelin's early twentieth-century work on dementia praecox, in which "paranoia replaced 'persecution mania,'" becoming a subset of dementia praecox (*Anxiety*, 72).

In *La Débâcle*, Maurice's reflections on the "degeneration of the [French] race" are both the product and the effect of his capacity for melancholic self-devouring. Magnan's work suggests in turn that the epidemic suspiciousness into which Maurice falls is likewise a sign of degeneration. Zola's novel can thus be read to contain within itself that structure of disavowal which Pick has located within the late nineteenth-century concept of degeneration. "We"—that is, Zola's contemporary French readers—are brought to the melancholy realization that we are fundamentally implicated in a "degeneration of the race" closely linked to Maurice's melancholy. At the same time, however, "we" persist in locating this degeneration within specifiable victims of the "corrosive suspicion," through a gesture of paranoid othering that effectively repeats the suspiciousness of those whom it others. To hold both of these positions at once, as the structure of disavowal suggests that "we" do, is to adopt a fundamentally ambivalent attitude toward the events represented, an ambivalence like that which Freud saw as characteristic of melancholia: "In melancholia the relation to the object is not a simple one; it is complicated by the conflict due to ambivalence" (11:256). To fully acknowledge, as a reader, the play of melancholia and paranoia endemic to the character of Maurice Levasseur is thus, in itself, a melancholic gesture.

In order to track more closely the ways in which this melancholic acknowledgment gets written into the ending of *La Débâcle,* I will turn briefly to a distinction that Melanie Klein elaborated on the basis of Freud's work in 1935—the distinction between the so-called depressive and paranoiac positions. As Klein formulates them, both positions presuppose the ego's anxious confrontation with the "psychical fact that its loved objects are in a state of dissolution—in bits" (124). In the "depressive position," the ego strives to overcome the anxiety and remorse triggered by the disintegration of its ambivalently loved objects through attempting to unite those objects "into a whole," to "save the good objects both internalized and external" (127, 124). In the "paranoiac position," by contrast, the disintegrated object or objects are transformed into a "multitude of persecutors," in a way intended to preserve not the good objects, however ambivalently understood, but the ego itself (127, 124). Arguing that the depressive state is "based on the paranoid state and genetically derived from it," Klein nonetheless goes on to speak of paranoid fears and suspicions as a mode of defense against depressive anxiety, which she would increasingly come to see as the very basis of "all sublimations," including love, reparation, and altruistic feeling (130, 129, 125). As is true of melancholy in that play of melancholia and paranoia we have tracked thus far, Klein's depressive position effectively straddles its paranoid counterpart in the developmental process, since it names both that gesture whereby the infant (at four to six months) joins together good and bad images of the mother and the psychically mature attitudes of love and fellow feeling.

How might we understand *La Débâcle*'s ideological development in light of Klein's distinction? By taking its reader from the specific confusions of the days leading up to the battle at Sedan (part I of the novel), through the aestheticized confusion of that battle itself (part II), to the ideological bric-a-brac of the Paris Commune (part III), Zola's novel charts a general course from the enactment of depressive anxiety to a denunciation of its paranoid reaction. And yet, while *La Débâcle* clearly portrays revolutionary violence as fundamentally aberrant, stripped of that epic promise which one finds (for example) in the earlier *Germinal*, one might also argue that Zola's plotting partakes of a paranoid defensiveness much like that which the novel denounces in the Commune. There is perhaps no better example of this than what the ending threatens to do to the mythic confusion of Jean and Maurice, as Maurice's death paves the way for a reaffirmation of normative heterosexuality (in the persons of Jean and Henriette) and for the rebirth thematic on which the ending so patently insists (621):

> Then Jean felt an extraordinary sensation. It seemed to him, as day was slowly dying over this burning city, that a new dawn was already breaking.
> . . . Beyond the still roaring furnace, undying hope was reviving up in that great calm sky so supremely limpid. It was the sure renewal of eternal nature, eternal humanity, the renewal promised to all who hope and toil, the tree throwing up a strong new shoot after the dead branch, whose poisonous sap had yellowed the leaves, had been cut away. . . .
> The ravaged field was lying fallow, the burnt house was down to the ground, and Jean, the most humble and grief-stricken of men, went away, walking into the future to set about the great, hard job of building a new France. (911–912/508–9)

I have already suggested one weakness of this argument for paranoid emplotment. If Maurice's death allows for the coupling of Jean and Henriette, it is also precisely what stands in the way of that coupling. But there is another, more telling weakness, growing out of the fact that the argument for French rebirth through a return to reasonable and healthy peasant values is never made so forcefully as it is by Maurice himself:

> He was growing more delirious and paid no heed to the supplications of Henriette and Jean, who were terrified. In a raging fever he went on pouring out symbols and vivid pictures. It was the healthy part of France, the reasonable, solid, peasant part, the part which had stayed closest to the land, that was putting an end to the silly, crazy part which had been spoilt by the Empire, unhinged by dreams and debauches. And France had had to cut into her own flesh and tear out her vitals, hardly knowing what she was doing. But the blood-bath was necessary, and it had to be French blood, the unspeakable holocaust, the living sacrifice in the purifying fire. Now she had climbed the hill of Calvary to the most horrible of agonies, the nation was being crucified, atoning for her sins and about to be born again.
> "My dear old Jean, you are the pure in heart, the stout-hearted one . . . go and take up your pick and trowel, turn over the soil and rebuild the

house! . . . As for me, you did the best thing when you cut me out, for I was the ulcer clinging to your bones!''

He raved on [*il délira encore*]. . . . (907/504)

What are we to make of the fact that the novel here articulates one of its most fundamental thematics—that of expiation and rebirth—expressly in the mode of delirium ("He raved on")? To argue, as Lucienne Frappier-Mazur has done, that Maurice's delirium "serves to guarantee the truth of the assertion (as would visionary madness)" is to miss a paradoxicality essential to Zola's novel ("Guerre," 176). For if the general trajectory of Zola's plot moves from the anxious mourning for an ambivalently loved France to a paranoid rejection of that anxiety—both in the Commune and in the plot's apparent scapegoating of Maurice Levasseur—the novel as a whole strikes a note of depressive ambivalence, captured most poignantly by the suicidal self-sacrifice of its deliriously insightful protagonist. If Zola's novel contains an ethic, it is an ethic grounded in this depressive ambivalence, this melancholy that both encompasses and reflects upon the novel's play of melancholy and paranoia. Of all the confusions thematized in (and acted out by) Zola's *Débâcle*, this melancholic confusion of the reasonable and the feverish, of "us" and "them," is clearly the most significant.

3   *Mourning Triumphant: Hugo's Terrible Year(s)*

> No, the city of science cannot be led by ignorance; no, the city of
> humanity cannot be governed by the law of retaliation; no, the city
> of light cannot be guided by blindness; no, Paris, which lives in the
> clarity of fact, cannot live from confusion; no, no, no!
> The Commune is a good thing badly done.
>
> —Victor Hugo, *Actes et paroles, 1870–1871–1872*

Reading the two literary works of Victor Hugo most marked by the events
of 1870 and 1871—the 1872 poem cycle *L'Année terrible* and his 1874 novel-
ization of the Terror, *Quatre-vingt-treize*—involves a markedly different set
of frustrations than does the reading of *La Débâcle*. Where Zola's novel
mimics the anxieties of war by holding war's onset in maddening abeyance,
all the while claiming precise understanding of the root causes of the coming
disasters, *L'Année terrible* and *Quatre-vingt-treize* tend to withhold synoptic
cultural diagnosis as they threaten to submerge the reader in undigested detail and prophetic bombast.

Yet many of the core issues raised in my treatment of *La Débâcle* carry
over nicely to a reading of the Hugo texts. As I will demonstrate in the
course of this chapter, *L'Année terrible* attempts to parry a double mourning
triggered by the events of March 18, 1871, by constructing the poet as both
party and witness to a generalized cultural mourning. Just as Zola affirmed
his faith in a theoretical republicanism beyond the confusions endemic to
the Commune's cabaret theorists, so Hugo overcame his ambivalence with
respect to the Commune and the nascent Third Republic through repeated
expressions of faith in abstract, transhistorical values (truth, justice, reason,
and the like). Drawing upon an ambivalent, indeed *melancholic*, vision of
history that Hugo had developed long before 1870–71, *L'Année terrible* and
Quatre-vingt-treize serve as profound meditations on the moral paradox of
the historical Terror, which recurred with a vengeance in the Terrible

Year—the paradox that makes "triumphant mourning, full-blown murder . . . the conditions of our progress" (*Année,* 111).

I have argued that *La Débâcle* disavows confusion in two ways. It both profits from and repudiates the aesthetic richness of experiential confusion by positing the mastery of an analytic, yet still aesthetically sensitive, panoptic gaze. And it asks contemporary readers both to recognize and to deny their implication in that degenerate, melancholic confusion to which the Franco–Prussian War and Paris Commune reduce Maurice Levasseur.

Like Zola, Hugo clearly cultivates chaos to rhetorical effect. Hugo's adamant refusal of Parisian confusion notwithstanding, his texts from the early 1870s serve as apologies for confusion's moral stake as a necessary adjunct to the work of conscience and sentiment. In this sense, they can be read as case studies in the power of those confused yet profound images adduced by Lefebvre in his reading of the Commune (discussed in chapter 1).

This chapter begins by examining the place of melancholy and melancholic historicity in Hugo's texts on or around the Terrible Year, moves on to an examination of why confusion for Hugo is not something simply to be overcome through the cycling of history's melancholic spiral, then concludes with the question of whether Hugo's work of the period leaves room for revolution. The ineluctable ambivalence behind Hugo's pronouncing the Commune "a good thing badly done" leads him to posit, I will argue, a historical logic in a tripartite form, neither/nor/and yet. Unlike the neither/nor/but logics so common to late twentieth-century French theory, which typically find a way out of significant doublings through a third term largely excentric to the first two, Hugo's neither/nor/and yet logic does not step outside of pertinent doublings—between Versailles and Paris or the Vendée rebellion and the Convention—so much as it prophetically rewrites the historical second term.[1]

Symbolic Action

I will have occasion in a moment to address the function of mourning in *L'Année terrible.* In the case of the later Hugo, any discussion that thus implies the poet's psychic interiority, and the relative sincerity thereof, quickly runs afoul of the fact that the poet had long since become, in the words of Hugo's best recent biographer, "not just a real person with several masks but a limited liability company of egos, each feeding off the other and maintained by an army of commentators" (Robb, 217). No discussion of the traces of mourning in Hugo's post-Commune works, in other words, can fail to address the multiple ways in which the poetic self was fundamentally constituted through what Priscilla Parkhurst Ferguson has called Hugo's "politics of performance" (*Paris,* 158).

On December 11, 1851, just days after Louis-Napoléon's coup, Hugo fled Paris on a night train to Brussels, beginning an exile that would last until the fall of the Second Empire in September 1870. Settling first on the island of Jersey, then on neighboring Guernsey, Hugo quickly became a living symbol of opposition to the empire. His clandestinely published volumes *Napoléon-le-Petit* (*Napoleon the Little*) and *Les Châtiments* (*Punishments*)—smuggled into France in all manner of ways—enjoyed spectacular commercial success, helping to cement Hugo's status as "arguably, France's first modern media hero" (Ferguson, *Paris,* 158). Glossing a well-known photo of Hugo seated atop the *rocher des proscrits* (rock of the banned) on Jersey and staring (one presumes) in the direction of France, Ferguson notes that, while Hugo ceased writing for the theater after the 1843 failure of *Les Burgraves* (*The Burgraves*), he

> never gave up drama. He staged and performed his exile. Arguably, it was his best drama—certainly the one with the longest run and with the greatest effect. (*Paris,* 158)

The drama that was Hugo's exile finally closed on September 5, 1870, when Hugo returned to Paris, to be greeted by large crowds singing the Marseillaise and reciting from *Les Châtiments.* Over the next several months, Hugo would show his support for the nascent republic through a series of largely symbolic acts: writing impassioned, yet fundamentally naïve, appeals to the Germans, the French, and his fellow Parisians; holding public readings of *Les Châtiments,* and encouraging other such readings by renouncing his rights as author; lending his name to cannon and a postal balloon; finding his image in popular photographs and even (in a classic reductio ad absurdum) on the back of a flyer advertising sewing machines (Rosa, "Politique," 173, 184). Summarizing Hugo's appeal in the early months of the republic, Guy Rosa writes:

> He was the point of dialogue and unity for all shades of republican commitment, for a still larger antidespotic and progressivist sensibility, and for all the social strata participating in these.
>
> Thus Hugo's name, person and work served as catalysts, up until the Commune, for a sort of concrete unanimity that was Parisian, if not also national. ("Politique," 185)

Or, as Hugo himself remarked, playing on the derivation of the word "re-public" from the Latin *res publica*: "I am a public thing" (quoted in Rosa, "Politique," 186).

As a result of the elections of February 8, 1871, Hugo briefly found himself representing Paris in the National Assembly, sitting at Bordeaux. "On the 8th of February," Rosa notes, "Paris voted for the Republic and for the war, but against the Revolution, exactly along the lines set out by Hugo" ("Politique," 174). As one reads through Hugo's speeches to the Assembly, and especially his March 8 defense of Garibaldi, which led a Monarchist delegate to complain that France's greatest living poet "does not speak French," one is tempted to conclude, with Ferguson, that Hugo's off-and-on political career failed because the politics of performance "ill serve the practice of everyday politics," though Hugo's specific situation in 1871—as a radical deputy in a nominally Republican government dominated by Monarchists—was by no means conducive to long-term success ("Actes et paroles," 249; *Paris,* 160).

The final three poems in the March 1871 section of *L'Année terrible* chronicle an uncanny coincidence, of the sort that Hugo was otherwise prone to fabricate. On March 18, the consensus date for the beginning of the Commune following the French army's retreat to Versailles, Hugo attended the funeral of his eldest son, Charles, victim of a heart attack and a massive hemorrhage, brought on by "obesity, over-indulgence and the long winter nights spent manning the guns on the ramparts of Paris" (Robb, 462). Convinced that the revolution had come too soon, as a by-product of the Prussian invasion and the siege of Paris, and that its leadership was a liability—"bad timing, bad choice of men"—Hugo fled to Brussels on the pretext of needing to settle Charles's estate and thus assure the future of his grandchildren ("Actes et paroles," 256).

Much has been written about Hugo's decision to effectively sit out a revolution he had helped inspire. What is clear from the documents collected in his *Actes et paroles* (*Deeds and Words*) for the period is that Hugo conceived of himself as a potential mediator in the struggle between Paris and Versailles, calling repeatedly for concord and reconciliation ("Actes et paroles," 251). Finding grave errors and indeed madness on both sides of a conflict that pitted "right" (the Commune) against "the law" (Versailles), Hugo especially feared "the law's victory over right" ("Actes et paroles," 262). "The law's using universal suffrage to destroy that which is right," he writes, "is like a daughter using the father to destroy the grandfather" ("Actes et paroles," 263). In an attempt to reconcile his belief in the long-term power of democratic self-determination with his short-term mistrust of its effects, as evidenced by both the government and the Commune, Hugo pronounced himself "for the Commune in principle, but against it in practice" ("Actes et paroles," 253). Much like Zola some years later, Hugo staved off disillusionment by finding hope in the future of the Republican idea: "On both sides, madness. But France, Paris and the Republic will make it through" (quoted in Rosa, "Politique," 181). Nowhere is the full ambivalence of Hugo's take on the Commune more succinctly captured, however, than in this phrase of a letter from Brussels: "Sooner or later, Communal Paris (*Paris Commune*; note that he is *not* saying "the Paris Commune" [*la Commune de Paris*]) will impose itself" ("Actes et paroles," 257).

To the extent that melancholia presupposes an impoverishment of self, there is good reason to consider a poet whose crest bore the words *Ego Hugo* the least melancholic of men. Yet Hugo's specific indecision in the face of the Commune–era conflict between "right" and "the law" is nonetheless indicative of a passing melancholia. "Hugo appears," Rosa writes of the sojourn in Brussels, "to be unable to take sides, to get wrapped up in a web of competing motives" ("Politique," 180). This moment of irresolution was short-lived. On the night of May 27–28, following Hugo's offer to open up his house in Brussels to all asylum-seeking Communards, a mob attacked that house with stones and a battering ram, demanding that the poet be strung up on the nearest lamppost.

Expelled from Belgium shortly thereafter, Hugo took up residence in the small Luxembourgian town of Vianden, renewing his calls for clemency and writing verse after verse in defense of "those who are trampled upon":

> . . . . je défends
> Terrassés ceux que j'ai combattus triomphants. . . .
> Certes, je n'aurais pas été de la victoire,
> Mais je suis de la chute; et je viens, grave et seul,
> Non vers votre drapeau, mais vers votre linceuil,
> Je m'ouvre votre tombe. (*Année* 180, 184)

> I defend, struck down, those whom I battled in their triumph. . . . Surely, I would not have been a party to victory. But I am to the fall; and I come, solemn and alone, not to your banner but to your shroud; I let myself into your tomb.

The horrendous reprisals inflicted on defeated Communards thus allowed Hugo to rejoin that high ground of symbolic, humanitarian protest on which he had long felt most comfortable.

How did the Hugo of 1871, the melodramatic champion of an unpopular clemency, become the national hero of 1885, whose state funeral was attended by over two million mourners, more than the entire population of Paris at the time? Hugo's very failings as a practical politician, Ferguson argues,

> made him an even more powerful symbolic figure. . . . Hugo stood for the broadest ideology of the republic. Precisely because he could not be restricted to any particular political party or program, he could be appropriated by a Third Republic that had begun under such inauspicious circumstances and that needed legitimacy in a continuing context with both the right and the left. (*Paris*, 161)

Hugo's specific ambivalences with respect to the Commune as pivotal event, his long-standing embodiment of a literary and political revolutionism unshackled by any specific revolutionary agenda, thus helped the Third Republic to "convince France (and the world) that, while fulfilling the promise of the Revolution, it was not itself a revolutionary regime" (Ferguson, *Paris*, 178). In short, Hugo was precious to a regime that started out monarchistic (just as he himself had) because he stood as a shining example of how to both avow and repudiate the revolution.

Spectacles of Grief

Over the course of a long life, Hugo had occasion to bury both of his parents, his wife, and three of his four children (excepting only the troubled Adèle). Mourning is thus everywhere in Hugo's poetry, yet one is frequently struck by the poet's having, in the words of Graham Robb, "escaped the clutches of grief" (93). This sense arises in part from the fundamentally performative nature of Hugo's poetic self, whose pretense to simple sincerity so commonly takes the form of an "exaggerated naïveté" (Guerlac, 32). In part, it is the product of Hugo's way of exuding vitality in the face of his loved ones' demise. Edmond de Goncourt, for example, reports of his profound unease at an 1873 dinner where Hugo's "powerful and robust health" stood in marked contrast to the pallor of his dying son, François-Victor (*Journal*, 2:548).

An exemplary instance of Hugo's capacity to turn loss to account was the 1843 death by drowning of his pregnant daughter Léopoldine and her husband, Charles Vacquerie. After first interpreting his daughter's death as a divine reprimand for his womanizing ways, Hugo went on to compose a series of poems that were "calm, soft-hearted celebrations of life" (Robb, 243). Indeed, as Graham Robb forcefully demonstrates, Léopoldine's death turned out to be "one of the great opportunities of [Hugo's] career," since it laid the groundwork for Hugo's realization that the universe is "formed from the same substance as the human mind" (243). The crucial question is thus not whether the poet's mourning was "sincere," although Hugo's later redating of life-affirming poems composed shortly after his daughter's death suggests he was worried about the perception it may not have been (Robb, 355). Rather, it is what work the gesture of mourning might do within Hugo's project as a whole. It is with this question in mind that I now turn to *L'Année terrible*.

The poems of Hugo's collection chronicle a succession of turbulent events from the plebiscite of May 8, 1870; through war against Prussia, the siege of Paris, and the Commune; to the eventual reprisals against defeated Communards. From the beginning of the volume, and despite Hugo's obvious grounds for celebrating the demise of an empire that had forced him into exile, *L'Année terrible* constructs its poet–narrator as both party and witness to an ambient mourning: "France! O mourning! . . . . / This century is at the helm and I am its witness" (33).[2] This mourning is professedly militant in both nature and effect. In a verse from the December 1870 section of the cycle, the poet endeavors to convince the German people that the power of such (ostensibly French) humanitarian ideals as Liberty and Justice is such that they, "our conquerors," are in fact "our conquered" (84). He then goes on to claim that

> nos regards de deuil, de colère et d'effroi
> Passent par-dessus vous, peuple, et frappent le roi! (84)

> our gazes of mourning, anger and terror pass over you, people, and strike your king!

This inscription of mourning in a pattern of historical irony whereby victory is loss, and loss, victory, returns in a poem on the bombardment of Paris, in which the poet tells Versailles that "it is mourning that springs from your success" (131). When the Commune itself appears as a catalyst to mourning, it tends to do so indirectly, through the relay of a mourning for Charles: "Blow on top of blow. Mourning on top of mourning" (126). This asymmetry arises from the Commune's implication in principle, albeit not in practice, in a progressive pacification of the world, a historical movement toward what Hugo calls "the principle of human inviolability," the interruption of which served to trigger the poet's mourning ("Actes et paroles," 264).

In Hugo's treatment, the concepts of mourning and melancholia—*deuil* and *mélancolie*—are frequently interchangeable, as witness the passage below from "Les Deux Trophées" (The Two Trophies). This poem's essential conceit, evoked by its title, is a juxtaposition of Versailles's bombardment of the Arc de Triomphe and the Commune's toppling of the Vendôme column—both embodiments of "sovereign people" and prime instances of those Parisian landmarks Hugo sought to make his own. This juxtaposition then sets up a vision of the people, "the France [that] is one," as a unifying force transcending "two forms of chaos in the wrong" (142–43):

Sur ce hautain métal et sur ce marbre altier
Oh! comme on cherchera d'un oeil mélancolique
Tous ces fiers vétérans, fils de la République.
Car l'heure de la chute est l'heure de l'orgueil;
Car la défaite augmente, aux yeux du peuple en deuil,
Le resplendissement farouche des trophées. (142)

On this haughty metal and proud marble, oh how our melancholy eye will seek out those proud veterans, sons of the Republic. For the hour of the fall is the hour of pride; for defeat magnifies, in the eyes of the people in mourning, the trophies' fierce splendor.

However much mourning and melancholia might thus slide into one another in Hugo's work, melancholia retains a long-standing privilege by dint of its implication in the poet's vision of history as Manichaean struggle. In the 1827 *Préface de Cromwell* (*Preface to Cromwell*), Hugo speaks of the historical shift from antiquity to modernity, and the related displacement of epic by drama, as a function of the double destiny or divided nature of modern, Christian man—split between corporeal and immortal life, subject to the play of good and evil, darkness and light (36). Most interesting for our reading of its Commune–era analogue is Hugo's insistence that modern melancholy originates in an upheaval wrought by Christianity, such that misfortunes of the state (theretofore restricted to the ruling classes) could now touch the lives of all (*Préface,* 39). Contemporaneous with the rise of this "new sentiment," Hugo sees a new "spirit of examination and curiosity" and a new sense of poetry—"true poetry, complete poetry"—said to reside in "the harmony of opposites" (*Préface,* 39, 64).

It is then that, its gaze fixed on events that are both laughable and formidable, and under the sway of this spirit of Christian melancholy and philosophical critique . . . poetry will take a great, decisive step. . . . It will begin to act as nature does, to mix (without confusing them) shadow with light, the grotesque with the sublime—in other words, the body with the soul, the animal with the spiritual—for religion's point of departure is always that of poetry as well. It all hangs together. (*Préface,* 41)

Like so much of Hugo's work, *L'Année terrible* and *Quatre-vingt-treize* repeatedly evoke forms of chaos endemic to a Manichaean conception of human history: "O mankind! Light and night! Chaos of souls" (*Année,* 26). In a poem designed to contrast truly epic struggle with the venal war of the emperor-as-pickpocket, Hugo writes:

> Nous rêvions ces chaos de colère et de bruit
> Où l'ouragan s'attaque à l'océan, où l'ange,
> Étreint par le géant, lutte, et fait un mélange
> Du sang céleste avec le sang noir du titan. (45)

> We were dreaming these chaoses of anger and noise, where the hurricane takes on the ocean, where the angel struggles in the giant's grip and mixes celestial blood with the black blood of the titan.

As they work to sublime effect, such representations of historical chaos and its attendant disorientation repeatedly serve to justify the poet's expressions of faith in suprahistorical abstractions such as truth, right, justice, fraternity, and reason. These abstractions in turn underwrite *L'Année terrible*'s faith in the idea of the French nation; in Paris, "soul of the earth"; or in "an ideal Europe" (55, 86).[3] Hence lines such as this, from the poem "Paris incendié" (Paris Burned): "Where the sphinx says: Chaos! Paris says: Liberty" (150).

This transcendence of struggle notwithstanding, Hugo's vision of history remains ambivalent in at least three respects. First, the very movement toward transcendence through abstraction presupposes that neither of the polarized forces in conflict is allowed to prevail, that each holds the other perpetually in check (Baudoin, 268). Second, Hugo's conception of history privileges revolutions in general, and episodes of terror in particular, inasmuch as they manifest a fundamental (here prosopopoeic) ambivalence of affect:

> Les révolutions parfois versent le sang,
> Et, quand leur volonté de vaincre se déchaîne,
> Leur formidable amour ressemble à de la haine. (189)

Revolutions sometimes spill blood, and, when their will to vanquish is unleashed, their formidable love looks like hatred.

Finally, history for Hugo is ambivalent because it implies suffering freely embraced in the interest of human progress.

Writing in his notebook of a November 1870 visit to wounded soldiers at an ambulance near the Porte-Saint-Martin, Hugo reports of having told the soldiers, "I desire nothing more on earth than one of your wounds" ("Carnets," 1062). This conception of the poet as Christic martyr permeates *L'Année terrible*. In a poem that juxtaposes his mourning for Charles ("Sweet Martyr") with the earthly paradise apparent in Charles's children, Hugo writes:

> Car à faire saigner je ne suis pas hardi;
> J'aime mieux ma blessure. (213)

> As for making others bleed, I am not audacious. I prefer my own wound.

More pointed still is the passage in which the poet, "wild old prowler of the sea," offers up to Paris the figurative heart that is *Les Châtiments* with the words, "Eat my heart"—a gesture that prompts Yves Gohin to refer to Hugo as "the poetic Host of heroism" (53; Gohin, 9).

In the broad sweep of *L'Année terrible*, this, the poet's identification with the suffering Christ, plays itself off an equally poignant conception of maternal suffering as agent of human progress.[4] Thus, in the same poem that evokes the revolutionary hatred-that-is-love, we read:

> Ce monde en mal d'enfant ébauchant le chaos,
> Ces idéals ayant des profils de fléaux,
> Ces émeutes manquant toujours la délivrance,
> Toute cette épouvante, oui, c'est de l'esperance. . . .
> La vie ouvrant de force un ventre déchiré,
> A pour commencement une auguste souffrance. (189–90)

> This world in the throes of childbirth sketching out chaos; these ideals with the profiles of plagues; these riots always failing to bring deliverance; all of this terror, yes, is hope. . . . Life forcibly opening up a rent belly has its beginning in majestic suffering.

In short, in those poems in which Hugo sought to work through the traumas of the Terrible Year, we find a melancholic ambivalence of history— "The future is a monster before being an archangel"—conjoined, on the one hand, to a Christic martyrdom tightly associated with the figure of the poet and, on the other, to the sufferings of childbirth more loosely associated with "life" and the "world."

Melancholic Historicity

All three of the grounds for ambivalence mentioned above—the counterbalancing of polarized forces, the play of contrary affects, and the insistence on suffering as an agent of progress—come together in one of *L'Année terrible*'s most important poems, "Loi de formation du progrès" (The Law of the Formation of Progress), to whose opening lines I allude in the title of this chapter:

> Une dernière guerre! Hélas, il la faut! oui.
> Quoi! le deuil triomphant, le meurtre épanoui,
> Sont les conditions de nos progrès! Mystère!
> Quel est donc ce travail étrange de la terre?
> Quelle est donc cette loi du développement
> De l'homme par l'enfer, la peine et le tourment? (110–11)

> A final war! Alas, yes, it is necessary! What! Triumphant mourning, fullblown murder are the conditions of our progress! Mystery! What is this, the earth's strange labor? What is this law of man's development through hell, pain and torment?

Given the centrality of this mystery of progress through suffering to Hugo's thinking about the Commune, one would expect "Loi de formation du progrès" to have been written expressly for the February 1871 section of *Année* in which it appears. In fact, Hugo wrote the bulk of the poem during the winter of 1857–1858 as part of "Le Verso de la page" (The Back of the Page), one of two unfinished poems on the Revolution destined for *La Légende des siècles* (*The Legend of Centuries*).[5] The seemingly uncanny prescience of "Loi" is in large part an indication of how thoroughly Hugo's reading of the Commune was mediated by a reading of the Terror. Just as *Quatre-vingt-treize* engages the Commune through the Terror, with only the slightest explicit acknowledgment of that engagement (e.g., "We have seen a return of these ways" [243/160]), so "Loi de formation du progrès" interrogates the Terror through the more general mystery of progress through suffering, as if in anticipation of the Commune.[6] Indeed, Hugo's decision to situate this poem in the month immediately *prior* to the outbreak of the

Commune suggests a revisionist desire to proleptically parry the coming trauma through an expression of faith in the principle, further developed by *Quatre-vingt-treize*, that "catastrophes have a somber way of arranging things" (*Quatre-vingt-treize,* 251/165).

Having thus set forth his poem's central quandary, Hugo follows with a passage that claims for the poet–thinker a right to productive suffering like that enjoyed by the mother in childbirth:

> Que la douleur est l'or dont se paie ici-bas
> Le bonheur acheté par tant d'âpres combats;
> Que toute Rome doit commencer par un antre;
> Que tout enfantement doit déchirer le ventre;
> Qu'en ce monde l'idée aussi bien que la chair
> Doit saigner, et, touchée en naissant par le fer,
> Doit avoir, pour le deuil comme pour l'espérance,
> Son mystérieux sceau de vie et de souffrance
> Dans cette cicatrice auguste, le nombril;
> Que l'œuf de l'avenir, pour éclore en avril,
> Doit être déposé dans une chose morte. (111)

That pain is the gold with which we pay on this earth for the happiness bought by so many bitter struggles; that every Rome must start in a cave; that all childbirth must rip open the belly; that ideas in this world, like the flesh, must bleed and, touched at birth by the brand, must have, for mourning as for hope, its mysterious seal of life and of suffering in this august scar, the navel; that the future's egg, to hatch in April, must be laid in a dead thing.

After cataloging humankind's attempts to master the elements, whose sirenlike song enthralls the "great hearts" of human discovery, with their "gloomy love of martyrdom," Hugo goes on to evoke history's obscure spiral in a passage that, more than any other in the poem, looks both backward to the Terror and forward to the Commune:

> Destin terrifiant! tout sert, même la honte; . . .
> Ce qu'on aime naît de ceci qu'on déplore.
> Ce qu'on voit clairement, c'est qu'on souffre. Pourquoi? . . .
> Le genre humain gravit un escalier qui tourne
> Et plonge dans la nuit pour rentrer dans le jour. . . .
> Le meurtre est bon; la mort sauve; la loi morale
> Se courbe et disparaît dans l'obscure spirale. (113)

Terrifying destiny! Everything is of use, even shame. . . . That which we love is born from that which we deplore. What we see clearly is that we suffer. Why? . . . Mankind climbs a turning stair that plunges into the night to return to the day. . . . Murder is good; death saves; moral law bends and disappears in the obscure spiral.

This insistence on the salvational force of death clearly echoes vitalist biology of the early nineteenth century, according to which the life and death of particular organisms function reciprocally to ensure the systemic continuity of life itself.[7] The filial drama of *Quatre-vingt-treize* will engage this vitalist dialectic by suggesting that the pitiless Cimourdain and the merciful Gauvin represent "one death, the other life," with the crucial proviso—common to Hugo's antitheses more generally—that these figures "so absolutely opposite, were at the same time extraordinarily united" (290/*194*). "Loi de formation du progrès" likewise appeals to the vitalist commonplace of death's necessity to the furtherance of life in a context where the historical Terror clearly resonates:

> Toute fleur est d'abord fumier, et la nature
> Commence par manger sa propre pourriture;
> La raison n'a raison qu'après avoir eu tort;
> Pour avancer d'un pas le genre humain se tord. (113)

Every flower is manure at first, and nature begins by consuming its own rot; reason is reason only after having been wrong; to advance by a step mankind writhes.

Inherent in Hugo's vision of human history as an obscure spiral leading inexorably, if paradoxically, toward light and truth is the assumption of a vantage point from which history's paradoxes can be seen to fall away:

> En même temps, l'infini, qui connaît
> L'endroit où chaque cause aboutit, et qui n'est
> Qu'une incommensurable et haute conscience,
> Faite d'immensité, de paix, de patience,
> Laisse, sachant le but, choisissant le moyen,
> Souvent, hélas! le mal se faire avec le bien;
> Telle est la profondeur de l'ordre; obscur, suprême,
> Tranquille, et s'affirmant par ses démentis même. (115–16)

At the same time, the infinite, which knows where every cause leads, and which is nothing more than an incommensurable and lofty consciousness,

made up of immensity, peace and patience, knowing the end, choosing the
means, often allows, alas, the bad to be done with the good; such is the depth
of its order—obscure, supreme, tranquil, and affirming itself in that which
denies it.

This infinite consciousness, whose sovereign tranquillity contains within
itself all that is good and evil, and whose workings are effectively proven by
all that would belie it, is of course Hugo's God. In thus adopting a divine
vantage, Hugo's poem would elevate the lyrical "I" to a position from
which the apparent distinctness of good and evil, life and death, triumph
and mournful loss *cannot but* appear blurred.

This being the case, the gesture of apparent retrenchment on which "Loi
de développement du progrès" ends is a curious one:

Que cette obscure loi de progrès dans le deuil,
Du succès dans la chute et du port dans l'écueil,
Soit vraie ou fausse, absurde et folle, ou démontrée;
                    [. . .] le certain
C'est que, devant l'énigme et devant le destin,
Les plus fermes parfois s'étonnent et fléchissent. (118)

Whether this obscure law of progress in mourning, of success in the fall, of
the port in the reef, be true or false, absurd and mad, or proven. . . . what is
certain is that, standing before enigma and destiny, the firmest of men are
sometimes astonished and give way.

Whereas so much of Hugo's poem had traced a fundamental movement
that subsumes the "sad and deformed mixture" of history's competing principles into the eventual conquest of life itself, the poem shifts its ground by
insisting on a fundamental incompletion:

Pas de principe acquis; pas de conquête sûre;
A l'instant où l'on croit l'édifice achevé,
Il s'écroule, écrasant celui qui l'a rêvé. (117, 119)

No principle is acquired, no conquest sure; at the very instant we feel the
edifice to be complete, it crumbles, crushing him who had dreamed it.

On the far side of a vision of history driven by a melancholic ambivalence
it clearly points beyond, a vision that rescues divinity from the "chaos of
forces" that appears to have engulfed it in order that the lyrical self might
espouse that divinity's perspective, "Loi" finds a renewed inevitability of

historical ambivalence, most strikingly concretized by the construction of the poet as martyr (114). Here are the poem's final lines, beginning with a pair of verses Hugo added in 1872:

> Fête du nord; c'est la mort du midi qu'on célèbre.
> Europe, dit Berlin, ris, la France n'est plus!
> Ô genre humain, malgré tant d'âges révolus,
> Ta vieille loi de haine est toujours la plus forte;
> L'évangile est toujours la grande clarté morte,
> Le jour fuit, la paix saigne, et l'amour est proscrit,
> Et l'on n'a pas encor décloué Jésus-Christ. (119)

> Fête of the north; it's the south's death they celebrate. "Europe, laugh," says Berlin, "France is no more!" O mankind, despite so many ages gone by, your old law of hatred is still the strongest; your gospel is always the great, dead clarity; the day flees, peace bleeds, love is banished, and Jesus Christ has not yet been lowered from the cross.

What remains of this persistent ambivalence, and what falls away, will be the focus of my reading of *Quatre-vingt-treize.*

Quatre-vingt-treize *and the Necessity of Confusion*

Despite their extraordinary synoptic breadth, both *Les Misérables* and *La Légende des siècles* had studiously avoided engaging the French Revolution. Hugo began outlining a novel to fill this gap in 1862–1863, but the definitive impetus to what would become *Quatre-vingt-treize* came only as an effect of the Terrible Year.

Begun in December 1872 and completed the following June, *Quatre-vingt-treize* addresses the problem of the Revolution by setting a series of fictionalized events from the Royalist rebellion in the Vendée against the backdrop of the Terror. In classic novelistic fashion, the conflict between Royalist "whites" and Republican "blues" is couched as a struggle between the Marquis de Lantenac, a Royalist patriarch smuggled back onto native ground to lead the peasant armies of the Vendée, and the ex-priest Cimourdain, the Committee of Public Safety's delegate to Republican forces in the region. Caught between these two figures is the young Republican commander Gauvin—grand-nephew of Lantenac, yet the spiritual son of Cimourdain, his childhood tutor.

In the draft of a preface to this novel, Hugo writes, "I wrote a book titled *Les Misérables*; this one could have been titled *Les Inexorables* [The Inexorable Ones]" (*Quatre-vingt-treize*, 501).[8] Hugo's novel addresses the events of *l'année terrible* by pitting political inexorability—variously represented in the novel by Lantenac and Cimourdain, and clearly suggestive of the reprisals of 1871—against a spirit of clemency embodied in the saintlike Gauvin. *Quatre-vingt-treize* is chock-full of specifically atmospheric echoes of the Commune: scenes of revolutionary festivity, class confusion, and fits of "public madness"; evocations of the revolutionaries' fear that they might be working for the Germans, "who are at the gates"; even signs of a certain melancholy—"a strange and haughty weariness of life" (147/*87*, 168/*103*, 144/*85*). Above and beyond these, however, there echoes throughout the novel the larger, moral question of whether the new Third Republic could rise above the inexorability of its origins (in the Terror, as in the Commune's repression) to embrace an amnesty for the vanquished Communards.

I alluded in the opening of this chapter to the challenges that Hugo's Commune–era works pose through their proliferation of more or less undigested detail. To a significant extent, this proliferation was a legacy of Romanticism. Nearly fifty years earlier, the director of the Académie Française, Louis-Simon Augier, had castigated the Romantic movement, of which Hugo was fast becoming the leading light, with this most pointed question:

> What would one say of a painter who omitted the foreground, in which everything must be distinct, and reduced his landscapes to those distant backgrounds in which everything is vaporous, confused and indeterminable? (quoted in Robb, 111)

By the 1870s, Hugo had thus long since learned to cultivate obscurity as a rhetorical effect. In the case of *L'Année terrible*, a relative paucity of reference to specified historical events leaves the reader with "a certain sense of fragmentariness, of structured chaos" (Coombes, 368). Similarly, *Quatre-vingt-treize* is the product of a master gleaner, skilled at appropriating suggestive details without integrating them back into a historical narrative of any but the most sweepingly prophetic sort.

And yet the specific confusions inherent in the events treated in *L'Année terrible* and *Quatre-vingt-treize* clearly accentuated Hugo's penchant for sublime chaos. Emblematic in this respect is Hugo's treatment of that "epic accumulation of antagonisms" which was the revolutionary Convention (215/*138*). Largely tangential to the novel's plot, part II of *Quatre-vingt-treize*, "The Convention," is a brilliant compendium of political and architectural detail, in which epic lists vie for prominence with laconic sublimities before giving way to a fictional encounter of the three lions of the Revolution: Danton, Robespierre, and Marat. As critics often remark, the net effect of Hugo's vision of the Convention is to convey a sense of "perpetual motion, of effervescence, a sense of movement, not of site"—an effervescence accentuated by the fact that the novel gives us historical information only in fragmentary form, as though gathering up "the scattered remnants of a torn-up work" (Ferguson, *Paris,* 172–73; Rosa, "Critique," 331).

In one of Hugo's rhetorical registers, the literary enactment of historical chaos sets the stage for the coming of a quasi-divine enlightenment. Thus the narrator of *Quatre-vingt-treize* notes of the Convention: "From that chaos of shadows and that tumultuous flight of clouds came immense rays of light parallel to eternal laws" (214/*136*). But the sublimity of enlightenment is not always so grandiose. In a letter to Edgar Quinet dated March 2, 1874, Hugo speaks of using his novel to extricate the revolution from its association with horror: "I want to cast a calming ray onto that frightening number, 93" (quoted in Petrey, 50). If *Quatre-vingt-treize*'s various storms, tempests, and hurricanes—both meteorological *and* political—are sublime because they are awe-inspiring, they exist in part to give way to an equally sublime abatement or pacification:

> L'ouragan, l'océan, la tempête, l'abîme,
> Et le peuple, ont pour loi l'apaisement sublime. . . . (*Année,* 139)

> The hurricane, the ocean, the storm, the abyss, and the people have sublime appeasement for their law.

One of *L'Année terrible*'s more frankly sentimental poems recounts the story of a young boy, captured on a barricade and destined to be shot, who asks permission of an army officer to take a watch to his mother, promising to return. Although convinced that the boy will flee, the officer grants his request. When the boy reappears, the flabbergasted officer sets him free, at which point the poet writes:

> Enfant, je ne sais point, dans l'ouragan qui passe,
> Et confond tout, le bien, le mal, héros, bandits,
> Ce qui dans ce combat te poussait, mais je dis
> Que ton âme ignorante est une âme sublime. (176)

> Child, I do not know, in the hurricane that passes and confuses all—good and evil, heroes and brigands—what pushes you into this struggle, but I say that your unschooled soul is a sublime soul.

Here, as so often in these works, history's sublime confusions serve to trigger their overcoming in a naïve, often infantile sublimity.

Quatre-vingt-treize takes this mechanism a step further by linking this sublimity of innocence to a hidden harmony, evocative of a capacity for pity inherent in the universe itself. This linkage is most strikingly realized in a scene that is without question the novel's moral center, the so-called "Massacre of Saint Bartholomew."

As the scene opens, the Marquis de Lantenac finds himself trapped with eighteen remaining soldiers in the medieval tower of his family's ancestral chateau, La Tourgue. In order to hold Gauvin's besieging forces at bay, Lantenac has placed three young hostages—the children of the peasant woman Michelle Fléchard—in the chateau's library, which he has threatened to torch should Gauvin's forces attack. A literal reference to the 1572 slaughter of French Protestants instigated by Catherine de Medici, the scene's title foreshadows the Fléchard children's destruction of a venerable old volume supposed to be the gospel according to Saint Bartholomew. Just what relation this childish destruction might have to the Whites' eventual destruction of the library itself is one of the principal moral puzzles with which the novel confronts its readers.

The "massacre" begins at dawn, with the waking of twenty-month-old Georgette, whose prattle is likened to a bird's song:

> A child babbles what a bird sings. It is the same hymn, an indistinct, stammered, profound hymn. . . . This confused murmur of thoughts that are not yet anything more than instinct contains a kind of unconscious appeal to eternal justice. (330/*223*)

The pages that follow detail the innocent games of Georgette and her older brothers, René-Jean and Gros-Alain, whose feeling of oneness with nature—the blue sky and "honest trees" they see out the library windows, a passing sow bug, and a curious bee—gives them a dramatically ironic sense of security (331/*223*). When the children hear the faraway din of the Republican army preparing for battle, that "confusion of fierce sounds" becomes "a kind of harmony," to which the children listen, enthralled; "'It's God [*mondieu*] who's doing that,' said René-Jean" (337/*228*). Asking what ideas are floating half-formed through the children's minds, the narrator answers this for René-Jean:

> In that sweet, pensive head there was a mixture of God, prayers, clasped hands, and a tender smile that had been seen in the past and now was seen no more, and René-Jean whispered, "Mama." (337)

This scene is an illustration in miniature of the ways in which Hugo's confusion is not something simply to be overcome through a cycling of history's spiral. The novel's opening scene, in which the Red Cap battalion mistakes Michelle Fléchard and her children for an enemy ambush, is awash in specific confusions, most notably Fléchard's when the soldiers quiz her (to no avail) on her political sympathies. As the novel unfolds, however, the confusions of this emblematic mother give way to a more universal, sentimentalist confusion, linked to a protective maternity ostensibly inherent in creation itself.[9] Hence the following passage from the massacre's end, as the three children fall asleep:

> Space was calm and merciful, everything was radiant, everything was growing quiet, everything loved everything; the sun was giving its caress of light to all creation; one could sense that harmony which is given off by the colossal sweetness of things; there was a maternity in the infinite . . . it seemed that one could feel someone invisible taking those mysterious precautions which, in the formidable conflicts between men, protect the weak against the strong. . . . (346/234)

This scene clearly plays on a dramatic irony subtended by what we earlier saw to be the melancholic spiral of history; the children feel protected by the motherly force of infinite creation, at the very moment they are most threatened by a death inscribable in a paradoxical narrative of human progress through suffering. But the conjunction here of mystery, harmony, maternal sweetness, and sublime calming also suggests that such dramatic irony opens out, ironically, on the far side of irony itself. The tonal difficulty posed by the reading of this scene involves keeping in play both its ironies and its transcendence of irony, in a manner sensitive to the novel's essential ambivalences.

As my description of the scene will have made apparent, the massacre of Saint Bartholomew is haunted by a fourfold violence. Through the relay of the scene's title, the "carnage" that the children inflict in reducing a magnificent volume to shreds, which are then borne away like butterflies in the breeze, alludes both to the Saint Bartholomew's Day massacre of 1572 and to the martyrdom by flaying of the apostle Bartholomew, "so that history could say that Saint Bartholomew, having been flayed in Armenia, was quartered in Brittany" (342/231). But that "carnage" also anticipates the violence of the battle to come, whose inevitability is underscored by Hugo's decision to introduce La Tourgue to his readers as a spectral ruin—"cracked, disabled, scarred, dilapidated"—seen through the eyes of an unidentified traveler circa 1830 (299/*200*).

Given this inscription of the children's "tragic" destruction of a "majestic book" within a series of historical or quasi-historical acts of destruction, one is surprised at the lengths to which Hugo's readers have gone in disassociating these events (343/*232*). Consistent with his general thesis that *Quatre-vingt-treize* conveys "the single message that human beings must refuse the imperatives put by *historical* existence in order to realize their full *moral* potential," Sandy Petrey argues that Hugo's novel

> forcibly inserts [the signifiers Saint Bartholomew and Ninety-three] into a representational system hermetically cut off from human events. . . . Dehistoricization of meaning is accomplished by dissolving the names of a political massacre into a pastoral expression of "on ne sait quel appel inconscient à la justice éternelle" [a kind of unconscious appeal to eternal justice] (*History*, 13, 93–94)

Victor Brombert takes a similar tack in suggesting that the import of the historical violence to which the massacre alludes is "somewhat deflated" by the children's games—not to mention Hugo's "humorous cultural allusions to Virgil and Dante" and his "parodic echoes of Boileau's *Le Lutrin*" (216). However much the children's dismemberment of the book might raise "the specter of the self-destructive core of revolutionary ideology," Brombert argues, *Quatre-vingt-treize*'s "real substance is elsewhere," as evidenced by the shredded volume's disseminatory flight into an azure sky:

> Georgette thoughtfully looked at those swarms of little pieces of white paper dispersed by every breath of air and said, "Butterflies."
> And the massacre ended with the bits of paper vanishing into the azure sky. (Brombert, 217; *Quatre-vingt-treize*, 345)

These readings are by no means entirely wrong. Rather, they are reductive of an ambivalence crucial to Hugo's portrait of the Fléchard children as agents of a specifically melancholy historicity:

> To tear apart history, legend, science, miracles true or false, Church Latin, superstitions, fanaticism and mysteries, and to rend a whole religion from top to bottom, is a task for three giants, and even for three children. (344–45)

To relegate the captive children to a moral domain essentially separate from historical realities, or to see their games as tending to minimize the violences they double, is to fail to see how their "appetite for destruction" might in

fact subtend what Jeffrey Mehlman rightly calls Hugo's "depressingly sentimental celebration" of them (344/233; *Revolution*, 67).[10] Rather than assume
that a full appreciation of the children's destructiveness would effectively
undermine the scene's obvious sentimentality, we need to entertain the
thought that sentimentality is precisely what emerges on the far side of the
massacre's doublings.

In a suggestive reading of *Quatre-vingt-treize*, the critic David Denby has
placed the novel within the lineage of Enlightenment sentimentalism. This
he understands as a mode of representing personal misfortune, made visible
to an observing subject through external signs (such as tears, gestures, or
facial expressions), within a generalized "aesthetic of the tableau" (7). For
Denby, the rhetorical effect of Hugo's novel depends upon and continues a

> language of sentiment and interiority [that] attains public status as a
> normative language in the latter part of the eighteenth century: in the Calas
> affair, in Rousseau's *Émile*, in the debate over poverty, in the language of
> Revolutionary debate, in the work of Germaine de Staël, the discourse of
> sympathy is closely related to a discourse about justice and equality. (7)

The vision of the Revolution that one finds in *Quatre-vingt-treize*, as in Mi-
chelet's *Histoire de la Révolution Française* (*History of the French Revolution*), is
thus "a continuation and development of many aspects of sentimentalism:
the Revolution is the historical enactment of solidarity and sympathy, the
beginning of the triumph of the people, the recognition of the power of the
weak, the consecration of the state and of law as agents for their defence
and protection" (8).

From this perspective, the novel's most patently sentimental scene is that
in which a haggard Michelle Fléchard watches helplessly as flames consume
the chateau where her children stand imprisoned. Fléchard's quintessentially
maternal "cry of inexpressible anguish," which prompts a fleeing Lantenac
to return and free the children at the risk of his own capture, is but the
auditory equivalent of this sentimentalist tableau (411/281). The marquis's
transfiguration, in which "the high divine law of forgiveness, abnegation,
redemption and self-sacrifice" wins out over ostensibly Satanic political
concerns, triggers an internal debate on the part of a "thoughtful Gauvin"
(432/296). Should Lantenac be set free, as both a sentimentalist conception
of justice and familiality (biological *and* Revolutionary) would dictate? Or
should the needs of the nation prevail, on the grounds that "Lantenac's life
would mean the death of a host of innocent men" (438/300)? Faced with

this sentimentalist double bind, Gauvin chooses to free Lantenac, forcing Cimourdain to condemn him to death in Lantenac's stead.

The final chapters of *Quatre-vingt-treize* demonstrate plainly how a certain lack of clarity remains essential for Hugo's sentimentalism. I have argued that Hugo's vision of history, both before and after the Terrible Year, was marked by a melancholic ambivalence, traceable to the perception that progress comes only at the cost of enormous suffering—be it that of the Christic martyr (most clearly evoked here by the death of Gauvin) or of the mother in childbirth. As Gauvin is buffeted about by his conscience, by "these dizzying spirals of a mind turning in upon itself," this melancholic ambivalence—inherent in human history but epitomized by the Revolution—appears to break down (439/*301*). In pitting Gauvin's vision of futurity against Cimourdain's, in answering a purely logical revolutionism with a higher, more spiritual form, Hugo's novel opts for an ineluctable complexity in a way that (at least provisionally) minimizes ambivalence:

> Destiny had arisen: sinister before Cimourdain, formidable before Gauvin.
> Simple before the first; multiple, diverse and tortuous before the second.
> (441/*303*)

Glossing these lines, Suzanne Guerlac rightly speaks of a bending of "the straight line of reason" by pity, understood as "the addition of sentiment to reason"—a bending that "divides the sublime itself into a sublime of terror and a sublime of pity" (28).

To the question of why that complexity and obscurity fundamental to the work of sentiment should prove more powerful than linear reason, Hugo answers:

> Reasoning is only reason, sentiment is often conscience; the first comes from man, the second from a higher source.
> That is why feeling has less clarity and more power. . . .
> Cruel perplexities. (441/*302*)

As Hugo had made clear in Jean Valjean's trial by conscience in "A Tempest Beneath a Skull," *Les Misérables*'s pendant scene to *Quatre-vingt-treize*'s "Thoughtful Gauvin," the confusion that haunts human conscience in moments of high moral perplexity functions as a sign of divine presence; "in my conscience in me," he writes in *L'Année terrible*, "I have God for a guest" (220). That which comes from above as vertiginous spirals of moral conscience serves to ground a "human absolute" far above the "revolutionary absolute" (*Quatre-vingt-treize*, 428/*293*). Paradoxically, the result of such trials by confusion is a certain clarity, not of logic but of vision, as Gauvin discovers when, at the end of his ordeal, he says this of the work of the Revolution: "The visible work is fierce, the invisible work is sublime. I can see everything clearly now" (466/*320*).

A Place for Revolution?

Such a conception of the Revolution poses a pair of questions with which every reader of *Quatre-vingt-treize* must grapple. Does the supremacy of transcendental values to which the ending of the novel clearly points include, in Sandy Petrey's words, "a place for Revolution" (*History*, 30)? And what survives of that sacrality which Hugo expressly attaches to the Convention as "history's highest point"—"Everything that is great has a sacred horror"—in the wake of Gauvin's transpolitical sublimation (192/*121*)?

For a sizable body of readers, a great deal of the Revolution's glory does in fact survive. While complaining of the novel's "metaphysical abstractness" and its preference for "large decorative and rhetorical contrasts" over the "inner movement" of more dialectical emplotments, Georg Lukács reads *Quatre-vingt-treize* as "the first important historical work to attempt to interpret the history of the past in the new spirit of protesting humanism" (256). Despite its residual romanticism, the novel wins praise for its "glorification" of the French Revolution at a time when it was considered "particularly modern" to slander that Revolution (256–57).

In a manner that more closely tracks Hugo's conception of history's spiral in texts such as "Loi de formation du progrès," Priscilla Ferguson argues that *Quatre-vingt-treize* "contains the Terror . . . by proposing a cosmology in which evil is a temporary but vital, even positive, element in the good that necessarily follows" (174; cf. Clark, *Literary France*, 153). In making this argument, Ferguson advances a causal claim of a sort that is oddly lacking in Hugo's historical fiction: "Gauvin's vision of the future republic is already written in the terrible events of the present, the republic of compassion originates in the republic of terrible justice, that is, *where it first becomes a necessity*" (*Paris*, 171; emphasis added).

Early in his remarkable *History in the Text:* Quatre-vingt-treize *and the French Revolution*, Sandy Petrey pointedly questions the assumption that Hugo's novel makes a provision for revolution in any but the most ethereal of senses. Arguing that Gauvin's cry of "Long live the Republic!" as he goes to his death "cannot exist in history," Petrey claims that Hugo's ending transmutes a heretofore ambivalent real-life Revolution into a "wholly evil" one (33). Or, more precisely, the novel's conclusion splits the Revolution into its largely "evil" historical manifestations, represented by Cimourdain, and "a timeless component unpolluted by its occurrence in history," represented by Gauvin (97). In this more expressly categorical mode of Petrey's argument, Cimourdain's "desperately unexplained suicide" (more on this claim in a moment) is seen to indicate "the global failure of historical visions of the world in *Quatre-vingt-treize*" (22).[11]

This dichotomy with a transcendental twist helps explain Petrey's seemingly contrary pronouncements on the question of the novel's Manichaeanism. In a chapter on the novel's allegorical negotiations with the categories of moral judgment, Petrey writes that Gauvin

> embodies only half of the Revolution, the good half. The bad half is Cimourdain, a severance which eliminates ambivalence by keeping good and evil, life and death, as properly apart in the world as in semantic structure. (*History*, 86)

Several pages later, however, Petrey absolves *Quatre-vingt-treize* of the characteristic sin of modern revolutionism—that of "attempting to separate revolutionary goats from revolutionary sheep so as to keep only the good half"—by suggesting that Hugo's novel wholly "disengages its characters from the Revolution" (98).

Having argued that *Quatre-vingt-treize* effectively "eliminates ambivalence"—either directly or by subjecting the good to a mystical sublimation above the quagmire of human history—Petrey then paves the way for ambivalence's return by noting the inevitable failure of that transfiguration. Seen in its entirety, *Quatre-vingt-treize* becomes "an obsessively ambivalent exercise in historical and ahistorical signification," because historical meaning's claims on our attention are so pressing that "the attempt to void [such meaning] necessarily fails" (*History*, 105, 32). In his final chapter, Petrey brilliantly shows how the novel's ambivalence toward history tracks Hugo's own ambivalence with respect to the Commune. On the one hand, the pastoral withdrawal and affirmation of family so characteristic of the novel's ending retroactively justifies Hugo's refusal of the Commune's ambiguities and his consequent flight to Brussels, while Gauvin's spectacular successes on the battlefield serve as a compensatory rectification of "history's deafness to Hugo the prophet" (105). On the other hand, the persistence in *Quatre-vingt-treize* of an "authentically revolutionary vision" reflects Hugo's growing sense of the bathetic inefficacy of his eternalist rhetoric and his awareness, beginning in Vianden, that "the Communards' *historical* situation had shut them off from humanity's *eternal* condition" (109, 112–13). In sum, Petrey writes,

> [t]he pastoral component of *Quatre-vingt-treize* manifests the repugnant complacency with which *ego Hugo* often viewed, judged and pronounced on the acts of ordinary mortals. Its historical component demonstrates on the contrary an admirable ability to throw off complacency, look directly at events, and move towards acceptance of a human world not subject to the same processes which bring the dawn every day and the spring every year. (*History*, 105)

What, then, are we to make of the novel's ending? Having cast the deciding vote to condemn his protégé Gauvin to death on the guillotine, Cimourdain puts a bullet through his heart at very moment of Gauvin's beheading. Variously characterized to this point as Gauvin's spiritual father and his intellectual mother—"the mind suckles; intelligence is a breast"—Cimourdain attains a sisterly parity with Gauvin in the mystical Assumption of the novel's final lines: "And those two souls, tragic sisters, soared away together, the darkness of one mingled with the light of the other" (157/95, 482/332). The novel thus concludes with a single, *transhistorical* image that both contains and sublates that melancholic *ambivalence of history* which Hugo elsewhere links to the figures of Christ (whom both Gauvin and Cimourdain suggest here) and of the mother in the throes of childbirth (Cimourdain, approximately).

To argue, as Petrey does, that Cimourdain's suicide goes strikingly unexplained is to miss the ways in which Hugo's novel builds toward this final sublation. How better to parry the effects of a terrible year that calls into question the necessarily progressive nature of history's melancholic spiral than to assume melancholic ambivalence into a single, transhistorical image? Cimourdain's death cannot be a function of the specific failure of historical vision, moreover, because—to a degree that Petrey's argument cannot recognize—Cimourdain expressly doubles the poet's visionary persona. Although characterized as a partisan of "the straight line" and the "republic of the absolute" (153/92, 466/321), Cimourdain shares Hugo's visionary faith in an unspecified future ("he loudly called for the future" [150/89]), his concern for the plight of the downtrodden ("he had a special pity, reserved only for the poor and the wretched" [151/91]), his penchant for symbolic action (e.g., Cimourdain's suggestion that the arm of Louis XV be taken to Latude, "the man who had been buried in the Bastille for thirty-seven years" [153/91]), his sublimity "in isolation, in lofty remoteness" (156/94), and his status as substitute father (157/95). Above all, Cimourdain speaks to God's revolutionary function in ways that belie any simple dichotomy between his revolutionism and Gauvin's. In his exhortation to Lantenac's besieged forces, Cimourdain evokes a time when the Revolution's enemies, their children, or their grandchildren will know that "in Revolution there is God," a time when "all fanaticism, even ours, will vanish . . . when the great light will appear," then goes on to express this Christlike (and perforce Hugo-like) wish: "I ask you to do me the favor of destroying me in order to save yourselves" (375/255).

I have spoken of Hugo's discomfort with both the Communards and their governmental adversaries, prior to the reprisals that made victims of the Communards and pushed the poet squarely into their camp. This historical *dos à dos* finds its echo in the world-historical confrontation with which the third and final part of *Quatre-vingt-treize* opens, that of the feudal fortress and torture chamber, La Tourgue, with the guillotine as modern-day agent of death. This confrontation gets personified in turn as one between the Marquis de Lantenac and the abbé Cimourdain:

> Equal on the scales of hatred. . . .
>
> Let us point out that these two men, the marquis and the priest, were to a certain extent the same man. The bronze mask of civil war has two profiles, one turned toward the past, the other toward the future, but both equally tragic. (317/213)

As Petrey rightly notes, the confrontation of La Tourgue and the guillotine, Lantenac and Cimourdain, pleads "the necessity of a third choice" (*History,* 26). This third choice is not wholly excentric to the first two, but rather is implicit in (and a regeneration of) the historical second. If *Quatre-vingt-treize* does indeed make a place for revolution, it is in the specifically ambivalent space of a concessive third term. Neither Lantenac nor Cimourdain, the novel argues, and yet . . . "there was a glow of dawn on Cimourdain's fateful brow" (317/213). What is this tonal complexity if not a final instance of *Quatre-vingt-treize*'s negotiation with historical melancholy and its deep-seated investment in a fundamental confusion?

4   *Science and Confusion: Flaubert's* Temptation

We lack science, above all. We flounder like savages in barbary.
  —Gustave Flaubert, *Correspondance* (December 12, 1857)

My *only* distraction is to see the Prussian gentlemen pass, from time
to time, beneath my windows, and the only thing that keeps me
busy is my *Saint Anthony,* on which I work constantly. This
extravagant book keeps me from thinking of the horrors in Paris.
  —Gustave Flaubert, *Correspondance* (May 3, 1871)

Flaubert speaks often in his letters of a desire to make criticism, literary style,
and even politics "scientific." Yet critics habitually assume that the meaning
of Flaubert's "science" lies elsewhere than in the practices of the natural
sciences as he and his contemporaries would have known them. When
Raymonde Debray-Genette writes, for example, "All that Flaubert truly
takes from science is the idea of a probable generality," she implicitly subsumes science to an aesthetic category, to a "documentary *verisimilitude*" that
justifies—or, better, *authorizes*—prior acts of the imagination ("Science,"
44).[1] Likewise, there has long been a tendency among Flaubert's readers (especially of *Madame Bovary*) to see in science a threatening, if often ridicu-
lous, discourse of power inscribed in the young Gustave's oedipal conflict
with his father, the doctor. Here is Jean-Paul Sartre, from *L'Idiot de la famille*:

> Science is the demonic gaze that cuts lies "to pieces" and leads the hysteric
> back to his reality; in short, it is the *realizing* gaze of the Father and his power
> to decompose imaginary orders, to pin his younger son down, reduced to
> his naked impotence. (3:596/5:555)

Given Flaubert's lifelong commitment to a practice of writing informed
by meticulous erudition, his rhetoric of science must ultimately be brought
to bear on our understanding of the processes behind the Flaubertian text.[2]

But I would argue that only by postponing this subsumption, only by looking first at the nineteenth-century science behind Flaubert's rhetoric, can one see how Flaubert's work is at once tempted by science as an institution of power and drawn to confusion, the very negation of science and its ruses. In the first part of this chapter, I read the motley bustle that is *La Tentation de saint Antoine* to show how Flaubert wrote the contradictory temptations of science and confusion into the third and final version of that text (completed in 1872, but not published until 1874). And I argue for the inevitability of the temptation of confusion, given the model of science to which Flaubert in his middle years actively subscribed.

To make the argument solely in these terms, however, is to risk missing the historical embeddedness of the 1874 *Temptation*. First drafted in a three-year period straddling the February Revolution (1846–49), and put into final form around the time of the Franco–Prussian War and Paris Commune (1869–1872), *La Tentation de saint Antoine* served Flaubert as an aestheticized repository for his historical hopes and, more often, his historical fears. In September 1871, as he rewrote the book's march of the gods sequence, Flaubert spoke of his lassitude with "the vile worker, the inept bourgeois, the stupid peasant and the odious ecclesiastic" as the reason for his "losing [him]self," as best he could, in antiquity (*Corr.,* 4:372).[3] And yet Flaubert's version of fourth-century Alexandria echoes contemporary France in multiple ways. Witness the similarity between certain of its passages and passages from the contemporary correspondence in portraying times of transition, decaying values, and incipient boorishness:

> JUPITER: "I have no more use for [the souls] of men! . . . For now they live like slaves, oblivious of insults, of ancestors, of vows; and on all sides what triumphs is the mob's imbecility, the meanness of the individual, the hideousness of every race!" (130/*190*)[4]

> As for me, I am nauseated, *heartbroken,* by the stupidity of my compatriots. The incorrigible barbarism of mankind fills me with blackest gloom. (*Corr.,* 4:211/*2:151*)

> What grieves me most deeply is: 1) the stupid ferocity of men . . . 2) I am convinced we are entering into a hideous world, where those like us will no longer have a reason to live. Everyone will be utilitarian, military, stingy, small, poor and abject. (*Corr.,* 4:257)

Whereas the first part of this chapter explores Flaubert's debt to natural history and his reinscription of contemporary vitalist biology, the second part examines the specifically melancholy cast of the *Temptation*'s vitalism by inscribing it in the context of Flaubert's contemporaneous rants against the invading Prussians, the Paris Commune, and the early Third Republic. The chapter then concludes by revisiting Jean-Paul Sartre's account of Flaubert's crisis of 1870, and specifically Sartre's claim that the fall of the Second Empire occasioned Flaubert's "historical death" (*Corr.* [Conard], 8:94; *Idiot*, 3:471–72).

Science

My analysis of the function of "science" in Flaubert's *Temptation* begins with chapter 5—specifically, with the march of the idols and gods that Antony's onetime student, Hilarion, orchestrates as a demonstration of the ephemerality of religious belief. When a mourning Isis says of Osiris, torn to bits by the hideous Typhon: "We have found all his members. But I don't have the one that made me fertile,"

> ANTONY is suddenly furious. He flings stones at her, shouting abuse. "Shameless woman! Clear off! Clear off!"
> HILARION "Respect her! It was the religion of your forebears! You wore her amulets in your cradle." (124/*183*)

Antony's immediate and violent denial of the phallus, and of the Egyptian cult of fertility for which it here stands, is presented as the denial of that which is heretical and "shameless" to the Christian mind. At the same time, it is a denial of Antony's personal history, intended as a synecdoche for the history of Christian belief as a whole. Hilarion's response is perfect. What he appears to see is that Antony's surprisingly violent condemnation of Isis is not so much a reaction to an apparent shamelessness as an effort to put distance between himself and an un–Christian belief that nonetheless belongs to his personal past. Ethical rejection here masks the effort to purify the history of a belief.

Good Christian that he is, Antony must qualify as monstrous or unnatural all pre-Christian beliefs, all idolatries. To him, the history of his belief is a history of revelations; revelations and history itself all originate in the truth of the divine intervention.[5] Hilarion, on the other hand, has profited from the nineteenth century's continuing interest in comparative religion, historical anthropology, and (as we shall see) natural history; he knows that Antony's truth resembles—and probably originated in—so-called error:

You can find the Trinity again in the mysteries of Samothrace, find baptism with Isis, redemption with Mitra, a god's martyrdom in the feasts of Bacchus. Proserpina is the Virgin! . . . Aristea Jesus! (129/*88*)

In a curiously anachronistic fashion, in other words, Hilarion senses that the world of fourth-century Alexandria functions as "the emblem of a belated syncretism of old, displaced beliefs" (Donato, *Script,* 81). He speaks as the contemporary of Renan, who wrote this in a description of the Gnostics:

> The tremendous confusion of ideas which reigned in the Orient brought with it the strangest sort of syncretism. Small mystical sects in Egypt, Syria, Phrygia, and Babylonia took advantage of apparent resemblances with Church teaching and were able to claim to be part of it in order to anticipate Jesus and claim him as one of their adepts. (Quoted in Donato, *Script,* 97)

One would misunderstand the *Temptation* if one failed to see that Flaubert intended Hilarion's argument to be irrefutable. In the battle between historiography on the comparative model and a history based on myth and revelation, the former will always win. To Hilarion's brilliant display of erudition, Antony can only give what appears as the stupidest of responses: he says the Nicene Creed, "the symbol of Jerusalem . . . letting out with each phrase a long sigh" (129/*88*).[6]

Consider the following two passages from Flaubert's correspondence. The first dates from 1863, the second was written ten years earlier; yet we can read in the margin of both the future, final version of the *Saint Antony:*

> History, history and natural history! These are the two muses of the modern age. It is with them that we will enter into new worlds. Let's not return to the Middle Ages. *Let us observe,* that is the key. . . . Every religion and every philosophy has claimed to have God to itself, to measure the infinite, and to know the recipe for happiness. What pride and nothingness! (*Corr.,* 3:353)

> Who, until now, has done history as a naturalist would? Have we classed humanity's instincts and seen how, at a given latitude, they have developed and *must* develop? Who has established scientifically how, for a given need of the spirit, a particular form must appear, and who has followed that form everywhere, into the various human kingdoms? Who has generalized the religions? Geoffroy Saint-Hilaire said: the skull is a flattered vertebra. Who has proven, for example, that religion is philosophy become art, and that the brain that beats therein, namely superstition, religious feeling in itself, is made of the same matter everywhere, despite its external differences; that it

corresponds to the same needs, responds to the same impulses, dies by the same accidents, etc.? *(Corr.,* 2:378)

Both the character of Hilarion and the comparative tactic by which he tries to overcome Antony's faith in the uniqueness and necessity of Christianity are new to the 1874 text.[7] My thesis here is that Hilarion stands in the final *Temptation* as a fictionalized answer to the question Flaubert had posed twenty-one years earlier, "Who has generalized the religions?" For this reason, I cannot help but think that the name Hilarion—particularly when applied to a character who explicitly doubles the protagonist–*saint*— was associated in Flaubert's mind with the name Geoffroy Saint-Hilaire, on the model of whose work he had conceived the project of generalizing the religions in the first place.[8] I do not, of course, intend to use the correspondence, and its mentions of a specific natural historian, as a key to the "truth" of the literary work, as if the *Temptation* were a roman à clef and the character of Hilarion a thinly veiled Geoffroy Saint-Hilaire. As Gisèle Séginger has recently shown, it was Flaubert's practice progressively to write out such direct allusions to a scientific or philosophical intertext ("Fiction," 136). My purpose is, rather, to let the letters and novel/drama read one another. I hope to show that the text of the final *Temptation* glosses the earlier letters as thoroughly and convincingly as the letters themselves gloss that text.

In considering the exemplarity of natural history as one of the "muses to the modern age," let us start with the principle of the "unity of organic composition" (or, more precisely, the "theory of analogues") for which Étienne Geoffroy Saint-Hilaire was best known and to which Flaubert's letter of July 7–8, 1853, implicitly refers. In his *Philosophie anatomique,* Geoffroy presented that principle in this way:

> Nature constantly employs the same materials and is only ingenious in
> varying the forms they take. [Compare Flaubert's "the religious feeling in
> itself is made of the same matter everywhere, despite its external
> differences."] As if beholden to what she's been given, she always tends to
> bring forth the same elements in the same order, in the same circumstances,
> and with the same connections. (Quoted in Jacob, 122)

Unlike Cuvier, who distinguished four "principal forms" of animal life (Vertebrates, Mollusca, Articulata, and Radiata), Geoffroy Saint-Hilaire propounded a single "general plan" for all the animals (quoted in Flourens, 720). To this end he published articles comparing the opercular series of the fishes to the ossicles of the middle ear in the terrestrial vertebrates and arguing that insects "live within their spinal columns as mollusks live within their shells" ("Application," 117; "Mémoire sur l'organisation des insectes," quoted in Jacob, 122). In the course of his celebrated debate with Cuvier in February and March 1830, Geoffroy conceded that the expression "the unity of composition" could better be rendered as "the unity of the system in the composition and arrangement of the organic parts"; by "the unity of the system" he means the unity of nature itself such as the anatomist can deduce it (quoted in Cahn, 200). Geoffroy posited a law of "organic balance" whereby the hypertrophy and atrophy of an organ in a given region of an organism would necessarily lead to the atrophy or hypertrophy, respectively, of other organs in that same region. This law of "organic balance," together with the idea that a species' circumstances help explain the hypertrophy or atrophy of given organs, allowed Geoffroy to account for the fact of difference while still attempting to reproduce,

> as a fact that one comes to *a posteriori,* an *a priori* idea that is the fundamental mother-idea of Leibniz's philosophy, which this great genius captured in the expression, variety in unity. (Quoted in Gaudant, 67)

It would be quite impossible to perceive such a unity of the system of nature without recourse to a process of comparison that sought to reduce the apparent diversity of natural phenomena to a more fundamental sameness. The first explicit comparison between religions in chapter 5 of the *Temptation* comes from Antony himself: "all of which [the practices of the barbarian idols] is no more criminal than the religion of the Greeks, the Asiatics and the Romans!" (107/*162*). For Antony, error is error, and no one error is more criminal than another. To say that one non-Christian belief is closer to the truth than another is to admit that the truth can be shared and that Christianity itself is not absolute. Hilarion, of course, rejects the distinction between truth and error, but he maintains the logic of the formula by which the Christian relativizes the other: religious sentiment is religious sentiment, and no one practice is more criminal than another. His first interventions in the march of the gods serve purely to make this point:

> But the gods always demand torture. Your own indeed wanted. . . .
> Why do you perform exorcisms? . . .
> Father, Son and Holy Spirit likewise make up a single person! (108–9/ *164–65*)

When Hilarion murmurs lines of Scripture as a running commentary to the Buddha's life story, he enacts the style of reading that the march of the gods demands; from inside the text he creates that text's proper interpretation. Thus, as the march continues, the function of comparison can become more implicit and more beholden to information given directly by the gods (e.g., Ormuz saying of his cult, "Water was used for purification, loaves were offered on altars, crimes were confessed out loud" [118/*176*]) or by the curiously narrativized stage directions that Jeanne Bem has called the countertext (the Buddha's "halo"; "Antony thinks of Jesus' mother") (Bem, 246). Comparison becomes, as it were, embedded in the very fabric of the text.

To this point, however, there appears no reason to privilege the comparative gestures of natural history over those of comparative religion or mythology. Why, then, was the project of generalizing the religions associated with the anatomical work of Geoffroy Saint-Hilaire and not with the historical relativism, say, of Quinet's *Le Génie des religions* or of Bötigger's *Die Isis-Vesper*, from which Nerval's "Isis" had been drawn, if not exactly stolen?[9]

It was Balzac's "Preface to *La Comédie humaine* [*The Human Comedy*]" that, in 1842, definitively introduced the theories of Geoffroy Saint-Hilaire to the world of French letters. After presenting the theory of the unity of composition and singing the praises of Geoffroy Saint-Hilaire, Balzac writes:

> Convinced by this system before the debates to which it has given rise, I saw that, in this respect, society resembled nature. For does not Society modify man, according to the milieus in which he acts, into as many different men as there are species in zoology? . . . Social species have thus always existed, and will always exist, just as zoological species do. (8)

At the risk of schematizing a complex essay, we may say that Geoffroy's "unity of composition" allows Balzac to treat society as a totality, as a unified system on the order of nature, and that the idea of the social species lets him claim for literature an ease of representation long accorded to the natural historian on the basis of the recognizable, structural distinctions between one species and the next.[10] Balzac wants to write the one work about the one society that is Restoration France; he wants to paint "the portrait of Society, modeled, so to speak, on life itself"; the writer's task is that of "copying all Society" ("Avant-propos," 7, 9).

In his pronouncements on the exemplarity of natural history, the young Flaubert clearly shared Balzac's interest and faith in the possibility of representing, in language, phenomena of the seemingly extralinguistic world. When he says (in a passage I will turn to shortly), "Criticism must proceed as natural history does, *without moral ideas*," Flaubert assumes that the process of representation is not inherently problematic, even though particular representations may be tainted by "moral ideas" (*Corr.*, 2:450). Even as late as 1863, at a time when his novelistic practice increasingly questions the delimited unity of the object-in-the-world upon which classical representation depended, Flaubert still conceives of natural history as a domain of pure, untainted representation.[11] Thus the injunction, "*Let us observe*, that is the key," is a call above all to a certain kind of writing, that same writing with one's impartial eye which had made natural history a "muse to the modern age."

From the beginning, however, Flaubert's claims for the impartiality of natural history give as much the impression of a will to believe as of real conviction. Consider what follows the "absence of the moral idea" claim in his letter to Louise Colet of October 12, 1853:

> Criticism must proceed [Flaubert has in mind a projected history of the poetic sentiment in France] as natural history does, *without moral ideas*. It is not a matter of holding forth on any given form, but rather of showing what composes that form, how it relates to another, and how it *lives* (aesthetics awaits its Geoffroy Saint-Hilaire, that great man who demonstrated the legitimacy of monsters). When we have become accustomed to treating humanity with the same impartiality as the physical sciences bring to the study of matter, we will have taken a huge step forward. . . . Well, I believe this is doable. Perhaps it is only a matter, as in mathematics, of finding the right *method*. This method will be applicable, above all, to Art and Religion, those two great manifestations of the idea. (*Corr.*, 2:450–51)

That Flaubert was not wholly comfortable with his claim of exemplary impartiality for natural history is clear from his recourse here to the "physical sciences" that study "matter," and later to mathematics, as the ultimate methodological examples. Natural history as it is presently done must serve as the model for a new historical criticism because natural history has a *method* of representation; it eschews judgments of value in favor of "impartial" description, contextualization, and functional explanation. Yet behind this model there are—inevitably, it would seem—the models of the more justifiably "impartial" physical and mathematical sciences. What the Flaubert of 1853 perhaps already knows, but seeks to deny in deference to a certain will to believe ("Well, I believe this is doable"), is that the writing of history as a causally linked series of events is an invitation to be partial, and that the best of geological histories—to take an example from *Bouvard et Pécuchet*—can easily turn into "a fairy story in several acts, with man as its apotheosis" (143/*88*).[12] Interestingly enough, this particular history is signed "Cuvier."

Allow me to bracket for a moment Flaubert's will to believe in the impartiality of the methods of natural history in favor of a closer look at the particular method that proved the "legitimacy of monsters." Étienne Geoffroy Saint-Hilaire and his son Isidore were not the first, as Flaubert implies, to have shunned the moralizing rejection of the monstrous for the sake of a scientific study of the monster's place in a natural order.[13] Nor were they first to suggest that monstrosities resulted from abnormalities in the process of embryonic differentiation. What the Geoffroy Saint-Hilaires did was to demonstrate that the monstrous organism grows according to the same complex but regular developmental system as its normal counterpart. In other words, starting from the assumption that accidents of development, such as improper adhesions of the embryo to the placental wall or abnormal deliveries of blood to specific regions of the organism, lay at the heart of the problem of monstrosity, they went on to devise experiments showing that the monstrous growth was a regular and natural response to an initial accident (Cahn, 176ff.). The Geoffroy Saint-Hilaires could therefore reintegrate the monstrous organ into the system of nature by knowing three things: (1) "what it consists of" (i.e., the organ's present state as visible to the examining eye); (2) "how it is attached to another" (what connections or relationships of balancing it maintains with other organs); and (3) "how and by what it lives" (what nourishes it and for what function).

Hilarion, it is true, gives no explanations as to why given practices develop necessarily in given circumstances (under certain "climates," given certain "needs of the spirit"). But he does legitimate the monstrous belief by showing that what seems unnatural to Antony belongs, in fact, to a natural system with its own profound unity. He does to Antony's belief in the godlessness of idolatry exactly what Geoffroy implicitly does to the traditional Christian belief that monsters are "godless creations" (Chateaubriand) (quoted in Jacob, 140). He neither divinizes nor rejects the monstrous; he naturalizes it. For understanding alone mitigates the scandal of the "criminal form":

> Remember all those things in the Scriptures which scandalize you, because you don't know how to understand them. Just so, beneath their criminal shapes, these gods may conceal the truth. (126/*186*)

At the same time, Hilarion shows that the apparently natural beliefs of Christianity carry within them the unnatural idolatries from which they sprang. From the "scientific" point of view, it makes no sense to speak of the naturalness or unnaturalness of specific practices. All historical phenomena are in themselves mixed, heteroclite, even monstrous. Nature resides in the system as a whole; it is not the phenomenal world either wholly or in part. Rather, like the religious sentiment in itself, nature stands above the obvious diversity of phenomena as a creation of a scientific intelligence that in the pursuit of impartiality effectively validates its will to power.

Notice in passing that science's greatest ruse is also its most stringent demand. The pursuit of a scientific impartiality can satisfy an individual's will to power only so long as that will to power never announces itself as such. At the end of the march, however, the figure of Science reveals its will to power for all to see:

> And in front of him is Hilarion—but transfigured, lovely as an archangel, luminous as the sun—and so tall that to see him ANTONY tilts his head back. "Who then are you?"
> HILARION "My kingdom has the dimensions of the universe; and my desire knows no bounds. I go on forever, freeing the spirit, weighing up worlds, without hate, without fear, without pity, without love and without God. I am called Science."
> ANTONY tilts his head back. "You're more likely . . . the Devil!"
> HILARION fixes him with his eyes. "Do you want to see him?"
> ANTONY . . . "The horror I'll feel will rid me of him forever.—Yes!"
> A cloven hoof appears.
> Antony has regrets.
> But the Devil has tossed him on his horns, and carries him off. (141–42/ 203–4)

Confusion

Hilarion names himself Science at the moment of his triumph over the last of the gods, "the Lord God"; he is "lovely as an archangel, luminous as the sun." But the eminent sublimity of this victory is vitiated inasmuch as, at the moment of his transfiguration, the moment of his *naming,* he takes on a divine and absolute character, a character equivalent to those which all his previous statements and demonstrations had sought to relativize. In other words, Hilarion victorious immediately becomes subject to scrutiny on the basis of those principles which had assured his victory in the first place. They are (1) that no one system of belief has an absolute monopoly on truth to the exclusion of other systems; (2) that all absolutisms, like all organic objects in a vitalist universe, are subject to an exhaustion inherent in the notion of life itself; and (3) that the true discourse never contradicts itself. I have already spoken to the first of these principles; the pages that follow consider the second and third.

Prior to Virchow's elaboration in the late 1850s of a cellular theory of reproduction and growth, so-called vitalist biology explained animal pro-creation by hypothesizing a process whereby brute matter was imbued with mysterious "vital principles" (quoted in Jacob, 140). As a result of that hy-pothesis, vitalists concerned themselves first and foremost with the fate of individual organisms as manifestations of the "vital properties," and espe-cially with the struggle against death that characterizes the particular life. "If life is a matter of death," wrote Cabanis in 1830, "death in turn gives birth to and immortalizes life" (quoted in Jacob, 140). In other words, this time of François Jacob, "If the vital properties are worn down in each individual being, they are conserved throughout the living world" (140). For the vital-ist, then, the life and death of particular organisms functioned dialectically to assure the continuity of Life as an attribute of the system as a whole.

In the final version of the *Temptation,* and in that version alone, Death and Lust take one another by the waist and sing a hymn to the vitalist dialectic:

—I hasten the decay of matter!
—I help to scatter the seeds!
—You destroy, for my renewing!
—You breed, for my destroying!
—Make me more potent!
—Impregnate me where I rot! . . .
ANTONY "Death is then a mere illusion, a veil, masking in places the continuity of life." (154–55/*220*)

Just such a dialectic of life and death lies at the heart of the march of the gods. Like natural historians watching the generation and dissolution of liv-ing beings, Hilarion, Antony, and we as readers consider a sequence of reli-gious beliefs and practices caught in the ebb and flow of vital properties. Just as the vitalist dialectic assures the continuity of life itself, so the successive destructions of individual expressions of the religious sentiment serve to demonstrate the unity and continuity of that sentiment in itself. Several pages into the march, Hilarion explains the multiple aspects and rapid trans-formations of the Indian gods by saying, "Life exhausts itself, forms wear out; and they must progress in their metamorphoses" (110/*166–167*). It is difficult to read the *Temptation* without reading "life exhausts itself, forms wear out" as an embedded commentary on the dissolution that overtakes all the gods the fiction presents, and that is explicitly thematized as dissolution in the case of the Latin gods.[14] It is equally difficult to imagine that "Science" later might be exempt from that very process of exhaustion it here proves to be inherent in the assumption of religious power.

As if to underscore science's newfound status as religion, in chapter 6 Flaubert shows its spokesman succumbing to the "pride and nothingness"—elsewhere reserved for "religion" and "philosophy"—of "claiming to have God to itself, to measure the infinite, and to know the recipe for happiness." The chapter begins with the Devil whisking Antony away and up into the skies.[15] Freed of weight and suffering, Antony learns—or relearns—the secrets of the Newtonian cosmos:

> THE DEVIL carries him among the stars. "They attract and at the same time repel each other. Each one's action results from the others and makes its contribution—without means of any auxiliary, by the force of law, the single virtue of order." (144/*207*)

But Antony suddenly lowers his gaze and asks, "What is the purpose of all this?" The Devil answers, "There is no purpose! How should God have a purpose? By what experience could he be taught, by what reflection determined?" (144–45/*208*).

By using the denial of finality as a simple point of transition between Newtonian physics and a bastardized version of Spinozist metaphysics, the Devil sets up the first of many contradictions that will riddle his learned discourse. In classical, mechanist physics, "there is no purpose" denotes the workings of nature as a closed system of inviolable laws; nature's order is the creation of a hypothetical Prime Mover who retired from the field once the initial act of creation was accomplished. Spinoza of course denies the God/nature dualism upon which this mechanist scenario is predicated. "God" and "Nature" are simply two names for the same infinite substance, the *natura naturans*; God is thus the world's immanent and perpetual cause, not just its transient first cause. Or, as the Devil himself says of God: "Since he exists eternally, he acts eternally" (145). In other words, the God of the Spinozist Devil is an "auxiliary force" such as the Newtonian Devil had denied on the previous page.

At the end of the chapter the Devil changes his tune again, denying philosophic access to the thing-in-itself:

> But things reach you only through the medium of your mind. Like a concave mirror it distorts objects—and you lack the means to make accurate checks. (148/*212*)

What follows is a syllogistic hodgepodge of Cartesian doubt, Heracleitean flux, and Renanian relativism whose conclusion—"Perhaps there is nothing"—evidently contradicts the Spinozist Devil's certainty that "there is no nothingness! There is no void!" (148/*212*, 145/*209*).

Note that the transition to this apparently most nihilistic of arguments is assured by the implications of the argument that precedes it:

> You will never know the universe in its full extent; consequently, you cannot form an idea of its cause, nor have any right notion of God, nor even say that the universe is infinite—for it would first be necessary to know infinity! (148/*212*)

The Devil operates here from the Spinozist premise that in order to have truly adequate knowledge of any physical object, one must possess in oneself all physical objects ("the universe in its full extent"); one must be the Infinite Intellect itself.[16] Because (he continues) you are not that Infinite Intellect—or "the universe in its full extent" *or* "God": the concepts are fundamentally equivalent—you can have no idea of the universe's cause, no accurate notion of God, nor even the certainty that the universe is finite. In other words, the Devil's discourse is constructed to suggest that contradiction or paradox lies at the heart of "Science," represented here by a philosopher whom Flaubert elsewhere calls "my old and triply great Spinoza" (*Corr.*, 4:505). Whether or not Spinoza's answers to this problem in his philosophy are convincing need not concern us.[17] It is more to my purpose to note the effect that the presence of such contradictory implications has on Science's claim to master the universe.

Earlier, in his guise as Hilarion, the Devil had cited the contradictions of Christian Scripture as proof of its fallibility:

> And yet the angel of the annunciation appears in Matthew to Joseph, whereas in Luke it's to Mary. The anointing of Jesus by a woman happens according to the first Gospel at the beginning of his public ministry, but according to the three others only a few days before his death. (58)

In making this argument, Hilarion appeals to a principle of noncontradiction by which nineteenth-century science would have distinguished itself from fourth-century exegesis, and to which Flaubert's contemporaries could have been counted on to subscribe. And yet, "the reader must be duped": this note, from a scenario to *Bouvard et Pécuchet,* applies equally to the hegemony of science in *La Tentation de saint Antoine.*[18] For in the midst of the cosmic voyage, the discourse of science itself becomes contradictory, repeating the very book against which it ostensibly struggles. "Science" foreshadows its own dissolution by proving itself just one more religious belief subject to the vitalist dialectic and its twilight of the gods.

I should be clear on one point, however. "Science" in the *Temptation* is not stupid by virtue of its contradictions. To Flaubert's mind, self-contradiction was the prerogative of God, as well as of that rare artistic genius who was so "penetrated" by the objective world as to be able to project that world in all of its confusion, in the form of what Frank Paul Bowman has called "a vision of ironic chaos."[19] Contradiction was also the sine qua non of Flaubert's political pronouncements and a dominant strategy of his humor. Insofar as "virtue" implied to Flaubert an attitude of stoic resignation doubled by a yearning for that very ideal one is resigned to not attaining, the appropriation of contradiction into one's manner of life was a largely virtuous gesture. It was an ironic acceptance of the modern condition and of "democratic confusion," an acceptance that nonetheless signaled one's desire for an ideal, originary, or noncontradictory realm of the spirit (more on this desire in chapter 5). In short, "Science" in the *Temptation* is not stupid because it is contradictory; it is stupid only by dint of its pretense to an absolute power over a doctrine it in fact doubles.[20]

Connaissance

From the moment, at the end of chapter 3, when Hilarion offers to lead Antony to a land where wise men live beneath gigantic trees, nourished by a "warm air," the temptation of knowledge appears preeminent among the temptations. "You shall listen to them," Hilarion promises, "and the face of the Unknown will be unveiled" (60/100). No figure in the *Temptation* better incarnates the temptation of *connaissance*—as both "knowledge" *and* "acquaintance"—than Apollonius of Tyana. Antony himself sums up the attraction of this half sage and magician, half tour guide and pimp, when he says, "His way of speaking about the gods makes one long to know them," and thereby sets into motion the march of the idols and gods (106/162). One offer of acquaintance particularly troubles Antony, and particularly exemplifies the ambivalence of Apollonian *connaissance:*

APOLLONIUS "What is your desire? your dream? In the time it takes for a wish. . . ."
ANTONY "Jesus, Jesus, come to my aid!"
APOLLONIUS "Shall I make him appear, Jesus?"
ANTONY "What? How?"
APOLLONIUS "It will be he and none other! He will throw off his crown, and we shall talk face to face!" (105/*159–60*)

The reference is of course to First Corinthians, which I quote first in its French translation:

> À présent nous voyons confusément dans un miroir, mais nous verrons alors face à face. À présent, partielle est ma science, mais je connaîtrai alors comme je suis connu. (13:12)

At present we see confusedly in a mirror, but then we shall see face to face. At present, my knowledge is partial, but then I will know as I am known.

Apollonius wreaks havoc with the subtle metaphorics of the biblical text. An image that in Paul stands for the perfect coincidence of knowledge and acquaintance ("face to face") becomes for Apollonius the mark of familiarity and a certain submission. If Christian history is a voyage with Christ to the perfect knowledge of Christ and the Father, the Christlike magician can offer that voyage, too, albeit in the most absolute spirit of parody. Not the end of history, the appearance of Jesus here would have been just one adventure among others, the diversion of a moment that quickly passes. For Apollonius, the voyage to knowledge is nothing more than a series of fantastic acquaintances, a project of exotic adventure endlessly rejuvenated for the pleasure of the voyage itself, and for the fundamentally equivalent pleasure of the narration:

> On the edge of the sea we met the Cynocephales gorged with milk, on their way back from their expedition to the island of Taprobane. . . . The earth, in the end, became narrower than a sandal—and having thrown some drops of the Ocean at the sun, we turned right, to come back. (98/*149*)

And now we must start the pilgrimage again! (103/*157*)

The Devil of chapter 6 succeeds where Apollonius had failed. He guides Antony on a voyage of knowledge through a marvelous universe, but he does so as heir to a conception of knowledge as acquaintance that dates from the intervention of the quixotic sage. Blithely assuming a perfect analogy between books and the world, the Devil reads and represents physical and

metaphysical systems as Apollonius read and represented the fantastic phenomena he had seen on his travels. What the Devil doesn't see, or doesn't
wish to see, is that philosophical discourse is subject to a principle of noncontradiction foreign to the travelogue. This blindness makes him as ridicu-
lous in his high seriousness as Apollonius, that prophet of the eternal return,
was serious in his ridiculousness.

If Hilarion's comparative tactics are more subtle than the tactics of Apollonius and the Devil, they are nonetheless based on a similar, antitheological,
and decidedly antimystical notion of knowledge as acquaintance. Once
again a text of Geoffroy Saint-Hilaire helps to render explicit a conception
that Hilarion's reticence—and Flaubert's effacing of his intertextual tracks—
must leave implicit. In his *Fragment sur la nature* (*Fragment on Nature*) of 1829,
Geoffroy presents the following account of the origin of human knowledge:

> But finally, having set out to *know* himself and that which exists around him,
> [man] comes to establish himself *as master* in the heart of creation. For soon
> he will be seen conceiving and pursuing the audacious enterprise of *taking
> all things in creation one by one*, so as to *submit to himself,* to *register,* and to
> *inventory* in a manner of speaking all of nature's possessions and riches, as
> though he were giving them to himself as pieces of his furniture. (25)[21]

For Geoffroy the acquisition of knowledge is a process composed of
three stages, the first two of which—the consideration one by one of all
created things and the establishment of records and inventories—he evokes
here. In the third and final stage, one "arrives at a deduction, a general idea
which includes and explains [observed] coincidences" (*Fragment,* 16–17).
By an effort of "intellectual reduction," one discovers the "general laws of
nature." The essay mentions two such laws: Kepler's law of universal gravi-
tation and Geoffroy's own principle of the unity of organic composition.

Knowledge for Geoffroy Saint-Hilaire is the appropriation and domestication of one's self and one's circumstances. The world is mastered when it
is shown to be saturated with analogy, and this on two levels. Above and
beyond the play of similarity and difference that allows for the inventory,
for the establishment (in the best Linnaean tradition) of a table summarizing
the universe's essential facts, Geoffroy perceives "philosophic resemblances." Organisms that are marked by the sign of difference on the level
of classification—vertebrates and mollusks, for example—can be shown to
be analogous by the intellectual effort of a "philosophical anatomy" capable
of distinguishing an underlying uniformity of organization. I have shown
how the Hilarion of the march of the gods manipulates a comparable notion

of the uniformity of religious sentiment, originally suggested to him by Antony himself. At the same time, it is Hilarion who appears most responsible, within the diegesis, for the work of classification that characterizes those chapters in which he plays a specifically demonstrative role. Thus he is responsible for introducing Antony first to problems of biblical exegesis, then to the heresies, and finally to the "false" gods (in chapters 3, 4, and 5 respectively). Hilarion should also be credited, in his capacity as knowing guide to the chaos of Antony's phantasms, with the implicit order perceptible within certain of these chapters. The heresies of chapter 4, for example, appear in topical groups treating the dualism of matter and spirit, devotions and mortification, the problem of evil and its origin, the humanity or divinity of Christ, persecution, and so on.

In another of his midnight letters to Louise Colet, Flaubert writes:

> One would have to know everything to write. . . . The books from which whole literatures have sprung, like Homer and Rabelais, are encyclopedias of their age. They knew everything, those good folks, and we, we know nothing. (*Corr.*, 2:544)

La Tentation de saint Antoine is both encyclopedia and anti-encyclopedia. It continues in the long tradition of encyclopedic narratives from the Bible, Cervantes, and Rabelais to Buffon and Goethe, borrowing heavily from each of these; yet it deconstructs the mechanism for the transfer of knowledge upon which the encyclopedia is predicated. When Hilarion organizes the panoply of human superstitions along thematic lines, he carries out an essentially encyclopedic task. As the book progresses, however, such implicit structure increasingly gives way to an anarchic comprehensiveness that makes the gesture of being encyclopedic without truly fulfilling the predicative conditions for the appropriation of knowledge. Such empty gestures of predication are particularly noticeable in the book's final chapters. When the text tells us in one such list that a "Mirag" is a "horned hare that inhabits the isles of the sea," it (strictly speaking) fulfills the promise of predication but without rendering the proper name perceptibly less strange, and thus less resistant to assimilation into the field of the reader's knowledge (162/ *229*). It does not *tame* the horned hare.

Knowledge, according to Geoffroy, is like furniture; it clearly belongs to you only when every piece of it has been recorded and inventoried. The lists that fill the *Temptation*'s final chapters play on this reassuring function of the inventory, yet—with the possible exception of the classically emblematic list of the Olympians (127–28/*186–87*)—all tend to be as unappropriable as the objects they contain, as resistant to domestication as "alligators' heads on roe-deer's feet, owls with snakes' tails, swine with a tigers' snouts," and so on (162/*229*). If, on the one hand, the plot of the *Temptation* charts a path of knowledge and science from the first century to Flaubert's day, from exegetical disputes through Newtonian physics to the cellular theory that informs the book's final pages, on the other hand it enacts a progressive disintegration of the possibility of knowledge's formation and transfer; Science's apparent victory is nearly contemporaneous with the noise of the lists and the indifferentiation of monsters in the book's final pages. As the earliest incarnation of "Science," Hilarion represents both the second and the third stages of knowledge in Geoffroy's scheme. He creates orders of identity and difference and still masters the "philosophic resemblance." His method is silent but efficient. The Devil follows Hilarion in the time of the diegesis, yet marks a curious regression to Geoffroy's first stage. He takes cosmologies and epistemologies "one by one," establishes analogies between them that allow him to fill the silence of the heavens with a discourse that is explicitly (but inefficiently) scientific. He cannot see "philosophic resemblances" because his science has not passed through the stage of the inventory. Because he cannot yet see difference (between Newton and Spinoza, for example), he cannot perceive the "philosophic resemblances" that may surmount it. His analogies are the simple, uncritical analogies of Geoffroy's primitive antiquarian. Rather than demonstrating that the philosophic sentiment is "of the same stuff everywhere" by observing philosophies from a critical distance, the Devil unwittingly parodies such a demonstration by enacting the indifferentiation of philosophies. Bouvard and Pécuchet themselves are never more stupid. Or, rather, they are never more enamored of the notion that knowledge is a matter of acquaintance, and as such can lead nowhere, can serve no purpose except to perpetuate desire and generate text.

The monster that is Flaubert's final novel exists already preformed in the germ of the Devil's discourse. What other passage of the *Temptation* better argues that writing is simply a processing or transposition (nearly a *copying*) of the already written? What other seems better to illustrate *Bouvard's* hypothetical subtitle, "On Lack of Method in the Sciences" (Oeuvres [Pléiade], 2:704)? In short, who but the Devil could have written *Bouvard et Pécuchet?*

Desire

At the moment he comes into his inheritance, Frédéric Moreau, the protagonist of Flaubert's *L'Éducation sentimentale* (Sentimental Education), faces a crucial choice. Should he buy stock, and thereby accede to the power of that network of capital—epitomized in the novel by M. Dambreuse—that quietly but effectively subtends Flaubert's novel? Or should he follow his inclination and buy furniture?

Read in conjunction with Geoffroy Saint-Hilaire's theory of knowledge, the *Temptation* implies that a similar choice lies on the route to cognitive power. You can strive for science, for a strategy of control masked by its fundamental reticence to say that it controls. Or you can, as it were, get stuck as a primitive antiquarian of uninventoried knowledge; you can remain in Geoffroy's first stage. Supposing one might willingly pass through that first stage, what might be the overriding appeal of undifferentiated *connaissance*? Why would the Devil, or Antony, *choose* confusion?

In the aftermath of the dance of Death and Lust, Antony exclaims:

> Death is then a mere illusion, a veil, masking in places the continuity of life.
>
> But since Substance is one, why are the Forms so varied?
>
> There must be, somewhere, primordial figures whose bodies are nothing but their image. If one could see them, one would know the link between matter and thought, what Being consists of! (155/*221*)

Antony goes on to say that he has seen such "primordial figures" painted on the wall of the temple of Belus in Babylon, that those who cross the desert encounter animals beyond description. The Sphinx and Chimera then surge into view. But Antony has made a phantasmatic mistake. These "primordial figures" are not those which can help explain why the Forms of a unique Substance are varied, nor in what Being itself consists. The Sphinx and Chimera episode is interesting as spectacle, but it is of little consequence in the process of temptation.

Flaubert once told Edmond de Goncourt that Antony's final "defeat" was "due to the scientific cell."[22] The scene is uncanny; Antony participates in a fantastic journey back through time where plants and animals start to resemble humans and the products of human artifice:

> And then the plants become confused with the rocks.
>
> Stones resemble brains, stalactites resemble nipples, iron flowers resemble tapestries ornate with figures. (164/*231*)

"At the end," as a marginal note from Flaubert's scenarios for the *Temptation* tells us, Antony is too far away, in an abstract land, having seen everything, having lost all consciousness of himself, having become nothing *more than a looking machine, a living contemplation.* . . . He does not know how to distinguish the Orders of Nature. (*Oeuvres* [Club], 4:366)

Antony has been witness to all creation; he has quite literally *become* the Impartial Eye. In fact, his status as an observer appears so plainly "scientific" that critics have been known to ask whether, in the passage that follows, Antony might not be looking through a microscope:[23]

He lies flat on his stomach, leaning on both elbows; and holding his breath, he watches.

Insects having lost their stomachs continue to eat; dried ferns recover their freshness; missing limbs grow again.

At last, he sees little globular masses, no bigger than pin-heads and garnished with hairs all round. A vibration quivers across them.

ANTONY deliriously: "O happiness! happiness! I have seen the birth of life, I have seen the beginning of movement. The blood in my veins is beating so hard that it will burst them. I feel like flying, swimming, yelping, bellowing, howling. I'd like to have wings, a carapace, a rind, to breathe out smoke, wave my trunk, twist my body, divide myself up, to be inside everything, to drift away with odors, develop as plants do, flow like water, vibrate like sound, gleam like light, to curl myself up into every shape, to penetrate each atom, to get down to the depth of matter—to be matter! (232)

There are countless ways for a reader to feel uncomfortable about this scene, many of them no doubt intended by Flaubert himself. To minds attuned to the idea of scientific progress, the contemporaneity of the represented science—cellular theory dates from the late 1830s; Haeckel's theories of creation, upon which Flaubert particularly draws, appeared in 1867—would have coincided disturbingly with the breakdown of the promise of predication upon which the transfer of knowledge depends. But the mythic journey back to the origin clearly fulfills Antony's search for "what Being consists of" since he reads the material cell in terms traditionally reserved for the soul, or for God: "I'd like to . . . divide myself up, to be inside everything, to drift away with odors, [etc.]." A new Spinoza, he has found "the link between matter and thought." It is tempting to claim that Antony's plunge to the origin also dramatizes a presupposition of all unity-of-plan theories—namely, the possibility of *speculatively* reconstructing an original moment when the unique Substance appeared indeed unique, a moment prior to the development of the so-called various Forms. Of Geoffroy Saint-Hilaire, Cuvier once wrote:

> Behind this theory of analogies is another, much older theory, refuted long ago, but which some Germans have recently revived in the name of pantheism—namely, that of the production of all species through the successive development of primitively identical embryos. (Quoted in Cahn 202)

In the *Temptation's* return to a hypothetical primitive state, however, everything seems naturally to resemble everything else.[24] Such a primitive similitude is in fact the death of simile as a willed rapprochement of fundamentally different entities, as the perception of "philosophic resemblances." Antony takes joy in becoming the Impartial Eye precisely because the indifferentiation of what he sees *precludes* the possibility of a scientific inventory on the basis of similarity and difference. At the origin, Flaubert's scenarios attest, willed analogy and the indifferentiation of phenomena are necessarily one and the same: "Antony's delirium in discovering this *rapprochement or rather this confusion,* because, in the end, one can no longer distinguish" (*Oeuvres* [Club], 4:364; emphasis added). Antony yields to a frenzied joy when circumstances force him to abdicate his judgment. In other words, he becomes a scientist on the model of Geoffroy Saint-Hilaire (the Impartial Eye) just as science on that same model becomes impossible.

In this final scene, the temptation of knowledge itself goes marvelously awry. Antony's wanting to become the cell is indicative of a desire for maximum *connaissance* that paradoxically kills the desire for *connaissance* in the stupidity of pure being. Not only does he want to know all, be acquainted with every remote corner of the material world, he wants to *be* all materiality ("to curl myself up into every shape, to penetrate each atom"). In thus acceding to the saintliness of the Flaubertian artist, who surpasses "individual restriction" by embracing "Nature's immensity," Antony effectively dies to his own desire, both cognitive *and* sexual (Séginger, "Artiste," 82).[25]

Christ's superbly anticlimactic appearance in the book's final paragraphs constitutes for Antony no real acquaintance in the Christian sense; His appearance is no milestone of history. But it does reestablish the desire for knowledge *as desire*:

> Day at last dawns; and like the raised curtains of a tabernacle, golden clouds furling into large scrolls uncover the sky.

There in the middle, inside the very disc of the sun, radiates the face of Jesus Christ.

Antony makes the sign of the cross and returns to his prayers. (164/*232*)

Antony returns to the same endless cycle of chores, prayers, and temptations with which the book began. Perhaps he has learned nothing. But we as readers at least have seen that what matters in temptation is not whether one resists or succumbs; Antony in fact repeatedly gives in to his temptations, only to be saved by an act of grace. What matters in temptation is that the structure of temptation itself be preserved, that desire itself persist.[26] In a text that plays so heavily on the confusions endemic to a highly syncretic moment in the development of Christianity, and in which the cognitive confusions of the saint's all-knowing guides lead ironically to a series of climactic confusions into and within matter itself, the last word goes to desire—to a desire that, like science's own, "knows no bounds" (141/*203*).

We have examined a series of specific additions to the third and final version of *La Tentation de saint Antoine* that allow it to enact the consolidation and disintegration of the power of a scientific method. These include Hilarion and his comparative tactic, the vitalist dialectic, "Science's" transfiguration, and the spectacle of cells. My analysis thus far suggests that the disintegration of science enacted in the 1874 *Temptation* stands as an implicit recognition that the appeal of what Flaubert in 1853 called "a method to be found" was precisely that it was too Promethean, too ideal, and never would be found. By their every action, Bouvard and Pécuchet show that the truth of science is a will to believe in it, a resolve to say with Flaubert, "Well, I believe this is doable," and that the lack of an infallible method is actually a precondition of that truth.[27] But Hilarion already implies as much. For while proving that there is no singular truth, Hilarion admits: "Our merit lies only in our thirst for the true" (57/*96*). As a quest for truth and method, science must fail in the *Temptation* because science, truth, and method are all unreachable desiderata. And as Flaubert himself wrote, just three years before his death, "desire makes one live" (*Corr.* [Conard], 8:94).

Melancholy and Boorishness

The danger in thus giving desire the last word, as did the original piece on which this chapter is based, is that one fails fully to appreciate the fundamental melancholy of desire in the late Flaubert. That sense of eternal return on which the 1874 *Temptation* so strikingly ends should thus be read together with a letter from April 1870, in which Flaubert tells George Sand, "I am overwhelmed by a black melancholy, which wells up in connection with everything and nothing, several times a day. *Then, it passes and wells up again*" (*Corr.*, 4:180; emphasis added). (Flaubert goes on to note that he wants to finish the death notice of his friend Louis Bouilhet so as to get back to the *Temptation*; "since it's an extravagant thing, I hope it will divert me."[28]) In what remains of this chapter, I return to Flaubert's correspondence, and to Sartre's reading thereof in *L'Idiot de la famille*, in order to examine the specifically melancholic resonances of that desire which "makes one live."

The profound melancholy of which Flaubert complains in April 1870 clearly deepened after France stumbled into war with Prussia.[29] In early August, some two weeks into the conflict, Flaubert writes to Sand again:

> I wallow in a bottomless melancholy, despite work, despite the good Saint Antony, who ought to distract me. Is it the result of my repeated griefs [the deaths of Bouilhet, Saint-Beuve, Jules Duplan, and Jules de Goncourt]? Perhaps. But the war has much to do with it. (*Corr.*, 4:218/2:155)

In late September, after the French army's defeat at Sedan and the resultant fall of the empire, Flaubert tells his niece, Caroline Commanville, "I consider myself . . . a man who is finished, emptied out. I am no more than a shell, a shadow of a man" (*Corr.*, 4:238). Finally, several weeks later, he writes this to Princess Mathilde (cousin of the deposed Napoléon III):

> I have the feeling it's the end of the world. Whatever happens, everything I've loved is lost. When the war is over, we shall fall into an order of things loathsome to people of taste. (*Corr.*, 4:251)

It is surely the case that Flaubert suffered bouts of melancholy throughout his life. In a January 1852 letter in which he advises Louise Colet to scratch herself because he has enshrined her in a louse-infested Orientalist niche, Flaubert submits that

> if I am hard on you, remember that it's the consequence of the melancholy, the bitter irritability and funereal languor that harass and overwhelm me. Deep inside me there is always the after-taste of my land's medieval melancholies. (*Corr.*, 2:33)

Moreover, just as the first *Temptation* would be associated in Flaubert's mind with the deaths of his sister Caroline and his childhood friend Alfred Le

Poittevin (to whom the 1874 version is dedicated), so too was the final version composed under the shadow of "the loss of my dearest friends" (as listed above) (*Corr.*, 4:252). The work "of my entire life" was thus, just as importantly, the work "of all my dead" (*Corr.*, 4:531).

But the melancholy that the events of *l'année terrible* inspired in Flaubert cannot be reduced to constitutional despondency, the effects of cumulative personal loss, or some combination thereof. On several occasions, Flaubert's letters detail hysterical symptoms provoked by the Prussian invasion, which led to the billeting of Prussian soldiers in Flaubert's family house at Croisset. "I consider myself a lost man," he writes to Caroline in January 1871. "Every day I feel my intellect grow weaker and my heart dry up. . . . It's as though all those Prussian boots had trampled on my brain" (*Corr.*, 4:269). Several months later, at the height of the Commune, Flaubert tells Princess Mathilde:

> For eight months, I too have choked with shame, grief and rage. I have spent nights crying like a child. I have been close to killing myself. I have felt madness take hold of me and the first symptoms, the first attacks of cancer.[30] But, by dint of having boiled my gall, I believe it's petrified. . . . After the Prussian invasion, I pulled a funeral shroud over the face of France. (*Corr.*, 4:318)

We know that several of Flaubert's friends and correspondents— including Edmond de Goncourt, Théophile Gautier, and, above all, George Sand—suffered acutely from the spectacle of the Paris Commune.[31] Having drawn his figurative pall over France in the wake of the Prussian invasion, however, Flaubert actually greets the Commune with relative equanimity:

> As for me, . . . I find that, *after* the invasion, calamities scarcely touch me. The war with Prussia struck me as a great upheaval of nature, one of those cataclysms that only happens every six thousand years. By contrast, Paris's insurrection seems to me a very clear, nearly ordinary thing. (*Corr.*, 4:308)

By Flaubert's own account, the Commune failed to traumatize because the Prussian invasion had already monopolized his full store of "despair" (*Corr.*, 4:313). Indeed, the burning of Paris was but the "fifth act" of a "tragedy" whose horrors, Flaubert writes, "are modeled on, and quite probably triggered by, Prussia's" (*Corr.*, 4:336).

This last argument—that the Prussians in some sense instigated the Commune—should of course give us pause. In casting the 1874 *Temptation*'s march of the idols and gods in terms of a vitalist dialectic, whereby the wearing down of vital properties in individual beings helps to preserve those properties in the system as a whole, Flaubert clearly fictionalizes an anxiety that already plagues him in the fall of 1870:

> Whatever happens, the world I belonged to has run its course. The Latins are finished! Now it's the turn of the Saxons, who will be devoured by the Slavs. And so on. (*Corr.*, 4:245)

Flaubert's letters repeatedly thematize the agony of the Latin race[32] as the demise of all elegance, a death of distinction in all its forms:

> What grieves me is . . . the conviction that we are entering into a hideous world, from which the Latins will be excluded. All forms of elegance, even material elegance, are done for. A mandarin like me no longer has a place in the world. (*Corr.*, 4:256)

As I suggested earlier, Jupiter's diatribe against a world where "what triumphs is the mob's imbecility, the meanness of the individual, the hideousness of every race!" is a thinly veiled allusion to contemporary France, to a death of the Latins this Latin god both enacts and explains (130/*190*). But in speaking of the Prussians as the instigators of a "tragedy" that culminates in the Commune, Flaubert fails to heed the lesson of the vitalist dialectic, aptly evoked by Sartre (albeit not in those terms) when he writes: "The Latin world bears its death within itself as the subject of history, doomed to future annihilation: the Prussians merely carry out the sentence, they are the agents of Destiny" (3:592/*5:552*).

Why, then, would Flaubert lay the responsibility for the entire "tragedy" of 1870–1871 at the door of the Prussians? More precisely, why did the Prussian victory come to stand in Flaubert's mind as a sort of historical shorthand for five related, though by no means equivalent, developments: "first, the disaster threatened by the opposition; second, the fall of the Empire; third, the advent of the Republic; fourth, the triumph of science over the dream; fifth, accession to power of those positive and serious young men who have fossilized him in advance" (Sartre, 3:471/*5:436–37*)? I would agree with Sartre that "Prussia is merely a cover for [Flaubert's] real target, *science*," but precisely how we are to understand "science" here needs working out (3:598/*5:556*).

L'Idiot de la famille is a notoriously unruly work. At once a case study in the construction of a self through the mediation of others and an exemplification of Sartre's progressive–regressive method, *L'Idiot* is by turns brilliantly insightful, maddeningly long-winded, and surprisingly reductive. At the risk of appearing reductive in turn, I should like to isolate two analytic registers in Sartre's study, exemplified by their quite different accounts of Flaubertian "science." In dubbing the first and most evident of these Sartre's "strong" register, I want ultimately—in a twist on the logic of "loser wins"—to make a case for the felicity of the "weak."

In his preface to *L'Idiot*, Sartre announces his desire to uncover the "profound homogeneity" of Flaubert's life (1:7). Isolating as a pivotal moment Flaubert's nervous crisis at Pont l'Évêque in January 1844, Sartre's "strong" account privileges Flaubert's oedipal relation with his father, Dr. Achille-Cléophas Flaubert. By justifying the abandonment of his Parisian law studies, and thus opening the way to a life of writerly retreat at Croisset, Flaubert's fall at Pont-l'Évêque allows the young exile from a familial ethic of bourgeois seriousness to dream of a specifically literary "reign of personal power," in which he might place his bourgeois readers "in the frying pan of his words and make them pop like chestnuts" (*Idiot,* 3:458/5:424; *Corr.,* 2:16/1:152). And yet, Sartre contends, "Gustave's profound intention in 1844 is not to liberate himself from his father but, quite the contrary, to become reintegrated with his family and live in it under the authority of the black Lord" (3:664/5:620). In his embrace of a personalized sadistic power, as in his preference for oneiric irreality over a bourgeois, scientific realism, the young Gustave thus "cries out in advance for" the regime of an emperor—Napoléon III—whom he would come to see as an amusing version of the Antichrist (3:463/5:428, 3:461/5:427).

Sartre's account of the melancholy into which the events of 1870 plunged Flaubert turns around the writer's quest for social distinction. Arguing that Flaubert "needs the Empire so that his own failure—the fall beneath the human—should find its reward in a false but indefinitely repeated ennoblement," Sartre speaks of the Liberal empire as Flaubert's "*optimal* society" (3:577/5:537, 3:447/5:413). By treating Flaubert as its "great writer," Sartre argues, the late empire conferred upon him a nobility that, despite Flaubert's professed scorn, "instantly liberated him from the bourgeois he was, beneath his skin" (3:468/5:433, 3:536/5:498). Sartre's answer to the question of what triggers Flaubert's melancholy is categorical: "There is no doubt that it is the Empire. The Empire, meaning himself, since Napoleon III is the Garçon in power" (3:501/5:465). Defeat at Sedan and the subsequent proclamation of the republic thus

destroyed the surly courtier in [Flaubert] as well as the change of class from above—which he took in general as fictive and *believed* to be true in August

'66—and plunged him back into his intolerable reality as a bourgeois "living on his income and occupying himself with literature." . . . The imaginary child learns, half a century after his birth, that the real is a plenitude that cannot be abandoned. (3:581/*5:541*)

The events of September 1870 were especially traumatic to Flaubert, Sartre suggests, because they restored "the primal situation," reinstalling "the gaze of the Father in Gustave" and reducing him to his childhood role of family idiot (3:597/*5:556*). Art's uselessness became once again "his original sin"; "he alone, the younger son, brother of idiots, children, and beasts, has been denied scientific understanding" (3:597/*5:556*, 3:600/*5:558*).

I obviously have no quarrel with Sartre's contention that the Prussians served to focalize Flaubert's discontent with the events of 1870–71 inasmuch as they enjoyed a particular relationship with science. On several occasions, Flaubert specifically bemoans a collapse of intellectual distinction implied by the bellicose behavior of the Prussian "scientists":

Is it possible to believe in progress and civilization in the face of all that's happening now? What good is science, since that nation, full of scientists, is committing abominations worthy of the Huns! And worse, because they are systematic, cold-blooded, deliberate, without the excuse of passion or hunger. (*Corr.*, 4:264/*2:164*).

I bear no hatred of the communards, for the same reason I don't hate rabid dogs. What continues to grieve me is the invasion of the learned doctors, shattering mirrors with pistol shots and stealing clocks—history has never known that. (*Corr.*, 4:342)

To suggest, however, that the fall of the empire returns Flaubert to his situation circa 1844, to a state in which "scientific understanding" is largely denied him, is to ignore Flaubert's engagement with the discourse of science up to and including the 1874 *Temptation*. In reducing science to a manifestation of "the *realizing* gaze of the Father," Sartre conflates the perspective of Flaubert's impersonal scientific eye with that of what he elsewhere calls the "technician of practical knowledge" (3:596/*5:555*).[33] In so doing, he reads the mirrors that the literate Prussians reportedly left shattered in their wake as versions of the Stendhalian "mirror that is carried as one walks along the road," such that their shattering figures "the destruction of works of art in the name of technology and science" (3:598/*5:557*). Given the intensity with which Flaubert would take on both the promise and the pratfalls of scientific method in the 1874 *Temptation*, I think it more plausible to suggest that what one would see in those mirrors, could they be reconstructed, is not the realist road but the countenance of the Flaubertian man of science.

I am all the more persuaded by this reading inasmuch as Flaubert repeatedly calls for a return to a skeptical scientific spirit in his reactions to the Commune. On March 31, 1871, in a letter where he speaks of returning to "my poor *Saint Antony*" in order to "forget France," Flaubert tells Sand,

> The French Revolution must cease to be a dogma, and become an object of scientific inquiry, like everything else that's human. If people had known more, they wouldn't have believed that a mystical formula is capable of creating armies, or that the word "Republic" suffices to defeat a million well-disciplined men. (*Corr.*, 4:300/2:172)

On April 30, Flaubert returns to this theme, in a passage whose full resonance will become clear in chapter 5:

> What are we to believe in, then? Nothing! Such is the beginning of wisdom. It is time to rid ourselves of "principles" and to espouse Science, objective inquiry. The only rational thing (I keep coming back to it) is a government of mandarins, provided the mandarins know something—in fact, a great many things. The people never come of age, and they will always be at the bottom rung of the social scale because they represent number, mass, the limitless. (*Corr.*, 4:314/2:176)

Sartre is not entirely wrong to suggest that Flaubert's frequent calls for a government of mandarins front for an underlying quest for social distinction. Witness that passage quoted above in which Flaubert bemoans the passing of "all forms of elegance, even material elegance," then goes on to note that "a mandarin like me no longer has a place in the world" (*Corr.*, 4:256). But to assume this is invariably the case is to prefer a homogeneous style of reading, grounded in the Oedipus complex, to a more nuanced form of "thick" description essentially, if not equally, characteristic of Sartre's text. *L'Idiot de la famille* is strongest, I would argue, in its "weak" register—precisely where it fails to live up to its quest to uncover the "profound homogeneity" of Flaubert's life. Alongside the official *Idiot*, in other words, I find a second text, brilliantly attuned to the subtle shifts in Flaubert's attitudes toward contemporary events, to the overdetermination of Flaubert's motivations, and to the play of his self-contradictions and self-deceptions. The passage quoted above in which Sartre details the five sociopolitical developments condensed, in Flaubert's mind, within the single threat of Prussian victory nicely exemplifies this "weak" register. So, too, does the following account of Flaubert's positions on the matter of who and what precipitated the "end of a world":

> In his letters from this period, Gustave takes three different positions without worrying about contradicting himself—now blaming the Prussians for destroying the "Latin world," now condemning the Empire for preferring Latin civility to science, now prophesying in horror that the Third Republic would undertake a systematic reform of education and of life that he reproached the Emperor for not even attempting. (3:603/5:563)

(To this list, one should add Flaubert's reproaching the Commune for preferring faith in abstract principles to an attitude of scientific scrutiny.) What Sartre's "weak" register opens up, in short, is the appreciation of an essential ambivalence attributable (as I argue in chapter 5) to Flaubert's practice of the virtuous pose.

If there is a single argument of Sartre's belied by my reading of *La Tentation de saint Antoine*, however, it is the contention that the fall of the Second Empire and the birth of the Third Republic provoked Flaubert's "historical death or, if you will, his purely biological survival in a society that excludes him" (3:471–472/5:437). Whereas the crisis of 1844 inaugurated a literary career founded on a "loser wins" logic, such that Flaubert's failure—his lack in the real—gets transformed into the imaginary plenitude of fictional creation, the crisis of 1870 offered only *"the failure of failure . . . a dead loss, a pure and simple abolition of the being he gave himself"* (3:472/5:437). In the ten-year span between what Sartre calls Flaubert's "social death" and his "physical death," all that remained for the "fossilized" being that Flaubert had become was to remain faithful to the *failure* of the empire (3:464/5:429, 3:447/5:413). Picking up on the willfulness of Flaubert's melancholy after 1870—"I toss and plunge in my sorrow," Flaubert tells Caroline in December of that year—Sartre likens him to a widower who, "having chosen to be inconsolable and henceforth to live only in his wife's memory, would energetically reject her resuscitation" (*Corr.*, 4:267/2:167; *Idiot* 3:505/5:469).

In order to make his argument for Flaubert's historical death after the fall of the Second Empire, Sartre is compelled to rely heavily on the scenarios for a trio of unrealized novels (*Sous Napoléon III* [*Under Napoleon III*], *Monsieur le préfet*, and *Un Ménage parisien sous Napoléon III* [*A Parisian Household Under Napoleon III*]), to the evident exclusion of the two longer works that most occupied Flaubert's final decade—*La Tentation de saint Antoine* and *Bouvard et Pécuchet*. But in theorizing the demise of a "loser wins" logic that ostensibly cemented Gustave's solidarity with the fallen empire, Sartre effectively misses an analogous logic inherent in what I am here calling melancholy vitalism. For just as vitalist biology sees the death of particular organisms as subsumable to the continuity of life in the living system as a whole, so did Flaubert see the passing of an age ("The Latins are finished") as evidence of an endlessly recurrent cycle of rise and collapse ("And so on").[34] As both the *Tentation* and *Bouvard* work hard to show, life and the "desire [that] makes one live" effectively reemerge on the far side of all deaths, including Flaubert's supposed historical death.

Sartre is surely not wrong to argue that Flaubert misreads Renan's conception of Science as "endless questioning" inasmuch as Flaubert portrays science as "solely negative," a means of abolishing "illusions *without replacing them with positive knowledge*" (3:606–7/5:565). "But above all," Sartre continues, "Renan sees an order in historical sequences; he seeks meanings in them, where Gustave sees only confusion and upheaval" (3:606–7/5:566). What Sartre does not see, because his hypothesis of Flaubert's historical death works to preclude it, is that Flaubert's representation of this "confusion and upheaval" in the late work implies a rebirth of life and desire, minimalist to be sure, on the far side of all death, all confusion, and all entropic collapsing of difference. Flaubertian science is neither technocratic nor positivistic. It is a quest for truth and method and, *as such*, the catalyst to a "desire [that] makes one live." Just how that desire sustains itself in the absence of those criteria for judgment on which science is habitually founded is a question for the following chapter.

5   *The Party of Movement: Flaubert's* Bouvard et
Pécuchet

I would it accept it all, and write straight from the democratic point
of view, according to which everything is for everybody, and that
the greatest possible confusion exists for the good of the greatest
number. I would try to establish *a posteriori* that consequently there
is no such thing as fashion, since there is no authority, no rule. In
the past it was known *who* set the fashions, and every fashion had
some *sense* to it. . . . But now there is anarchy, and everyone is free
to follow his own caprice. Perhaps from this a new order will
emerge.

      —Gustave Flaubert, *Correspondance* (January 29, 1854)

When I say "they are" [*on est*], I mean five or six petit bourgeois
who sit in the café.

      —Gustave Flaubert, *Correspondance* (October 21, 1875)

To set us on the track of the elusive Bouvard and Pécuchet, I have chosen
a series of quotations whose subject is *on*.[1] The first is from a letter that
Flaubert wrote to his niece, Caroline Commanville, shortly before his death
in May 1880: "From the moment you lift yourself up, *on* (that eternal and
execrable *on*) knocks you down. That is why authority is essentially hateful.
. . . Moreover, your good-natured uncle is revolutionary to the bone" (*Corr.*
[Conard], 8:335). In a second quotation he laments to Edma Roger des
Genettes, *"On* is an enormous collective fool. And yet, O misery, we work
to amuse this *on" (Corr.,* 4:866). Elsewhere, Flaubert will speak of "the Public" as "the eternal imbecile called *On" (Corr.* [Conard], S3:325). "By common agreement (it was his idea), du Camp and I have burned all our letters
so that they would not, later on, fall into the hands of the odious *On" (Corr.*
[Conard], S3:329).

    In another letter written in the early years of the Third Republic, not so
long after the Franco–Prussian War and its aftershocks had aroused the

wrath of this self-styled "rabid liberal," Flaubert remarks, "Truth is, *on* detests style. *On* means all forms of Power" (*Corr.*, 2:698; 4:771). Bouvard and Pécuchet will say as much at the end of their excursion through literature, when they decide, "*On* does not like Literature" (225/147). Perhaps it is no accident that what they hold in their hands as they decide this are pamphlets calling for universal suffrage.

Bouvard and Pécuchet actually take up the matter of universal suffrage on the tenth of December 1848, when "all the people of Chavignolles voted for Bonaparte" (242/159). Proclaiming his belief in "the stupidity of the people," Bouvard asks, "Why can't you make three thousand francs a year out of rabbits? Because overcrowding makes them die" (242/160). Bouvard's likening of universal suffrage to an illness that develops "by the mere fact of a crowd" recalls the terms in which Flaubert thanks Ernest Renan for standing up in opposition to "'democratic equality,' which seems to be an element of death in the world" (*Corr.* [Conard], 7:289).

This series of quotations points to an association of ideas that was central to Flaubert's thinking on matters of politics and art, both severally and together. We might present these ideas in the form of an equation: *on* = the electorate in a democracy = five or six petit-bourgeois = "an element of death in the world" = authority, which is "essentially hateful." This equation includes a fifth term, which implicates us directly: *on* = the literary public—that is to say, the ultimate authority in all literary matters.

As the first of my epigraphs attests, Flaubert associated that entropic leveling of which the *on* is both a result and a symbol with utilitarian democratism, a belief that "the greatest possible confusion exists for the good of the greatest number." From the "anarchy" that follows an ongoing dissemination of social authority, in fashion as in politics, a "new order" might emerge. Such compensatory logics are in fact common in Flaubert's letters to Louise Colet from the early 1850s. Consider what follows his prediction, in September 1852, of an imminent "frenzied awakening" of a human soul that is "at present sleeping, drunk on the words it has heard":

The soul . . . will no longer have anything to restrain it, neither government, nor religion, nor any formula. Republicans of every stripe seem to me the most primitive pedagogues in the world—they dream of organization, legislation, a society like that of a monastery. I believe, on the contrary, that all rules are on their way out, that barriers are crumbling, that all is being reduced to the same level. This great confusion will perhaps bring liberty in its train. (*Corr.*, 2:152/1:169)

If modern history is thus a process of leveling that tends toward anarchic "confusion," toward a maximally entropic state that Flaubert equates with the collective or the mass, what "new order" and/or "liberty" might emerge from that disorder? What values are to be found, paradoxically, in the negotiation with the odious *on*?

For the Flaubert of the 1850s, exemplified by the correspondence with Louise Colet, the act of recognizing an increasingly anarchic or bric-a-brac world sets the artist, like the natural historian, on the track of an ideal harmonization or adequation. In the continuation of my first epigraph, Flaubert attributes the current "anarchy" of French fashion to "the historicizing tendency of our age": "Thus in the space of less than thirty years we have seen vogues for the Roman, the Gothic, the Pompadour and the Renaissance, and something remains of all that" (*Corr.* 2:518–519/*1:213*).[2] He then goes on to ask:

> So, how to take advantage of this for *Beauty's sake*? . . . By studying what form, what color, is suitable for a given person *in a given circumstance*. This involves the ability to sense a certain harmony between color and line. (*Corr.*, 2:518–19/*1:213*)

By the 1870s, however, Flaubert had come to see the promise of an ideal harmonization on the far side of heteroclite phenomenality as largely hollow. In both *La Tentation de saint Antoine* and *Bouvard et Pécuchet*, this relentless apologist for the prerogatives of individual distinction implies that a fusion with confusion itself—with undifferentiated matter, but also with the library and the political *on*—could be the vehicle of a specifically artistic freedom, one that accrues to the author in the very absence of authorial agency. In the face of a generalized entropic leveling, in other words, the only liberty still open to this author-qua-"rabid liberal" grows out of a confusion with forces that increasingly *limit* individuality as the necessary condition of all claims to liberty.

A word on this chapter's title. The "party of movement" was a faction of progressive Orleanists, led by Jacques Lafitte, whom Louis-Philippe brought to power in an effort to channel liberal initiatives after the Revolution of 1830 to Orleanist ends. By borrowing that label for a reading of *Bouvard et Pécuchet*, I mean to underscore how Flaubert conjures the entropic threat he saw as characteristic of contemporary France by setting his text into motion, by enacting the quest for culture as a desiderative movement that is both of and in the text. In so doing, this chapter argues, Flaubert effectively implies *and subverts* a series of traditional liberal values—those of freedom, culture, judgment, and individual distinction—while nonetheless taking his "revenge" on those who would deny such values. After briefly considering how Flaubert's reprise of melancholy vitalism in *Bouvard* results in a form of what LaCapra has called "post-traumatic writing," the chapter concludes by examining two variants of the late nineteenth-century French Liberal response to an agonistic quality inherent in the era's mounting democratism, contrasting the melancholy ambivalence or double-voicedness of Ernest Renan's writings circa 1871 (his textualization of social prescription in the mode of either/or) with what I call the antiagonistic strategies of Flaubert's contemporaneous novels (their tendency to couch such prescriptive utterances in a logic of neither/nor).

The Motus Animi Continuus

> Nothing gives a better sense of the irresistible energy of the movement of ideas than the force with which humanity drags behind her the very ones who most boldly attempt to stop her.
> —Ernest Renan, "Du Libéralisme cléricale" (On Clerical Liberalism)

> You know the theory of liberty better than I. You even take the liberty of doing what is ordained.
> —Pissedoux to Père Ubu, *Ubu enchaîné* (Ubu Bound)

To Flaubert's mind, any act of rebellion against a principle of authority risks giving birth to a new, functionally equivalent authority in its turn.[3] Revolt against any conformism will be an unsatisfactory expression of the will to liberty insofar as the act of revolt itself helps to institute a new conformism. This would be one reason why, in a novel such as *L'Éducation sentimentale,* Flaubert expresses his authorial liberty by having his narrator embrace the authority of the collective, by merging his narrative voice—though ambiguously—into the voice of the *on.* Flaubert reveals himself as a consummate practitioner of what Pissedoux calls "the theory of liberty" by situating his narration squarely within the field of authoritative stupidities while bathing the narrative in an irony so generalized and ambiguous as to preclude its being read as a partisan act, much less an act of revolt.

In Flaubert's later works, and particularly in *Bouvard et Pécuchet,* the burden of producing such an irony is borne almost entirely by Flaubert's practice of "style."

If the *on* does not like Literature and execrates "style," then the pursuit of "style" can function as an act of defiance against that *on* which, Flaubert tells us, "means all forms of Power." Throughout his working life, Flaubert envisioned the work of style, or the quest for "an absolute manner of seeing things," as a way of flaunting his mockery of any bourgeois, utilitarian calculus of expenditure and return (*Corr.*, 2:31/*1:154*). "Style" was the search for a language that is rhythmic, palpitating, and sonorous, and for "a sustained energy that runs from beginning to end without abating" (*Corr.*, 2:303). To Flaubert, "style" denoted that great effort whereby the author wrests life and energy out of a language he finds poised on the brink of lifelessness. Art was thus life's protest against the death that is immanent in the language of the authoritative *on,* made from within that same language. Already in 1853 Flaubert would write:

> Life! Life! To have erections! That is everything! . . . All the power of a work
> of art lies in this mystery, and it is this primordial quality, this *motus animi*
> *continuus* (vibration, continual movement of the mind—Cicero's definition
> of eloquence), that results in conciseness, relief, form, energy, rhythm,
> diversity. (*Corr.*, 2:385/*1:193*)

By the time he sets to work on *Bouvard et Pécuchet,* Flaubert will have abandoned the specifically lyric style that is both the subject and the vehicle of this quotation in favor of a more abrupt and prosaic, ironic style. The extreme concision and deliberate "compositional clumsiness" of the writing in the late works function, as Jonathan Culler has argued, as signs of the author's distance from the language in which he writes (203). In the terms of our discussion, the work of style becomes all but inseparable from the ironization by which Flaubert attains a modicum of liberty in the very act of writing in the language of the collective. This merging of irony with the practice of style is most evident in the *Dictionnaire des idées reçues* (*Dictionary of Received Ideas*), that work in which Flaubert spoke most radically in the language of the *on,* and which he conceived of (ironically) as a way of entering into "the modern democratic idea of equality" (*Corr.*, 2:208/*1:176*). In the *Dictionnaire,* the irony that guarantees Flaubert's liberty as an author can rest on as narrow a foundation as two commas, separating three prepositional phrases.[4] Thus we read, under the rubric "Lathe": "Indispensable to have in your attic, in the country, for rainy days" (553/*314*).

Flaubert's development or, better, his progressive purification of ironic style on this level of tenuity represents one solution to his lifelong program of securing his liberty as an author and narrator in an age when conformism was the basis of authority. The ironic style allowed Flaubert to write against the *on,* as the institutionalized absence of difference or desire, without actually writing *against* the *on,* which would limit his freedom. By committing Flaubert to no party other than that of irony itself, the ironic style served the same function in his writing as his wild and obviously theatrical expressions of opinion served in his correspondence and social life. In his novels, Flaubert could never play the role of "revolutionary to the bone," at least not directly, because he knew that in literature the antiauthoritarian gesture tends to be read as an act, as a taking of sides, and not as a social gesticulation that has no real counterpart in practice. The ironic style is thus the literary equivalent of a *pose,* in precisely the sense suggested by this note from a scenario for *Bouvard:*

> THE POSE—why is it condemned? What we now call "pose" used to be called "virtue" and "greatness." (*Bouvard* [Cento], 163)

The ironic style allowed Flaubert to express hatred, which is a virtue, he says, and hence also a pose:

> We must forget nothing, neither kindness nor offense. This leveling out of good and evil, the beautiful and the ugly, this inane gentleness, this universal blessing is one of the plagues of our time. Hatred is a virtue. (*Corr.,* 4:610)

In short, the ironic style was this author-as-rabid-liberal's best weapon against the threat of indifferentiation, the cognitive equivalent of that moral indifference which he spoke of as a plague on his contemporaries.

Yet, as Flaubert well knew, this very weapon against the threat of indifferentiation was itself apt to create an *effect* of indifferentiation. And this for two principal reasons. First, the halting rhythms, logical ellipses, and lapidary sentences that form the basis of Flaubert's late ironic style tire the reader by incessantly calling attention to themselves as linguistic effects. Second, the generalized, antagonistic strategies of irony that one finds in *L'Éducation sentimentale* deny the pertinence of situational conflict and thus rob the novel of that most traditional motor force of the novelistic plot.[5] We know that the relative failure of *L'Éducation sentimentale* weighed heavily on Flaubert, and that he attributed that failure to the fact that "the reader finishes the book with the same impression he had at the beginning" (*Corr.* [Conard], 8:224). This novel, which Flaubert clearly intended as a warning against moral inertia, was seen to fall, paradoxically, into an inertia of style. For in purging his writing of the lyricism that had been native to it, distilling what was left into an ironic essence that was strategically antagonistic, Flaubert had also robbed his style of that *motus animi continuus* that he had earlier recommended as the protest of Art against the entropic tendencies of bourgeois life and language.

To the series of problems I have raised thus far—How can Flaubert maintain his liberty in a conformist age? How can he write against the *on* without actually writing *against* the *on,* which would limit his freedom? How can he do all this and, at the same time, entertain the *on* as the source of his authority as a novelist?—we must now add one more: How can Flaubert write in and "against" the voice of the *on,* the voice of "democratic equality," without falling into that indifferentiation or "element of death in the world" against which he is compelled to write? Taken together, these questions delineate a problematic space within which no one style of writing, particularly in Flaubert's time, could feel totally at home. They define a sequence of dilemmas to which each of Flaubert's novels must be read as proposing a provisional solution—provisional for the reason that any new displacement in the problematic space of the dilemmas raises new problems to replace those which the displacement itself was intended to solve.

Agon

> There exists no truth so refined, so nuanced that it cannot be understood by all.
>
> > —Ernest Renan, "L'Instruction supérieure en France" (Higher Education in France)

> We cannot very well set about to contrive opponents who will do us the service of forcing us to become more intelligent, who will require us to keep our ideas from becoming stale, habitual and inert. This we will have to do for ourselves.
>
> > —Lionel Trilling, *The Liberal Imagination*

Bouvard et Pécuchet tells the story of two petit bourgeois who retire from their positions as copy clerks to embark on a grand tour of human knowledge and experience. Its protagonists belong, as Hugh Kenner puts it, to a generation "untainted by the least memory of a time when knowledge, which is power, was the preserve of the few" (8). The ease with which Bouvard and Pécuchet take on "the status of engineer"—"Very well!" they say, "we shall do so!"—is comic, but it is nonetheless indicative of an ongoing democratization of access to knowledge and power (148/92). Bouvard and Pécuchet can dream of belonging to learned societies, and even of running for deputy, with an earnestness their grandfathers could have scarcely imagined. On the basis of a naturalist doctrine that reads as a pastiche of Flaubert's own aesthetic—"One should write as one speaks and then all will be well, so long as one has felt and observed"—Bouvard and Pécuchet can even judge themselves "capable of writing" (218/*142*).

In their very essence as fictional characters, therefore, Bouvard and Pécuchet are products of a democratic age. Yet they also represent that ostensibly free subject beloved of classical liberalism in its struggle with the homogeneous mass: the "eternal and execrable *on,*" whose power in matters of politics and art was also undeniably an outgrowth of the democratic spirit. In a prescriptive note that found its way into the dossier for *Bouvard,* Flaubert wrote: "Protests for the Rights of the Individual against the Mass and against the gendarme should be felt throughout" (*Oeuvres* [Club], 6:433). Given that authority is "essentially hateful" because the force of authority tends to deny all individual distinction, given that the *on* is a leveling principle par excellence, then Bouvard and Pécuchet must, in their own bumbling way, stand for individual freedom and difference. They must do so in spite of the fact that, as desiring beings, they are repeatedly shown to be defined *by one another.* It is liberalism's ethic of individual difference through personalized desire, an ethic that clearly fostered the growth of our modern consumer societies, that provokes such a blindness to the social nature of desire.[6]

From the moment they arrive in Chavignolles, Bouvard and Pécuchet are objects of scrutiny:

> Meanwhile the bourgeois of Chavignolles were eager to know them, and came to look at them through the fence. They closed the openings with planks, which upset the locals. (76/*40*)

Curiosity about these unlikely Parisians quickly metamorphoses into the absence of true curiosity—an attitude of surveillance. Their maid spies on them. Rumors begin to circulate: they are hiding a body in the house (the "body" is in fact an artificial cadaver, an adjunct to their study of anatomy); they have nocturnal communication with the Devil, or may even *be* the Devil (when they try to bring back the spirit of Bouvard's father) (119–20/*70,* 296/*200*). "We know you! We know you! [*On vous connaît!*]" the Abbé's servant tells them (396/*274*).

This voice of the *on* merges almost indistinguishably into the voice of the state's power. "They [*on*] put people in jail who are not as bad as you"; the "Mass" comes to speak with the voice of the "gendarme" (126/*76*). As the novel progresses, the punitive mechanics of the state become increasingly apparent. Thus, when Bouvard and Pécuchet, now philosophers, start to "undermine basic principles" by questioning "the honesty of men, the chastity of women, the intelligence of the government, the good sense of the people," the mayor "threaten[s] them with prison" and "calumnies [are] invented" (319/*217*). Such threats only spur Bouvard and Pécuchet on to ever greater liberties of opinion. Against a Christian orthodoxy said to be composed of "those truths on which everyone agrees," Bouvard defends polygamy and Pécuchet, Buddhism (343/*234*, 364–65/*251*). When the two are finally summoned into court for insulting a gamekeeper, in a scene I shall return to in a moment, Pécuchet turns sublimely defiant:

> And he gave the impression of mocking the court.
> "Gentlemen," said Coulon [the justice of the peace], "I am amazed that people of intelligence. . . ."
> "The law dispenses you from having any," replied Pécuchet. "The Justice of the Peace sits for an indefinite period, while the judge of the supreme court is deemed capable up to the age of seventy-five, and the judge of first instance only up to seventy." (402/*278*)

The Desire for Judgment

> A sacrosanct Institution, which considers itself essentially superior, the State fetters the dynamic nature of the perpetually mobile and creative Self.
> —Henri Arvon, on the philosophy of Max Stirner

> The universal exercise of private judgment is . . . unspeakably beautiful.
> —William Godwin, *Enquiry Concerning Political Justice*

Flaubert died just as he was to begin the closing scene of *Bouvard's* first volume. But in his plan for that scene, we see that the exacerbation of Bouvard and Pécuchet's subversive tendencies was to have forced the arrival of the gendarmes with a warrant for their arrest: "They are accused [*on les accuse*] of offences against Religion, public order, incitement to Revolt, etc." Meanwhile, "the public gradually invades their house" (413/*287*). Superimposed on that sequence of failed inquiries which gives *Bouvard* such a sense of drifting repetitiveness, therefore, is a plot that opposes the clerks to their neighbors and the state, and that steadily builds to the climactic "tutti" of the final scene.

Examination of Flaubert's dossiers for *Bouvard et Pécuchet* suggests that each of the novel's secondary characters was intended to represent an aspect of the hostile *on*: its hatred of literature or love of authority, its hypocrisy or its avarice. Such a representative function is particularly evident in the following note: "Show how and why each secondary character abhors Science, Truth, Beauty, Justice—1) instinctively, 2) out of self-interest" (*Bouvard* [Cento], 175). We might sum up the relation of conflict that subtends the plot of *Bouvard et Pécuchet* by saying that the two former clerks represent a passion for "Science, Truth, Beauty, Justice," and for those "Rights of the Individual" which Flaubert invariably associated with that passion, against an *on* deemed hostile to those values by instinct and interest. In other words, Bouvard and Pécuchet incarnate a spirit of constant critical vigilance in opposition to the mental inertia of those around them. We can be sure that, unlike Professor Dumouchel, for example, they would never wish the Institute to "draw up some sort of [historical] canon to prescribe what is to be believed" (191/*123*). In short, Bouvard and Pécuchet stand for that act of judgment whereby the individual expresses his liberty of thought, and hence also—the equation is crucial for Flaubert—an essential ethic of liberty.

Yet rarely have fictional characters possessed faculties of judgment more sporadic than theirs. And even in their moments of critical lucidity—as in their excursion through philosophy, which ends with their developing the "lamentable faculty . . . of noticing stupidity and finding it intolerable" (319/*217*)—the force of Flaubert's novel is to deny the very faculties and criteria upon which any act of judgment must be founded. Consider the scene in which Bouvard and Pécuchet examine, in succession, common sense, the data of the senses, reason, morality, self-evidence, and revelation—rejecting them all as bases for judgment, and with arguably good cause in every instance (307–8). What Flaubert's novel gives with one hand, it takes away with the other: judgment is the greatest ethical protest against the inertia of the *on,* but judgment is intermittent, if not outright impossible. The only way out of such a dilemma is to find meaning in the desire for judgment rather than in its attainment. Even if judgment were strictly impossible, even if no amount of critical vigilance could help distinguish the true from the false, the beautiful from the ugly, and so on, the very movement of the quest for judgment would still serve to defy the relative stasis of the system of powerful convention. Liberty of the spirit is a protest of desire, expressed as energy in its purest and most futile form, against the entropy inherent in the closed system of the authoritative *on*.

This thematizing of authority as tending toward stasis might lead us to believe that, in *Bouvard et Pécuchet,* the most substantial protest against the pressures of established authority is that which expresses itself through the mobilization of desire. Standing before the police court, for instance, Bouvard and Pécuchet "defend" themselves by claiming (1) that they had not insulted the gamekeeper; (2) that "the words offence, crime and misdemeanor are meaningless"; (3) that the penal code is irrational; (4) that fines are not proper punishment for rich men; (5) that justices of the peace are dispensed from the prerequisite of intelligence; and so on (401–2/*278*). Such a movement of unconstrained desire fosters in turn a particularly lively textuality. It is in fact by mimicking the continual movement of its protagonists' desiring minds, their continuous passion, that Flaubert's text ultimately rejoins the lost stylistic ideal of the *motus animi continuus:*

> Aroused by Pécuchet, [Bouvard] went into a frenzy about fertilizer. In the compost pit were heaped up branches, blood, intestines, feathers, anything he could find. He used Belgian liqueur, Swiss "lizier," washing soda, smoked herrings, seaweed, rags, had guano sent, tried to make it—and, carrying his principles to the limit, did not tolerate any waste of urine; he did away with the lavatories. Dead animals were brought into his yard, and used to fertilize his land. Their disemboweled carrion was strewn over the countryside. Bouvard smiled amid all this infection. A pump fixed up in a farm cart spread out liquid manure over the crops. If people looked disgusted he would say: "But it is gold! gold!" And he was sorry not to have still more dungheaps. How fortunate are those countries with natural caves full of bird droppings! (89/*48*)

Eugenio Donato recognizes in the images of excretion and putrefaction that overflow this paragraph "the very metaphors of the history in which [Flaubert's] work is inscribed" (74). He goes on, pertinently, to quote an early letter to Louis Bouilhet: "We are dancing not on a volcano, but on the rotten seat of a latrine. Before long, society is going to drown in nineteen centuries of shit, and there'll be a lot of shouting" (*Corr.,* 1:708/*1:129–30*). "Poetry, like the sun," Flaubert later tells Maupassant, "gilds manure"; the art of fiction is an art of locating stories—dubious stories that keep on desiring—within a history that is ruthlessly entropic or on the stage of a society rotting out from underfoot. On the rotten floorboards of the world's latrine, *Bouvard et Pécuchet* dances; the novel is, almost quintessentially, "the dancing of an attitude" (Kenneth Burke's characterization of symbolic acts in general is nowhere more fitting than here) (9).

If the realist project of finding new life in decay is inherently ironic, however, this irony will be of less interest for our purposes than the irony of desire itself as a temporal rhythm—an irony that is fully actualized here in Flaubert's final novel, but is already implicit in the metaphorics of the 1853 passage on "style" where Flaubert says: "Life! Life! To have erections! That is everything!" (*Corr.*, 2:385/1:193). In mimicking the movement of its protagonists' desires, so as ultimately to present itself as the (writing of the) writing of desire, Flaubert's text, we shall see, becomes a braid of ironic rhythms—between life and death, expansion and contraction, protest and acquiescence, freedom and constraint.

The Fall into Belonging

The bulk of *Bouvard et Pécuchet's* projected second volume was to have consisted of their "Copy," a compilation of discursive idiocies of all sorts. At the end of that volume, while sifting through a pile of old papers they had bought by the pound, Bouvard and Pécuchet were to have discovered the draft of a confidential report from Dr. Vaucorbeil to the local prefect, saying that Bouvard and Pécuchet are not "dangerous madmen," only "two harmless imbeciles" (*Bouvard* [Cento], 125). Vaucorbeil, in other words, would have refused to exercise his prerogative (as a medical authority in an age of sanatoriums) to exclude Bouvard and Pécuchet from bourgeois society. As "harmless imbeciles," his letter implies, they belong *among us*. His judgment subverts the agon between the clerks and the citizens or institutions of a theretofore hostile society, thus setting up a highly conventional comic ending.

But of course Vaucorbeil's benevolent diagnosis is ironic in the context of the novel as a whole. In denying Bouvard and Pécuchet their "madness," thereby guaranteeing them a certain freedom of movement, it also denies them liberty in the form of an irreducible difference between themselves and the conformist *on*. Bouvard and Pécuchet had found ethical value in the endless game of overstepping the limits of prescribed belief. And in this sense, as in so many others, we might read them as embedded figures of the author—of Flaubert himself, but also of the author in general at a moment in history when, as Foucault has argued, the very notion of an author tended to reflect society's need to mark all literary discourse as potentially trans-gressive.[7] Vaucorbeil's diagnosis, however, tends to erase that line of demar-cation over which any such game of overstepping as Bouvard and Pécuchet's must take place. In the world of Chavignolles, it suggests, *every-one* is a bourgeois, even the *bourgeoisophobe*.

Or, in other words, in *Bouvard et Pécuchet, on est tous bourgeois;* the render-ing "they are all bourgeois" can only provisionally preclude the more collo-quial rendition, anticipated by Flaubert's ironic logic: "*we* are all bourgeois." That gesture of self-exclusion from the entropic authority of the collective, which founds both Bouvard and Pécuchet's ethic of constant vigilance and Flaubert's own (paradoxically absolutist) notion of style, is thus at every moment threatened by a fall back into the symmetry of social be-longing. And yet, as Lacan's work on aggressivity in the Imaginary surely suggested, one cannot live with such symmetry; the *on* will inevitably return in the guise of an agonistic other. In Derridean terms, the relation between "they" and "we" in *on est tous bourgeois* is that of a *différance* between an ethical claim of difference-from-the-other, on the one hand, and the per-petually redeferred acknowledgment of symmetry, on the other. To the ex-tent that liberal ideology mandates both a pursuit of individual distinction through the acquisition of culture and the overcoming of social schism through a mutual tolerance grounded in "a common cult of justice and the good, inseparable from that of the fatherland" (Renan), this differential play—like that ambivalence toward which my reading of *La Débâcle* tends—is itself quintessentially liberal (*Questions,* 27).

The Novel as Revenge

> "Since the bourgeois are savage, the workers jealous, the priests servile, and the people will accept any tyrant, so long as he leaves their snouts in the trough, Napoleon has done well! Let him gag them, trample them, exterminate them! Nothing will ever be too much for their hatred of the law, their cowardice, their ineptitude, their blindness!"
>
> —Pécuchet

In October 1872, Flaubert writes a letter praising Edma Roger des Gen-ettes for being "proud and valiant, or rather stoic" in a time of "universal flabbiness." He then adds, speaking of *Bouvard*: "I am contemplating a thing in which I shall *vent my wrath*. Yes, I'll finally rid myself of all that is suffocating me. I shall vomit on my contemporaries all the disgust they inspire in me" (*Corr.*, 4:583–584). A month later he tells Turgenev that he is overwhelmed by the present state of society and inundated by "public stupidity":

> Everything I read by my contemporaries makes me quiver with indignation. A fine state to be in! Not that it's preventing me from preparing a book in which I'll try to spew out my bile. . . . 1870 drove many people insane, made imbeciles of others, and left others in a permanent state of rage. I'm in that last category. It's the *right* one. (*Corr.*, 4:604–605/*200–1*)

In December of that same year, he speaks of the writing of *Bouvard* as a purgative, but also advises George Sand against taking too seriously "my exaggerated ire" (*Corr.*, 4:624).

In what sense was *Bouvard* "the book of vengeances," as Flaubert was reported to have told Maxime du Camp?[8] Behind this question I hear two others. Against whom or against what would Flaubert have taken his revenge? And what form did that vengeance ultimately assume?

However traumatized Flaubert may have been by the Prussian invasion, the principal object of his vengeful wrath was clearly not Prussia but contemporary France. Two letters to George Sand from the fall of 1871 help circumscribe that rage. In the first, dated September 8, Flaubert echoes the rhetoric with which this chapter began in speaking of "the crowd, the mass, the herd"—or what he elsewhere calls the *on*—as "always detestable" (*Corr.*, 4:375–76/*2:180*). As a result of " 'free and compulsory' education," the degrading influence of the popular press, and, above all, universal suffrage, he sees the line that once separated the bourgeoisie from "the good 'People' " as fast disappearing (*Corr.*, 4:376/*2:180*). The second letter, dated October 7, continues this thought: "The entire dream of democracy is to raise the proletariat to the level of bourgeois stupidity. That dream is partly realized! They read the same newspapers and share the same passions" (4:384/*2:182*). And yet, as this letter unfolds, Flaubert singles out mandatory primary education for special opprobrium. If the Prussian universities fueled Prussia's victory, and if French secondary education produced the men of the Government of National Defense, he tells Sand, "primary education gave us the Commune" (*Corr.*, 4:385/*2:183*).

To Flaubert's mind, the remedy for this state of affairs was twofold: to have done with universal suffrage, "that insult to human intelligence," and to recognize the claims of a "*natural aristocracy*" (*Corr.*, 4:376/*2:180–81*;

4:384). Thinking of the work of Ernest Renan (to which I will return in a moment), Flaubert envisions a state where power might fall to a small class of "mandarins," highly educated men capable of overcoming France's long-standing propensity for metaphysical sentimentalism—the revolutionary doctrine of equality, Flaubert writes, is "an essentially Christian idea"—and thus open a way for "Critique, that is to say . . . the examination of all things" (*Corr.*, 4:376/2:180). As Sartre notes, Flaubert's exemplary "men of character" are individuals who look beyond the narrow self-interest typical of Second Empire individualism in their aristocratic devotion to higher entities, such art, mysticism, or war (*Idiot*, 3:623–24/5:581). For all his allegiance to ostensibly natural hierarchies, however, Flaubert is not entirely blind to what might ferment in the *on*. "The mass must be respected, however inept it may be," he writes, "because it contains seeds of incalculable fertility. Give it liberty, but not power" (*Corr.*, 4:384/2:183).

The specific catalyst to Flaubert's vengeance in *Bouvard* was thus an entropic social leveling variously attributable to universal suffrage, increased educational opportunity, and the rise of a popular press—a leveling very much implicit, I have argued, in Flaubert's shorthand phrase "l'*on*." But how did he in fact take that revenge? He did so by giving the reader of *Bouvard*, as representative of the *on*, precisely the sort of freedom of judgment few contemporary readers would have wanted. Pace Maxime du Camp, in other words, it was not just *Bouvard*'s second volume that Flaubert had in mind when he spoke of his "book of vengeances" (quoted in Flaubert, *Oeuvres* [Masson], 1:35).

We commonly think of the nineteenth-century reader as having looked for meaning in novels within the bounds of what Roland Barthes once called a "more or less parsimonious plurality" (*S/Z*, 12/6). By an implicit pact, the reader agreed to a partial suspension of his critical faculties in exchange for an assurance that the story would make a certain sense in the end—not too much sense, perhaps (for literariness was at stake), but not too little.[9] Thus the reader's access to the power and pleasure of authoritative interpretation presupposed his willingness to submit, at least in part, to the author's effort to limit his interpretive freedom.

When Flaubert speaks of fiction as the art of illusion, or when he presents the interventions of the *on* in *Bouvard et Pécuchet* in a way that cries out for thematization, he implicitly conceives of the act of reading in all its habitual innocence. Still, *Bouvard* as a whole militates against such innocence, and against the silent pact whereby writer and reader worked to elaborate a mutual authority. For in *Bouvard*, as Gothot-Mersch nicely puts it, "everything is constructed to make us lose our footing"; the novel's highest ambition, it often appears, is to leave its readers dazed and confused ("Introduction," 36). The reader retains a near perfect liberty of interpretation, but Flaubert's strategies of thwarting any impulse to order, to digest or to judge the various episodes of the encyclopedic voyage, deny him access to interpretive power. "Give it liberty, but not power": Flaubert's 1871 dictum on the mass in politics, the political *on*, applies equally to the *on* that is the public reading *Bouvard et Pécuchet* (*Corr.*, 4:384/*2:183*).

In the recent heyday of *Bouvard* criticism, from the mid-1970s well into the 1980s, critical attention was largely focused on the techniques whereby Flaubert invests his account of Bouvard and Pécuchet's journey through knowledge and culture with an essential ambiguity. Accordingly, any discussion of such techniques will tend to fall into the realm of the already-said, through which (following Flaubert's own lead) I should now like to move quickly.

Bouvard et Pécuchet is characterized by an extension or intensification of disorganizing techniques already present in Flaubert's previous works. Thus we find in the novel familiar ambiguities of pronoun reference, syntax that unhinges descriptions which otherwise call out for visualization, and incomplete résumés that partialize the phenomena they are intended to resume. We also find a heady manipulation of technical terminologies reminiscent of *Salammbô*, such that, like Bouvard and Pécuchet, we wrestle with "orthosomatic sticks"; "as for the peach trees," we, too, get "tangled up in the upper mother branches, the lower mother branches, and secondary lowers" (96/*54*).

By far the most important of Flaubert's disorganizing techniques, however, deal with problems of voice and judgmental context. In making it difficult for the reader to decide who is speaking at a given moment, Flaubertian style effectively prohibits her from molding her interpretations on those of narrators or characters whose judgment tends to be sound. We encounter the problem of voice in a relatively simple guise whenever the text offers a judgment that we expect the narrator knows to be false:

> Obviously [Mme de Noaris] loved [Pécuchet]; they could have been married; she was a widow and he did not suspect this love, which might perhaps have brought happiness to his life. (354/*242*)

More vertiginous manifestations of the problem of voice include those which make us wonder whether the habitual distinction between direct and indirect discourse has any meaning to it, as in this passage where Bouvard actually speaks in a syntax that we associate with the narrative voice in moments of free, indirect discourse:

> Bouhours accuses Tacitus of lacking the simplicity required by history. A professor, a Monsieur Droz, criticizes Shakespeare for his mixture of serious and farcical, Nissard, another professor, considers André Chénier as a poet to be beneath those of the seventeenth century. The Englishman Blair deplores Virgil's picture of the Harpies. (221/*144*)

If this is how Bouvard speaks, how can we hope to distinguish the narrator's voice from that of the focalized characters in the process of reading free, indirect discourse? Faced with the report of an opinion, how are we to know that the apparent stupidity lies in what is reported and not in whomsoever does the reporting? Anthony Thorlby is precisely right when he says of *Bouvard et Pécuchet*: "Genuine absurdities in the activities and ideas of the day are compounded with the personal idiosyncrasies of Bouvard and Pécuchet in such a way that the perspective is lacking for any clear distinction to be drawn between them" (49).

It is Flaubert's syntax, together with the blurring of discursive origins, that bears the brunt of the work of denying the reader any perspective for judgment. Consider the passage I have just quoted. Some of the opinions that compose it may not be stupid (it would indeed be stupid to assume that they all are), but Flaubert's sentence piles them together in such a way as to cut each one off from any argumentative context by which it might be judged more or less intelligent. The syntax of Bouvard's little summary pushes us as readers to reject the opinions it contains en masse, which is precisely what Bouvard himself does in the end: "In short, all these people who compose books of rhetoric, poetics and aesthetics seem complete idiots to me!" (221/ *144*). Against the stupidity of this global pronouncement, the reader could undertake a meticulous evaluation of the various aesthetic pronouncements through reintroduction of their argumentative contexts, but at that rate she might never finish the book.[10] Or she could simply decide that Bouvard himself is an imbecile. My point here is not so much that the reader of Bouvard is caught in a sort of "imbecile's paradox" (what is the status of a valid judgment, for example, when it is expressed by an imbecile?) as that she has no way of mediating between the most particular and the most general statements of the text's meaning or significance. In this respect, *Bouvard et Pécuchet* continues in the lineage of *La Tentation de saint Antoine*; the practice of syntactical accumulation yields an image in miniature of the delirious encyclopedic narrative, a narrative that forces the reader either to make questionable global pronouncements about the intelligence, madness, or method of the perceiving subjects (Antoine, Bouvard and Pécuchet) or to pay exaggerated attention to details of the encyclopedic journey.[11] Ever since critics gave up trying to decide whether Bouvard and Pécuchet are imbeciles (they are, of course—brilliant ones), they have tended to produce tightly focused *partial* readings—readings that, like the book itself in its more radical, encyclopedic aspects, do not add up to anything like a unified whole.[12]

By way of a provisional summary, let us agree to define "judgment" in one of its traditional senses, as "the faculty that allows us to discriminate between the good and the bad in all things" (this from the *Grand Dictionnaire universel du XIXe siècle* [9:1075]). If this is what we mean by judgment, then the thematic of the hostile *on* that furthers the plot of *Bouvard et Pécuchet* clearly contains an implicit judgment: the two clerks represent "the good" because they stand for critical vigilance, a desire for knowledge over the lack thereof, movement over stasis.

At the same time, Flaubert's syntax and the syntax of his narration—his construction of the tale of the encyclopedic voyage—repeatedly serve to frustrate our judgment. Just as Flaubert's syntax works to prevent the differentiation between reported opinions, so does the syntax of *Bouvard's* narration tend to disallow the sort of generalizations of judgment that typically give readers the sense of having mastered a text. Strictly speaking, there is no one answer to the question of whether Bouvard and Pécuchet are imbeciles, not even the flippantly paradoxical one I just proposed. Likewise, there is no one answer to the question of whether they lack method, nor to the question of why they so often fail. Sometimes they lack method; at others, they have a surfeit of method. Sometimes they fail as a result of mistakes in judgment; at others, their judgment is sound but their projects are ruined by freak interventions of nature. And sometimes, in fact, they succeed. So great is our unspoken need for the generalizations of traditional, masterful interpretation, however, that we tend to read even their periodic successes as failures—specifically, as failures to fail.

On the one hand, it would seem, we have a plot that implies judgment; on the other, a textuality that threatens to block it. But even this proposition may be too schematic. For that quality which expresses the value of Bouvard and Pécuchet's struggle against the entropic *on*—the quality of thought-in-motion—is precisely that which Flaubert's text mimics so as to frustrate judgment on both the level of the sentence or paragraph and the level of the text as a whole. Consider the following passage, where I have italicized those words which signal a substantial change of perspective:

In connection with the barbarians Thierry demonstrates how foolish it is to enquire whether a prince was good or bad. Why not follow that method in examining some recent periods? *But* history must avenge morality; we are grateful to Tacitus for having torn Tiberius to shreds. After all, whether or not the queen had lovers, whether Dumouriez planned treachery from the time of Valmy, whether in Prairial it was the Mountain or the Gironde who began, and in Thermidor the Jacobins or the Plain, *what does it matter* for the development of the Revolution, whose origins go deep and whose results are incalculable? Therefore it had to take place, be what it was, *but* suppose that the king's flight had not been impeded, that Robespierre had escaped or Bonaparte been assassinated—chances dependent on a less scrupulous innkeeper, an open door, or a sleeping sentry—and the way of the world would have changed.

As regards the men and events of the period, they no longer had a single idea left standing. (187–88/*120–21*)

No doubt it was Flaubert's design that we, too, finish his book without "a single idea left standing." In one sense, this confusion is our punishment as representatives of the *on,* and the act of fostering it, an act of revenge. Yet this is punishment in the mode of "silly gentleness." Just as Vaucorbeil "punishes" Bouvard and Pécuchet for their transgressions by reintegrating them into the collective, so does Flaubert punish and forgive us our inertia by enrolling us as readers in the party of movement. The ambivalence of the gesture by which Flaubert tells his reader, "You are guilty of inertia, but you long for movement," is essential to the question of the novel's comedy, to which I will return at chapter's end.

A Politics of Pose

> Posing, affectation, humbug everywhere.
>
> —Gustave Flaubert, *Correspondance* (January 29, 1854)

Bouvard and Pécuchet were to have begun by copying everything that came to hand, but soon they feel a need to classify; the act of classification implies substantial judgment (*Bouvard* [Cento], 124). To take an example from Claudine Gothot-Mersch's reconstruction of Flaubert's compendium of stupidities—the so-called *Sottisier*—we might have found under a rubric such as "Contradictory Affirmations and Judgments" the following two quotations:

The Holy Spirit commands slaves to stay in the place, and does not compel their masters to free them. (Bossuet)

Without a doubt, no one has spoken for the enslaved, the poor, and the humble with as much courage and vigor as have our Ecclesiastical writers. (Chateaubriand) (468–69)

Commenting on a passage from the scenarios in which Bouvard and Pécuchet are said to copy contradictory statements one after the other, Claude Mouchard and Jacques Neefs have written, "The opposing statements are only a moment, a crucial one perhaps, but one that shifts our attention away from the problem of truth or value to a perception of attitudes" (192). On the one hand, by cutting off the contradictory citations they copy from any discursive context or habitual field of knowledge, Bouvard and Pécuchet refuse to decide (and make it hard for us as readers to decide) in favor of one quotation at the expense of the other; their "Copy" is plainly antiagonistic in this sense. On the other hand, the very juxtaposition of contradictory statements underscores language's function as a field of conflict par excellence. It makes each quotation what Mouchard and Neefs call "a gesture of thought-speech," implicated in an agon that appears gratuitous and silly (192). The "Copy" that Flaubert was to have written through Bouvard and Pécuchet would have made two antithetical gestures: a stoic gesture of renunciation (in deciding not to decide, for example, the relative merits of two opposing statements) and a concomitant gesture of indignation (both statements are stupid, and the conflicts that make up our culture are themselves stupid).

In making these two antithetical gestures, the "Copy" would have realized the two preconditions of a writing that is both "virtuous" and "free." Ironic style as Flaubert practices it, and would have practiced it in the second volume of *Bouvard,* proceeds from an irreducible tension between the attitudes of renunciation and indignation, both of which are inevitably *poses.* Antiagonism (Barthes's "neither-norism") is a pose, marking the limit of a desire made unrealizable by that threat of moral inertia or death inherent in true moral indifference. And indignation and hatred are poses, made strictly unattainable in Flaubert's practice of literature by his need to maintain his liberty. In short, if Flaubert's ironic style foregrounds the attitudes implicit in other preexistent acts of language, it does so in order ultimately to assure a differential movement between its own antithetical poses.

In seeking to account for this irresolvable tension between the gestures of indignation and resignation, we note that Flaubert's ironic style strikes the poses of freedom on the margins of society, while tending to confirm the status quo so as not to fall into the unfreedom of revolt. As such, it reflects a dilemma that had plagued French liberal doctrine, generally speaking, since the rhetoric of individual liberty that had furthered the bourgeoisie's pre–Revolutionary rise to power was first perceived as threatening to that power.[13] More specifically, liberal desire in the wake of the events of 1830, 1848, and 1871 implied a bourgeois quest for social distinction that could not announce itself as such without ceding the rhetoric of liberty to the forces of popular revolution, and thus perpetuating that same cycle of revolt which spurred Flaubert to develop his antiagonistic strategies. One response to this dilemma, and not the least effective, was to be found in the liberal ideal of the cultivated mind, according to which social distinction was not the reflection of membership in a privileged class so much as the simple result of individual talent and energy. It is not our opponents, Lionel Trilling writes, "who will require us to keep our ideas from becoming stale, habitual and inert. This we will have to do for ourselves" (x). Liberalism, as Flaubert clearly knew it, proposed an individualist ethic of vigilance and effort, dedicated to an unacknowledged quest for the power of what Bourdieu calls cultural capital.

There is no question but that *Bouvard et Pécuchet* valorizes the injunction to cultivate one's mind. Yet it ironizes it as well; for beyond the *on,* it is the stupidity of the two clerks that makes them their own best opponents. Once the ethical judgment of (liberal) self-distinction common to Trilling's precept and to the plotting of Flaubert's novel is recognized as unviable, however, it is Bouvard and Pécuchet's stupidity that has historically allowed value still to be conferred upon them. For their *bêtise* opens the door to irony in a sense that is both Romantic in origin and modern, even postmodern, in resonance—irony as what Friedrich Schlegel once called "the clear consciousness of eternal agility, of an infinitely teeming chaos" (148). If *Bouvard et Pécuchet* thus sets us on the track of thought-in-motion as both an instrument and an aim of modernist and postmodernist rhetoric, however, it does so as a direct response to a crucial breakdown in the underpinnings of liberal ideology.

The liberal subject is defined as a subject, as an individual, by the fact of her desire, most especially her desire for liberty. To the extent, however, that any one individual's desire will necessarily conflict with the desires of others, the question arises as to how a liberal social order might be brought forth from the chaos of conflicting desires, how authority—be it political, epistemic, or even narrative—might found itself on apparent anarchy. This problem is structural in a sweeping historical sense; that "sack of potatoes" to which Marx's *Eighteenth Brumaire* famously likened the French peasantry after Napoléon's coup is patently generalizable as an image of the liberal social order. Whether this structural anarchy was paradoxically aggravated in moments of high revolutionary tension (as bourgeois observers have tended to argue) or alleviated in the constitution of the revolutionary "fused group" (Sartre) is a question that has been, and will likely remain, a subject of debate.

Be this as it may, classical liberal discourse tends to assign the task of fixing, and therefore mastering, these fundamental confusions to a small number of hypothetical master forces, such as the "invisible hand" of capitalist theory or, in more overtly political contexts, the force of reason. In Zola's *Germinal,* for instance, at a moment of maximal political anarchy, Étienne Lantier hears "an astonished voice of reason, asking why all of this"; the novel then ends with the narrator speaking of Étienne's reason as having "matured": "he predicted that, one day, lawfulness would be more terrible still" (351, 501). This "voice of reason," presumed inherent in all liberal subjects, ultimately allows liberal ideology to precipitate social authority out of the anarchy of competing desires, while projecting an image of that authority as only benignly constraining. "The rational thing," Flaubert writes, in a passage previously quoted, "is a government of mandarins" (*Corr.,* 4:314/*2:126*).

In the essays collected in his 1868 volume, *Questions contemporaines,* Renan advocates a bipartite pedagogy in science and in virtue as the means of forming what he calls "a reasonable, enlightened nation" (24). Accepting the enlightened European public of his time as "the true intellectual sovereign power," Renan speaks of that public as an "incorruptible judge," won over only by "good reasons" (72). But Renan's faith in the progressive power of reason was clearly shaken by the events of 1870–1871. The essays in his subsequent *Réforme intellectuelle et morale* (*Intellectual and Moral Reform*) are infused with Renan's "profound sorrow" at the demise of his dream (which Flaubert clearly did not share) of a Pan-European alliance between Germany, England, and France, aimed at directing humanity "along the path of liberal civilization" (327). More to the point, the essays repeatedly argue that "reason's rights in the governance of humanity"—the philosophical rights of republican ideology—need to be counterbalanced by the implicitly monarchical rights of established custom, "the rights resulting from history" (357). In *Réforme's* final essay, composed before the Franco–Prussian War but published in its wake, we hear the echoes of Renan's liberal faith still resonating in the final moment of a patently dialectical process:

> Every day there grows in the very heart of France a popular mass that is
> devoid of religious ideals and rejects all social principles beyond what is

grounded in the will of individuals. The other mass, not yet permeated by this egotistic ideal, is diminished on a daily basis by primary education and the practice of universal suffrage. Against this rising tide of invasive ideas, however, . . . there stands a set of superior interests and needs, according to which society should be guided and organized by a principle of reason and science distinct from the will of individuals. (508–509)

Bouvard and Pécuchet, for their part, take pride in exposing reason as a liberal ruse, a universalist front for particular desires: "Reason offers more guarantees [than the evidence of the senses], since it is immutable and impersonal, but to be made manifest it must be incarnate. Then Reason becomes my reason" (307/*208*). More serious, perhaps, they run roughshod over the laws of rational argumentation that allow for legality as the basis for social authority. Witness the following passage, where the mayor, Foureau, comes to reclaim a baptismal font discovered by Bouvard and Pécuchet in the local cemetery and taken by them to be a basin used by the Druids to catch the blood of their sacrificial victims:

> "That's not the end of it, old fellows. You've got to give it back!"
> "But what?"
> "Funny joke! I know you are hiding *it*."
> They had been betrayed.
> They replied that they were keeping it with the curé's permission.
> "We'll see about that."
> And Foureau went off.
> He came back an hour later.
> "The curé says it is not so! Come and explain yourselves."
> They stood their ground.
> First, the baptismal font was not needed, and was not a baptismal font anyway. They would prove it by a mass of scientific arguments. Then they offered to acknowledge in their will that it belonged to the commune.
> They even proposed buying it.
> "And anyhow it is my property!" Pécuchet repeated. The twenty francs accepted by Monsieur Jeufroy was evidence of the contract and if they had to go before the magistrate, well, that was too bad, he would swear a false oath! (181/*115–116*)

The comedy of this scene depends upon Foureau's functioning as representative of authority in a double sense: he is at once the mayor, representative of civil law, and a stand-in for the logical norms that underlie such a legality, specifically for that law of noncontradiction which the two clerks here so jubilantly violate. In claiming that the font is their property just after proposing to buy it, in arguing that it is not a font before offering ultimately to acknowledge it as communal property (which it arguably would not have been as a Druidic basin), Bouvard and Pécuchet represent a certain free play of desire (more on this characterization in moment) in its confrontation with an authoritative agency[14] to whom such contradictory arguments as theirs are neither logically nor legally admissible.[15] Indeed, the mobility and mutual exclusivity of their arguments remind us of that story of the copper kettle that Freud so often told to illustrate the proposition that the "mutual canceling-out by several thoughts, each of which is in itself valid, is precisely what does not occur in the unconscious."[16] It is largely because liberal authority has tended to present itself as employing relatively benign tactics of coercion that liberalism fosters just such a comedy of desire, figured as a rhythm of emancipation and constraint.

One of the stories *Bouvard et Pécuchet* tells, as has often been remarked, is that of the inability of language and a rational process of categorization to master a fleeting, even rebellious, reality. When Bouvard and Pécuchet set out to study clouds using the Luke–Howard system of classification, for example, they find that "the shapes changed before they could find the names" (88/*48*). Deep into their medical studies, they are likewise surprised to find that

> sedatives are sometimes stimulants, and emetics purgatives, that the same remedy is suitable for various complaints, and that the same ailment may disappear with opposite treatments. (130/*79*)

It is tempting to say that *Bouvard's* comedy of defiance espouses disorder and drift, an irruption of the real into the domain of language, all the better to unburden us from the authority of that implicit order and logic which sets the domain of language apart from the material world. In this sense, the comedy of defiance would be one more manifestation of a will to "be matter," a desire for confusion figured by the process of fusing with (or confusion into) the material world. Yet this reading ultimately founders on the fact that, in *Bouvard*, language itself proves remarkably fluid, as the two clerks discover when they study verb agreement and spelling:

> The subject always agrees with the verb, except on those occasions when the subject does not agree. (217/*141*)

> Littré finished them off by affirming that there has never been positive orthography, nor ever could be. (218/*142*)

Lawrence Schehr is precisely right when he argues that the "figure of the *flou* [the hazy, the indistinct] in Flaubert's writing . . . is the *flou* of the un-fathomable and uncapturable gap of the world of representation," a world that precisely straddles both language and its referents (198).

It would, of course, be too simple to speak of the novel as implying a univocal critique of reason, since the careful weighing of opposing arguments that is constitutive of rational procedure lends itself here to a textuality in the mode of operative irony, defined by Henry James in his "Preface to 'The Lesson of the Master' " as that irony which "implies and projects the possible other case" (1229). It would be more accurate to say that *Bouvard et Pécuchet* consistently subsumes the laws of reason to the dictates of the *motus animi continuus,* respecting rational procedure only when it furthers the cause of continuing passion, of that continual movement of the spirit toward its object that we as moderns would call continuous desire. In *Bouvard et Pécuchet*, the sheer proliferation of contradictions and category mistakes, illogical summaries and paralogisms, inexplicable ellipses countered by grotesque abundances of detail, opaque signifiers, odd vocables, and unlikely homologues reflects the force of a desire that simply cannot be bothered with the standards of rational argument, or the code of *le bon style.* Unable as readers to distill such a textuality into concentrated, rational form, and blocked by the outrageous multiplication of Bouvard and Péchuet's desires from ascribing stable meaning to the history of any one particular desire, we are left with the impression of a desire cut loose from any particular object, including an infallible method or a totalizing absolute knowledge.[17] Moreover, the inscription of all possible values into a series of ironic rhythms—ironic rhythms of desire that more than anything else constitute the very substance of this novel—invites us to read Flaubert's tale of two ageless copy clerks as the story of desire itself or, perhaps, the story of writing as an expression of desire itself.

Traumatic Writing

In the final pages of the previous chapter, I sketched out a double danger that haunts the reading of Flaubert's texts and letters in the wake of 1870–1871. To give desire the last word, I suggested, is to risk failing to see how desire in the late Flaubert is fundamentally melancholic. (The earlier published iterations of this chapter and the last arguably fell into that trap.) But to focus on Flaubert's obvious melancholy is to risk missing (as Sartre in fact misses) how life and the "desire that makes one live" tend to reemerge in

Flaubert's texts on the far side of all deaths, confusions, or modes of entropic collapse. In the case of *Bouvard*, where the protagonists' return to copying functions so strikingly as an image of restricted but persistent desire, the risk of missing desire's attendant melancholia is clearly the more salient. I would argue, following Schehr's good analysis, that the critical tendency to find a certain freedom in the play of Flaubert's novel is founded on a widespread critical misprision, whereby that sense of liberation which the concept of textuality clearly brought to literary studies in the 1970s and 1980s was repeatedly found refracted as a property of given texts *themselves* (and perhaps none more so than *Bouvard et Pécuchet*).[18] Witness, in this regard, Jefferson Humphries' claim that *Bouvard* affords its readers "the very indeterminacy, the *freedom* of indeterminate desire," or my own suggestion above that the two clerks represent the "free play of desire" in their confrontation with the mayor, Foureau (160).

Recent work by Dominick LaCapra helps take this analysis a step further. In his *Writing History, Writing Trauma*, LaCapra argues that

> some of the most powerful forms of modern art and writing, as well as some of the most compelling forms of criticism (including forms of deconstruction), often seem to be traumatic writing or post-traumatic writing in closest proximity to trauma. They may also involve the feeling of keeping faith with trauma in a manner that leads to a compulsive preoccupation with aporia, an endlessly melancholic, impossible mourning, and a resistance to working through. (23)

Derrida is of course LaCapra's principal point of reference here, but his list of those who practice "traumatized or post-traumatic writing" includes Nietzsche, Mallarmé, Flaubert, Woolf, Blanchot, Kafka, Celan, Beckett, and Foucault (105).

The pertinence of LaCapra's analysis for our attempt to read *Bouvard*'s deployment of confusion as a response to the widely traumatic events of the Terrible Year is nowhere more clear than in the following passage:

> I would argue, or at least suggest, that undecidability and unregulated *différance*, threatening to disarticulate relations, confuse self and other, and collapse all distinctions, including that between present and past, are related to transference and prevail in trauma and in post-traumatic acting out in which one is haunted or possessed by the past and performatively caught up in the compulsive repetition of traumatic scenes—scenes in which the past returns and the future is blocked or fatalistically caught up in a melancholic feedback loop. (21)

Understood in this sense, the notion of post-traumatic acting-out helps account for the compulsive repetitiveness of Bouvard and Pécuchet's encyclopedic trajectory, not to mention the repetitiveness of the novel in which
they figure. LaCapra's delineation of a symptomatic confusion of self and
other under the pressure of traumatic experience nicely complements my
earlier, more expressly strategic reading of Flaubert's aims in merging his
narrative voice, albeit ambiguously, into that of the *on*. More telling still, the
return to brute, unreflective copying on which Flaubert's novel ends, entails
both an entropic collapse of value distinctions and a return to Bouvard and
Pécuchet's past as copy clerks, such that all futurity disappears into a form
of pure melancholic repetition:

> No thinking it over! Let us copy! The page must be filled, the "monument"
> completed—good and evil, the beautiful and the ugly, the insignificant and
> the distinctive must all be equalized. Only phenomena are true. (443)

Crucial to the ethico-political ramifications of LaCapra's argument is the
distinction he draws, following Freud, between acting-out and working
through. The essence of LaCapra's critique of Cathy Caruth's work on
trauma (and, in a more nuanced fashion, of Derrida) lies in the contention
that such work repeats, "whether consciously or unconsciously, the disconcertingly opaque movement of post-traumatic repetition in a seeming attempt to elucidate that movement" (184). Against a mode of criticism thus
given over to a transferential acting out of "processes active in the object of
study," LaCapra advocates a complex process of working through, of which
mourning and the various modes of critical and/or transformative social
practice are said to be component parts (36, 22).

As LaCapra understands it, working through entails three closely related
mental sets of particular interest for the analysis of *Bouvard et Pécuchet* as an
instance of post-traumatic writing in a democratic social frame. These include the making of distinctions, the affirmation of absence qua absence,
and the reinvestment in a necessarily agonistic civic life.

All processes of working through, LaCapra writes,

> involve the possibility of making distinctions or developing articulations that
> are recognized as problematic but still function as limits and as possibly
> desirable resistances to undecidability, particularly when the latter is
> tantamount to confusion and the obliteration or blurring of all distinctions
> (states that may indeed occur in trauma or in acting out post-traumatic
> conditions). (22)

Of the many necessary distinctions that surface over the course of LaCapra's argument—discriminations between self and other, victim and perpetrator, the "metametaphyisical" and the historical, and so on—two are of particular importance: the distinction between "past and present or future" (as evoked above) and that between absence and loss (151, 21).

For LaCapra's purposes, "loss" applies to specific historical phenomena (the events of the Shoah, for example). "Absence," by contrast, serves to designate absolute, transhistorical forms of lack (195, 52). Loss is thus closely related to "historical trauma"; absence, to "structural trauma," understood as "an anxiety-producing condition of possibility related to the potential for historical traumatization" (82). Much of the interest of LaCapra's distinction lies in the ways it gets blurred, in ways (we are told) that "bear striking witness" to the impact of (often unspecified) traumatic events (46). The conversion of absence into loss, LaCapra writes, is most fully emblematic of those "fundamentalisms and foundational philosophies" which posit a "fully unified community or *Volksgemeinschaft*" by projecting "blame for a putative loss onto identifiable others" (51, 56). On the other hand,

> when loss is converted into (or encrypted in an indiscriminately generalized rhetoric of) absence, one faces the impasse of endless melancholy, impossible mourning, and interminable aporia in which any process of working through the past and its historical losses is foreclosed or prematurely aborted. (46)

It is indicative of the very slipperiness of these conversion scenarios, however, that—several pages after situating the Derridean aporia on the side of generalized absence—LaCapra cites "generation of the aporia" as a narrative of loss, together with Rousseau's account of the passage from nature to culture and Lacan's version of the entrance into language—not to mention Heidegger's notion of *Geworfenheit*, Žižek's encounter with the Real, and Butler's theory of heterosexual melancholy (52).

The crucial question for our reading of *Bouvard et Pécuchet* is whether Flaubert's novel evinces a working through of absence *as absence*, a process which requires that one recognize "both the dubious nature of ultimate solutions and the necessary anxiety that cannot be eliminated from the self or projected onto others" (58). To what extent and in what ways, in other words, does the novel take upon itself the recognition that "full unity, community, or consensus" is necessarily lost or lacking (60)? If LaCapra is right to suggest (as I believe he is) "that the provision of modes of symbolizing difference and conflict—not full consensus or community—is basic to democracy and that the dialogic itself in a democratic context must have an agonistic component," to what degree is the ethos of Flaubert's novel democratic despite itself (60)? In order to address these questions, I should like to close this chapter by briefly contrasting the function of trauma, melancholy, and working through in Flaubert's posthumous novel with their role in a body of contemporaneous work of which Flaubert thought most highly, that of Ernest Renan.

Flaubert with Renan

There is no question but that Flaubert looked to Renan, in the wake of the Paris Commune, to articulate the various crises besetting contemporary France. "Free compulsory education will do nothing," he tells Sand in a letter from October 1871,

> but swell the number of imbeciles. Renan has said that superbly, in the
> preface to his *Questions contemporaines*. What we need most of all is a *natural*,
> that is to say a legitimate, aristrocracy. (*Corr.*, 4:384/*2:183*)

Several weeks later, he tells Edma Roger des Genettes (with typically confirming irony) that Renan's latest book, *La Réforme intellectuelle et morale*, is "very good, entirely in line with my thinking" (*Corr.*, 4:433).

Leaving aside for a moment the question of how Flaubert's paraphrases might simplify a strikingly nuanced series of arguments, his newfound sense of Renan as a kindred spirit is by no means difficult to understand. Like Flaubert, Renan conceives of science as a force of progress above political interest and personal gain (*Questions,* 74). Like the novelist, he bemoans a growing egalitarianism as the breeding ground for "egotism, mediocrity, isolation, coldness, the unlivable," and calls upon society to recognize "the fact of natural superiorities" (*Réforme,* 486, 362).[19] Or, to echo the quotations that opened this chapter, both writers see the many concessions made to the "superficial spirit" of the crowd or mass as democracy's "original sin"; both lament the fact that universal suffrage has handed France's destiny to "five million peasants, to whom liberal ideas are foreign" (*Réforme,* 467, 342).

This sense of a shared ethos notwithstanding, Renan's reaction to the events of 1870–71 is most useful for my purposes in the way it ultimately diverges from Flaubert's. To borrow Freud's significantly vexed distinction between mourning and melancholia, I would argue that whereas Flaubert repeatedly (and accurately) evokes a "bottomless melancholy" into which the events of 1870–71 had thrust him, Renan's tone in the wake of "these sorrowful weeks" is closer to that of mourning—mourning for the loss of what he liked to call "ancient rigor" and for the demise of his dream (but not Flaubert's) of a Pan-European alliance of Germany, England, and France, directing the world toward "liberal civilization" (*Réforme*, 325, 384, 327).

A remarkable series of pages from *La Réforme intellectuelle et morale* helps us situate this difference precisely. Having counseled a politics of "penitence" aimed at overcoming the failings of the Revolution, most especially a "taste for superficial democracy," Renan imagines the discourse of a certain "well-meaning patriot, more anxious to be of use to his fellow citizens than to please them" (373; cf. 514). This good patriot, who clearly echoes Renan in his more Germanophilic moments, calls for a multifaceted project of reform. France, we are told, must break out of that vicious circle which has doomed French republicanism "both to provoke social anarchy and to repress it brutally" (376). She needs to reestablish royalty and (in a certain measure) nobility—both understood to govern by historical, not divine right—through the reinstatement of a constitutional monarchy. Finally, she must be brought to understand that "the conscience of a nation resides in its most enlightened segment," hence an urgent need to buttress primary and secondary education (375).

Having developed these familiar views at some length, Renan breaks off, to begin a new section with these words:

> Happy are those who have found in familial traditions or in the fanaticism of a narrow mind that sense of assurance that alone resolves all doubts! As for us, too accustomed to seeing matters from all different sides to believe in absolute solutions, we would also grant that a very honorable citizen might speak as follows. (383)

Arguing that a nation's character exerts a strong inertial force, and that any project of reform which asks France to renounce her "democratic prejudices" is but a flight of fancy, Renan's upstanding citizen suggests that France is, and will remain,

> a country of amiable folk—pleasant, decent, upstanding, cheerful, superficial and kind-hearted, but utterly lacking in political intelligence. . . . France will sink deeper and deeper into the rut of materialism and vulgar republicanism into which the entire modern world, Prussia and Russia excepted, appears to be headed. (384)

Picking up on an argument that runs throughout Renan's text, the honorable citizen thus embodies a fundamental political realism attuned to the particularities of national cultures and supranational developments. However much one might want to bemoan, for instance, the modern decline of a warrior nobility, now restricted to Prussia and Russia, there is no way around the fact that universal suffrage has made France a "profoundly materialist," hence "essentially pacifist," nation (344, 346). For Renan's honorable compatriot, in short, it is good politics not to oppose the inevitable, but "to serve the inevitable and make use of it" (421).

As an epigraph to an earlier section of this chapter, I cited a passage from Renan's 1848 article on clerical liberalism, evoking the irresistible force of a progressive "movement of ideas" destined to sweep up even those, such as the Catholic Church, primed to resist it (*Questions,* 283). One way of understanding the effect of *l'année terrible* on Renan's work is to say that the events of 1870–1871 served to confirm his increasing sense of this movement as the catalyst for a mournful ambivalence that effectively tracks an ambivalence inherent in liberalism itself. "German liberalism nobly proposes as its object," Renan writes in the preface to *Réforme,* "not the equality of social classes so much as the cultivation and uplifting of human nature in general, though the rights of man also count for something" (329). If this passage, in Renan's own voice, clearly sites liberalism on the side of the well-meaning patriot, it is nonetheless significant that the honorable citizen himself goes on to situate the liberal on the side of the rights of man:

> Let France . . . brandish unflinchingly the liberal banner that has defined it for the past hundred years. That liberalism is often a source of weakness is in fact one reason why the world will come to it, for the world is becoming flabby and losing its ancient rigor. (384)

Renan's work of the late Second Empire and early Third Republic, in short, puts into play a mournful ambivalence made manifest—on the level of the sentence and beyond—through a practice of double voicing, a staging of the dialogic. This ambivalence, which pits admiration for the embattled rigor of a largely Germanic and Protestant elitism against the realistic acknowledgment of mounting democratic egalitarianism, largely mirrors an ambivalence intrinsic to contemporary liberalism, caught as it was between the prerogatives of a bourgeois elite and those of an increasingly exacting populace. In his 1864 essay "L'Instruction supérieure en France," Renan casts the historical coherence of French culture as itself ambivalent: intellectually serious *and* witty, politically glorious *and* wrongheaded. "France's greatness," he writes, "lies in her ability to contain opposing poles within herself" (*Questions,* 95). But in the wake of the Commune, this largely picturesque ambivalence gives way to a melancholic division within Renan's thought itself, the working through of which it will be the task of his writings to effect.

If Renan's work thus gives voice to social conflict in the mode of either/or, Flaubert's does so (we have seen) in the mode of neither/nor. Time and again in *Bouvard*, Flaubert deploys the agonistic divisions of modern French history in order ultimately to empty them of both historical content and affective power.

> As they chatted on about all this they became excited. Bouvard, liberal and sensitive, was for the Constitution, the Gironde, Thermidor. Pécuchet, bilious and inclined to authoritarianism, declared himself a sans-culotte and even for Robespierre. (186/*119*)

Just as often, I have suggested, Flaubert's practice of indeterminate voicing denies his readers any solid perspective for judgment, leaving them little choice but to reject all parties to a given discursive conflict. The force of Flaubert's late work, in other words, is to deny the very standing that would allow political positions to be formed into relations of ambivalence, such as those which permeate Renan's work of the period. But this gesture of denying argumentative standing, and the related denial of reason as a means of political adjudication, allow Flaubert, I have argued, to rejoin the liberal value of ideational movement on the far side of adjudication's apparent collapse. It is surely no accident that the passage I cited earlier as exemplary of *Bouvard*'s deployment of thought-in-motion ("In connection with the barbarians, Thierry demonstrates . . ." [187–88/*12*]) follows immediately upon the following, plainly antiagonistic paragraph:

> The Revolution is for some a satanic event. Others proclaim that it was a sublime exception. The defeated ones on each side are, of course, martyrs. (187/*120*)

Given the extent to which *Bouvard*'s indeterminacies of voicing thwart the making of distinctions or developing of articulations that LaCapra rightly sees as critical to the process of working through, it is tempting to read Flaubert's last novel as an elaborate acting out of the traumas of the Terrible Year designed to block readerly access to the instruments of a successful working through. Surely Flaubert's pronouncements on *Bouvard* as a novel of revenge militate in favor of such a reading. But there is another form of collapsed distinction worth bearing in mind here—one that points in the direction of a sociability more suggestive of working through. I have argued that while the plotting of Flaubert's novel clearly relies upon the fundamentally paranoid gesture whereby its protagonists attempt to maintain their distinction from others in the world, the novel also shows (through the interventions of Doctor Vaucorbeil) that Bouvard and Pécuchet are harmless imbeciles who belong among those others, among the *on*. Indeed, the two former clerks' commitment to social and civic life is curiously, but unambiguously, strongest in the novel's final completed chapter (on the education of Victor and Victorine) and in its unfinished conclusion (with their lectures on the future of Humanity). I read this commitment to a social life envisioned from within not only as an effective refutation of Sartre's thesis on Flaubert's historical death, but also as pointing toward that "necessary anxiety that cannot be eliminated from the self or projected onto others" which LaCapra sees as requisite to the process of working through. If this is the case, if a positive agonism essential to a democratic order persists on the far side of Flaubert's neither/nor, then *Bouvard*'s relation to a nascent democratism is not simply reactive and cranky, but also—if minimally—anticipatory.

These ladies, carried forward by the current . . . crept forward,
pressed so close they could hardly draw breath . . . and their satisfied
desire was gratified by this tedious approach which stimulated their
curiosity. It was a jumble [*pêle-mêle*] of ladies dressed in silk, petty
bourgeoises in cheap dresses, bareheaded girls, all lifted and
intoxicated by the same passion.

—Emile Zola, *Au Bonheur des dames*

This big baby known as the French people needed a toy; I gave
him universal suffrage. (You have seen how he has used it.) Poor
kid, who gives booboos to Mama Republic with the toys she
manages to get for him.

—Clovis Hugues, *Lettre de Marianne aux Républicains*

Unlike the literary texts with which I began this study, Émile Zola's *Au
Bonheur des dames* is not *about* the Paris Commune, either directly (*La Débâ-
cle, L'Année terrible*) or indirectly (*Quatre-vingt-treize*). Nor is its relation to
the Commune essentially reactive and symptomatic, as I have argued for
Flaubert's *La Tentation de saint Antoine* and *Bouvard et Pécuchet*. Rather, *Au
Bonheur des dames* evokes a revolutionary violence recently evidenced by the
Commune largely through its portrait of that specifically *commercial* revolu-
tion operated by Octave Mouret's eponymous department store.

Of the many commonalities that allow Zola to suggest political revolution behind and through its capitalist counterpart, none is perhaps more pivotal than the trope of confusion. The novel repeatedly refers to Mouret's
Bonheur as a *bazaar*—a word derived from the Persian for market or *souk*,
which by the late 1860s had come to signify "a disorderly place, where everything is pell-mell" (*Petit Robert*). As modern readers invariably note, the
Bonheur contains within its pages an entire theory of how department stores,

to our day, manipulate their customers' confusions to productive effect. By destroying the hitherto "intelligent arrangement" of his store—separating related departments, placing key high-turnover items far from the store's entrances, and using mirrors to disorienting effect—Mouret condemns his customers to "a constant toing and froing [that] . . . multiplies them and makes them lose their heads" (300/*233*, 302/*234*). Or, as the novel's quintessential impulse buyer, Mme. Marty, puts it: "There's no order in this shop. You lose your way, you do foolish things" (328/*256*).

In the *Bonheur's* great sale scenes (chapters 4, 9, and 14), this confusion inherent in the commercial ethos of Mouret's store tracks that confusion we have seen to be endemic to moments of high revolutionary drama. By selling low-cost "hung" goods just outside the Bonheur's doors, Mouret effectively mimics the disorderly crush of the revolutionary crowd: "First of all, there must be a crush at the entrance; from the street, it should look like a riot" (300/*232*). Inasmuch as "ladies" of all social classes prove equally subject to the new neuroses unleashed by the Bonheur, the experience of the riotous department store crowd is (like its revolutionary counterpart) profoundly egalitarian.

But in allowing revolutionary experience to resonate behind Mouret's innovations, Zola operates a crucial chiasmus. Whereas the demise of the Commune clearly yoked revolutionary disorder with death in the minds of Zola's contemporaries, in the world of the Bonheur, it is *order* that is death (witness the fate of Le Vieil Elbeuf) and disorder, life: "because life, [Mouret] said, attracts life, breeds, multiplies" (300/*232*).

As these echoes of the vitalist dialectic begin to suggest, *Au Bonheur des dames* remains marked by the experience of revolution through its insistence upon what Hugo saw as the melancholy logic of the historical Terror. Following a visionary nightmare in which she sees the remains of the old boutiques of the Saint-Roch quarter hauled away in tumbrels, like aristocrats to the guillotine, the novel's protagonist, Denise Baudu, comes to the realization "that this was good and that this dunghill of miseries was essential to the health of the Paris of tomorrow. . . . Yes, it was the debt of blood: every revolution needed martyrs and one could only go forward over the dead" (461–62/*368*).

This explicit articulation of a Terrorist spiral of history confirms the political resonance of those headless mannequins which so captivate Denise and her brothers upon first glimpsing Mouret's store. Clearly meant to suggest the seduction exercised by a traumatic vision of feminine castration, and in this sense analogous to that gaping hole into which Mouret's first wife,

Mme. Hédouin, falls to her death, the headless mannequins effectively pre-figure the Bonheur's capacity to make women (and occasionally men) "lose their head" (59/*28*, 320/*249*; cf. 498/*397*). Witness the following passage, which brings together several of the motifs I have discussed thus far—a de-mocratizing of luxury, the seductive decapitation of women, and the calcu-lated sowing of confusion for commercial ends:

> There was something for every taste, from wraps at twenty-nine francs to the velvet coat priced at eighteen hundred francs. The material swelled across the round bosoms of the tailors' dummies, broad hips emphasized their slender waists, and where the head should be, there was a large price tag, stuck into the red flannel of the neck with a pin; and mirrors on either side of the display were carefully positioned to reflect the dummies and multiply them endlessly, peopling the street with these beautiful women, all for sale, who bore their prices in fat figures in place of heads. (33/*6*)

What are we to make of images such as this? Zola's *Bonheur* plainly asso-ciates the democratizing logic of modern capitalism with violence against women, and especially with the seduction of women through such vio-lence. To read the novel at the dawn of the twenty-first century is to be sensitive to the ways in which the commercial machine that is Octave Mouret's department store elevates women of all social classes to the role of "queen of the house," all the better to violate and degrade them—in the interest, we are told, of their own *jouissance*. What the novel calls the "de-mocratizing" of luxury, in other words, is closely linked to a certain female masochism:

> By increasing their sales tenfold and democratizing luxury [the department stores] became a dreadful agent of expense, causing ravages in households and operating through the madness of fashion, which was constantly more expensive. And if in the stores woman was queen, adulated in herself, humored in her weaknesses, surrounded by every little attention, she reigned as a queen in love, whose subjects were swindling her so that she paid for each of her whims with a drop of her own blood. (116/*75–76*)

The repressive nature of this scenario is indisputable, but is not the whole story. The danger in focusing upon that fetishistic violence through which Mouret's store, and by extension Zola's novel, seeks to relegate women to the status of headless masochists is that one will miss the ways in which the novel also does violence to itself. Zola's *Bonheur* is inherently fetishistic not just because it caters to an explicitly male fetishistic gaze, which it clearly does, but also in the way it habitually disavows its own best insights (into the disintegrative effects of capitalism, for instance, or the essentially ungrounded nature of male mastery). Likewise, masochism here is not simply the libidinal penchant of the store's all-suffering "ladies"; it is also the very basis of a new, liberal democratic order longingly envisioned (albeit not in those terms) by Zola's novel.

My principal focus in this chapter will be on the masochistic suffering of the increasingly allegorical figure of Denise Baudu. What might appear to be an argumentative shift—from melancholy in previous chapters to masochism here—is in fact only the teasing out of a masochism inherent in the experience of melancholy, in which the object of the superego's wrath "has been taken into the ego through identification" (Freud, *Ego,* 51). In light of this diagnostic affinity, Denise's will to suffer can be read in two complementary ways. It functions as a displaced response to that sense of collective melancholy which *La Débâcle* (written nearly a decade later) would show to have followed the experiences of the Terrible Year. But it also places Denise squarely in the lineage, in ways to be examined here, of that all-suffering Mama Republic of which Clovis Hugues, founding editor of the Commune–era *La Voix du peuple* (*The People's Voice*), speaks in my second epigraph above. Denise's suffering, in short, both augurs and does the work of a certain social, even "socialist," futurity—as if answering in advance that melancholic bind to which *La Débâcle*'s Maurice Levasseur would come to be subject.

Confusion Disavowed

As a first step in this argument, I return to that model of disavowal evoked in chapter 2, as it helps to elucidate the *Bonheur*'s well-nigh obsessive quest to control an evacuation of meaning the novel quite plainly sets into motion. In the *Bonheur*'s sale scenes, the very frenzy of the desire for commodities repeatedly blurs the boundaries of gender and class, conflating bodies and commodities, and reducing individual bodies to a vertiginous whirl of (fetishistic) body parts. Consider the following passage from chapter 9:

> And this sea, these many-colored hats, these bare heads, blonde or black,
> flowed from one end of the gallery to the other, blurred [*confus*] and drab
> amid the sharp, vibrant colors of the materials. . . . Everywhere the mirrors
> extended the shops, reflecting displays with fragments of the public, faces
> reversed, portions of shoulders and arms, while to the left and to the right,

the side galleries opened up vistas . . . where the crowd was no more than human dust. (316/*246*)

Here, as so often in the novel, the hysteria unleashed by commodities upon the collective body of the store's shoppers gives rise to an equally hysterical dismemberment of that body. At the same time, female masochism is made manifest by yet one more instance (the crowd's reduction to a mass of "human dust") of the novel's clear tendency to link shopping with the desire for death.[1]

But just as surely as the novel evokes a confusion of hysterical *morcellement* under the sway of the death drive, so will it disavow that confusion by designating the space of a transcendent order. In Manoni's terms, the *mais quand même* of fetishistic belief depends, once again, upon a prior *je sais bien*. The very pressures that reduce the overwhelmingly female crowd first to body parts, and thence to dust, also tend to generate confusion's counterprinciple. In the sale scene of chapter 9, this counterprinciple appears in the (supposedly innocent) form of the Bonheur's bedding department—a vision of small iron beds draped in white curtains, reminiscent of a schoolgirls' dormitory, that "appeared to be suspended . . . above [the store's] confusion" (317/*247*). By the novel's final chapter, however, this transcendent space of exception has been filled by a resolutely mythic bed, now quite blatantly suggestive of the marriage bed into which Mouret (and Zola's novel) will lure the virginal Denise Baudu:

> It looked like a great white bed, vast and virginal, awaiting the white princess of the fairy tales, the one destined to come at last, all-powerful, wearing her white bridal veil. (487/*388*)

Several pages later, the reader encounters a remarkable fetishistic set piece, which begins with the comic voyeurism of a certain M. Boutarel, provincial husband extraordinaire (500). Couched in the form of an extended collective striptease enacted for the (implicitly male) reader's voyeuristic gaze—"as though a group of pretty girls had been undressing themselves from one department to the next" (501/*399*)—this passage speaks to the particular confusion of naturalist catalogs run amok as it reviews some of the manifold perversions endemic to the world of the Bonheur, as home to "an army of headless, legless dummies, . . . with the disturbing lewdness of cripples" (501/*399*). It suggests, moreover, that social leveling in Zola's novel implies first and foremost an equality of exposure to the scopophilic gaze: "woman laid open to view from underneath, from the petty bourgeoise with her uniform linen to the rich lady smothered in lace" (502/*400*). But above all the passage rehearses the birth of a fetishistic sacrality, endemic to the new commercial order, out of an eternally feminine "quivering mystery of skirts" (502/*400*).[2] It is of special interest, therefore, that the text's act of successively unveiling and reveiling the "mystery" that is the woman's sex should be seen to lead, as if naturally, to the mystery of procreation: "Then there was another room, baby clothes, in which the voluptuous white of women eventually became the pure white of the child: an innocence, a joy, in the mistress who is awakening to motherhood" (502/*400*). From this point forward, the entire store will be seen to evince the "milky pallor" of Denise Baudu's much "adored" body (506/*403*).

This final move is of course hardly innocent. For much of the novel, Denise has proven seductive precisely because she disrupts traditional gender roles. She is both sensual *and* reasonable, a sentimental guardian of domestic tranquillity *and* a passionate advocate for "the logical development of trade" (271/*207*).[3] Indeed, it this androgynous quality that makes Denise so "troubling" to Mouret:

> Denise, won over by his familiarity, . . . got quite excited, quoting examples, which showed that she was not only well informed, but full of farsighted, new ideas. . . . The girl had no doubt matured in the atmosphere of Paris and was becoming a woman. She unsettled him, this sensible and reserved woman, with her lovely hair heavy with passionate yearnings. (263–64/*200*).

Denise proves seductive because she embodies a contradiction inherent in the commercial order of the Bonheur, which must both "masculinize" its female workers (in the interests of social harmony and progress) and treat them as pure embodiments of a fetishistic womanliness to which it appeals.[4]

But in presenting the Bonheur's entire silk department as a trope on Denise's otherwise absent body, in elevating the shopgirl to the double status of universal mother and "benevolent queen of the shop," chapter 14 effectively undoes this contradiction (504/*401*). The sexual trouble occasioned by a figure who had appeared to be a walking category mistake is conjured away by a Cinderella plot that idealizes—indeed, fetishizes—the woman precisely because it has crippled her. Like the Chinese man of Freud's example, who mutilates the woman's foot and then reveres it, Zola's text appears "to want to thank the woman for her having submitted to castration" (Freud, "Fetishism," 219). In denying that contradiction endemic to woman in the new commercial order represented by the Bonheur, the novel thus builds a fetishistic split into its very structure.

Democracy and the Space of Power

If I may resume in a single formula the forms of disavowal at work in the passages discussed thus far, it would be this: Zola's text *knows very well* that, along with a "democratic" leveling of class distinctions, capitalism unleashes cognitive confusion, sexual perversion, and gender trouble, *but all the same* it acts as though such confusions can be mastered by means of a patently creaky, heterosexual, and patriarchal "happy" ending.[5] It is not just that the novel must do violence to its own best insights in order to attain significant closure and, in the process, assuage well-documented Third Republic anxieties about "the degeneration of motherhood, family life, and reproduction" (Pick, 98, discussing Nye, *Crime,* 160–61). Narrative mastery here is an illusion made possible by the prior positing of an unmasterable excess— that excess of cognitive and sexual confusion which it is the function of Zola's ending so massively to disavow.

One aspect of the *Bonheur* that my analysis thus far has not addressed is the novel's complex libidinal investment in the figure of Denise Baudu.[6] I would argue that this investment has everything to do with "democracy," understood in a sense somewhat larger than that of simple class leveling, which is what the novel's sole reference to "democratizing" (cited above) intends. In Althusserian terms, pursuing this argument will mean reading the novel's libidinal investment in Denise Baudu as the answer to a question the novel cannot yet pose as such—the requisite but absent question of the futurity of liberal democracy.[7]

To open up this argument, I would turn here to a theoretical commonplace extensively discussed by Claude Lefort, Slavoj Žižek, Chantal Mouffe, and Joan Copjec—the idea that, in democracy, "the *space of power* . . . is tacitly recognized as an empty space, which by definition cannot be occupied—a symbolic space, not a real one" (Lefort, 126).[8] "In pre-democratic societies," Žižek has written,

> there is always a legitimate pretender to the place of Power, somebody who is fully entitled to occupy it, and the one who violently overthrows him has simply the status of a usurper, whereas within the democratic horizon, *everyone* who occupies the locus of Power is by definition a usurper. (*For They Know,* 267)

In this view, that sacrificial logic to which democratic leaders of our day are so patently subject, their extraordinary susceptibility to scandal or assassination, is not so much a regrettable by-product of democracy as democracy's very guarantee.

For my present purposes, however, the crucial question is how societies of post–Revolutionary Europe might have protected the empty locus of power. Žižek suggests one answer when he speaks of the monarch in Hegel's *Philosophy of Right* as "an empty, formal agency whose task is simply to prevent the current performer of Power (executive) from 'gluing' on to the locus of Power—that is, from identifying immediately with it" (*For They Know*, 269). Precisely because one became a monarch only through the purely contingent mechanism of biological lineage, the role of monarch served as "nothing but a positivization, a materialization of the *distance* separating the locus of Power from those who exert it" (269).

The Paris Commune, as we have seen, represented an unprecedented attempt to forge a new social order in the absence of stable embodiments of social and political power. Beyond the inherent rudderlessness of the events that led up to the Commune (especially those of October 31 and March 18), and beyond the contingent absence of Auguste Blanqui (arrested, you will recall, on March 17), the Commune's "destruction of hierarchic investiture"—this is Kristin Ross, echoing Marx—"involved the displacement (revocability) of authority along a chain or series of 'places,' without any sovereign term" (*Emergence*, 45). Or, as Lissagaray writes, thinking of the Comité Centrale's assumption that their mandate to lead would expire with the Communal elections of March 26: "What could be said against this new-born power whose first word was its own abdication?" (123/*92*).

In an 1881 essay for *Le Figaro* titled "La Démocratie," Zola speaks of his "profound faith" in a democratic groundswell "[which] can only be an expansion of being, a wider engagement with and of the world" (650–651).[9] *Au Bonheur des dames*, I want to argue, thinks through the protecting of power's empty locus in the context of this coming democratization by borrowing a page from French Republican iconography of the mid-nineteenth century. In his classic study *Marianne au combat*, Maurice Agulhon speaks of a "spontaneous popular instinct" to represent the republic in the form of "a female allegory" (164–65/*128*). The iconic figures of Marianne and "the Republic" functioned as "abstract female sovereign[s]," pure symbols endowed with the dual task of personifying the republic and of keeping the locus of social power strictly open (Agulhon, 194/*152*). The very abstraction of these figures is in fact what gave them their remarkable symbolic plasticity. Here is Agulhon, glossing an 1856 *Lettre à Marianne* by Republican journalist and activist (and Lissagaray *bête noir*) Félix Pyat:

> Marianne is now the Republic, now the mother of the Republic and now the Endeavour that will build the future Republic; she is now a Virgin and now a Mother (not an ambivalence of Pyat's invention), now a Queen (by opposition to Napoleon) and now a Goddess (as it were an alternative Madonna). (164/*128*)

There is of course a great deal of this symbolic mobility in the figure of Denise Baudu. She is both virgin and mother, symbol of a new utopian order (as advocate of a moral harmony to be found within capitalism itself) and echo of the old (she is "queen")—the fitting analogue of a political order, that of the early Third Republic, paradoxically athwart a monarchical past and a republican future.[10] Denise incarnates, moreover, that standard of "impeccable, white virtue" to which Zola (in a journalistic apostrophe to the "Republic, my sweet") once spoke of the republic as held, "under threat of . . . being treated as a lost and licentious slut, whom decent souls cannot greet on the sidewalk" ("Vertu," 711). And in her role as "the woman destined to come," Denise becomes the subject of a waiting game much like the one in these lines from Eugène Poitier's Republican ballad, "Quand viendra-t-elle?" ("When Will She Come?," 1870): "Ah! I am waiting for her [for Marianne, a.k.a. the Republic], I am waiting—Will I have to wait much longer?" (405/*321*; quoted in Agulhon, 165/*129*).[11]

If, in her symbolic function, Denise thus owes a good deal to iconography of the republic, her ideological import, I would argue, is strictly liberal democratic. By "liberal democracy" here I mean a social order—both democratic *and* capitalist—grounded in the pursuit of two largely irreconcilable forms of freedom: the freedom of the capitalist market and the individual's freedom to best realize his or her particular capacities (Macpherson, 1–2). Denise is crucial to Zola's novel precisely because it is she, with her "sensitive, feminine ideas," who is seen as squaring some of liberal democracy's most recalcitrant circles (438/*349*). For not only does she attempt to show how the capitalist's pursuit of pure self-interest leads necessarily to a betterment of the workers' condition, and hence of their capacities for self-realization (438/*348*); she is also made to incarnate the sort of benevolent authority of which liberal democracy can only dream: "When Denise laid down the law, without raising her voice, not one of them resisted. Her very gentleness endowed her with absolute authority" (406/*323*).

One might argue that Zola's novel knows full well that Denise's authority is nothing without the power of Mouret behind it. To this extent, Denise would exemplify a principle articulated by Gay Gullickson, who notes that the effectiveness of female allegorical figures from ancient Greece onward "depended on . . . the exclusion of human women from the traits they embodied" (6).[12] But I see two critical qualifications to this view of Denise's authority as a masculinist alibi. Zola's novel not only wants to grant that authority great ideological weight in its own right; it also quite clearly implies that Mouret's power is *itself nothing* without the power of capital behind it.

This second point suggests another way of approaching the question of liberal democracy in relation to Zola's novel. In theoretical terms, what differentiates liberal democracy from simple representative democracy (with which in practice it is often associated) is the fact that in liberal democracy, the locus of power is doubly empty. Not only can the space of power never be fully and legitimately occupied by any one leader, party, or governing body (such is the sine qua non of representative democracy); capital itself, which in some important sense should fill that space, effectively cannot. As the *Bonheur* knows, capital can have power only through its circulation; to the capitalist enterprise, inertia is tantamount to death.

It is in this light that I would analyze the final chapter of Zola's *Bonheur*. Throughout the novel, Zola's narrator has taken great pains to insist upon Octave Mouret's mastery, his "male royalty" (492/*392*). Even Mouret's supposed femininity, evinced by his "delicate intuition" into woman's "secret being," is thematized as a ruse that allows him to reign brutally over his clients, "like the despotic king of chiffon" (124/*82–83*). The narrator once again insists upon this despotism near the end of chapter 14:

> They were starting to leave, the counters were littered with lengths of cloth, and gold pieces rang in the tills, while the customers, despoiled, violated, went away half undone, with the satisfied lust and vague shame of a desire slaked in the depths of some shady hotel. He was the one who possessed them in this way. . . . He reigned over them all with the brutality of a despot, whose whim destroyed families. (522/*415–16*)

I would argue, however, that there is a good deal of compensatory fantasy in the *Bonheur's* (quasi-hysterical) insistence upon the despotic sexuality of its leading man. In an important sense, the novel knows that Mouret is nothing without his ability to make capital circulate. The locus of power in this ostensibly progressive, liberal democratic world is indeed empty, and can be filled only by the plainly reactionary and symptomatic longing for a certain despotism.[13]

It is all the more ironic, therefore, that the very chapter which appears to confirm the despotic male in the space of power—chapter 14—is also that which most tellingly suggests why he can in fact never be coextensive with that space. For the chapter is punctuated, as it were, by two processions—the first by Denise in her role as "benevolent queen of the shop," the second by the million-plus francs earned on the novel's final day:

> On the first floor, ladies' wear, perfumery, lace and shawls were lined up devoutly as at the passage of the good Lord [in fact, it is the day's take]. From one to another, the clamor rose and swelled to become the roar of a people acclaiming the golden calf. (525/*418*)

The final chapter of the *Bonheur*, in other words, develops under the sign of two fetishistic entities—Denise as queen and the million—neither of which can fully occupy the locus of power and each of which serves to prevent Mouret from, in Žižek's words, " 'gluing' on to" that space. The fact that Denise is the quintessential Zolaesque woman—a "mobile unit," an "empty square par excellence," who "can be equated with the people, with the body, or money—with all that circulates and/or is repressed" (this is Naomi Schor summarizing a critical commonplace), in no way saves Denise from the destiny reserved for her by patriarchal society (*Breaking*, 29). What Denise's symbolic mobility does do is to guarantee an openness constitutive of that liberal democratic order for which she otherwise speaks, to assure that even the most despotic of masters can reign only as a usurper.

To return to that structure of disavowal so pivotal for my readings of Zola in this study, *Au Bonheur des dames* knows full well that the space of power in its world is inherently empty, since it could be fully occupied only by that which cannot in fact occupy it—capital itself. The figure of Denise likewise can never become coextensive with that space, since it enjoys symbolic power largely to the extent that it approximates capital's mobility. All the same, the novel wants to believe that the locus of power can indeed by occupied—by the despotic (and only mildly hysterical) man of genius. As in the earlier case of the novel's disavowal of the very confusion it so brilliantly exposes, there is an element of male "panic" here, much like the panic of the little boy who believes that he could lose his penis because his mother seems to have lost hers (Freud, "Fetishism," 215). In the economy of Zola's novel, narrative mastery and the closely related theme of Mouret's despotism are thus nothing more than simulacra, fetishistic supplements to knowledge the novel has not repressed but disavowed.

Masochistic Identification

It would be a mistake, however, to allow these rather classic forms of fetishistic disavowal to have the last word. For to do so would be to risk missing
a structure of disavowal equally central to Zola's novel, but more closely
associated with a certain traditionally female masochism. In a remarkable
piece on American television coverage of the first Gulf War, Laura Marks
writes of the masochism of the military wife, forced to sacrifice her individual fears and desires on the altar of country (61). National mobilization, or
the constitution of a "national family," depends, Marks argues, upon the
viewer's "masochistic identification" with the selflessness and coping strategies of what she calls "militarized femininity" (62, 59). The masochism of
the military wife, like that of so many other women who serve the military
behind the scenes, thus guarantees her an integral role in a structure that
ultimately effaces her (59). Her attitude is definable, in short, in terms of the
following specifically *masochistic* split: I know full well that war is cruel, both
to me and to my family, but all the same, the nation itself demands my
acquiescence.[14]

This split is easily recast into terms applicable to Denise Baudu. Denise
knows that she and hers have suffered at the hands of the new commercial
order epitomized by the Bonheur. A sense of mourning for the loss of the
small family businesses (such as her uncle's Le Vieil Elbeuf) that once
thrived in the Saint-Roche quarter clearly permeates Zola's novel, culminating in the two funeral processions—for Denise's cousin, Geneviève, and
her aunt, Mme. Baudu—that frame its penultimate chapter. Yet, from beginning to end, Denise persists in defending the new order on the grounds
that it is dictated by a certain "logic" of history and of "life":

> In secret, she was on the side of the department stores, out of her instinctual
> love of logic and of life. (252/*190*)

> Denise calmly set out her argument: . . . the logical evolution of trade, the
> requirements of modern times, the size of these new establishments, and
> finally the public's greater well-being. (271/*207*)

> Was it true, then, that the world must necessarily grow fat on death, in a
> struggle for life that raised creatures in the charnel-house of endless
> destruction? . . . She knew that this was good and that this dunghill of
> miseries was essential to the health of the Paris of tomorrow. (461–462/
> *367–368*)

The evident Darwinism of passages such as these in turn justifies an explicitly Terrorist logic: "Yes, it was the debt of blood: every revolution needed martyrs and one could only go forward over the bodies of the dead" (462/*368*). Submission to the force of commercial and social progress thus implies a form of what Dorinda Outram has called "Revolutionary Stoicism," an ethos of stoic dignity whose function in post-Revolutionary France was to affirm the sovereignty of the virtuous individual while validating "middle-class control of the public sphere" (81, 88). In Denise's case, this stoic ethos appears in a quintessentially reactive (read "female") form:

> Whereas the male heroes emphasize their non-reactivity, their remorseless control over body and emotion, women . . . react with warm and generous outrage, and through maternal or married love or family affection of other kinds, perform acts of courage and sacrifice. (Outram, 84)

Should we thus be content to diagnose Denise's attitude as post–Revolutionary stoicism of a patently "female" and pro-capitalist type? Should we perhaps, following Judith Butler's argument in *The Psychic Life of Power*, read Denise as a test case for the subject's passionate submission to subjection, that more or less universal process whereby the law "becomes an object of passionate attachment, a strange scene of love" (128)? What is in fact lost by *not* speaking of masochism in Denise's connection?

A great deal, I would argue. Denise's submission to "the necessities of modern times" plainly resonates with Freud's work on "moral masochism," and specifically with that page where Freud reads "Reason and Necessity" as tropes on the parental couple, source of the sadistic superego ("Economic Problem," 168). Moreover, Zola carefully aligns Denise's moral masochism with masochism in its more classic, "erotogenic" form ("Economic Problem," 168).[15] Throughout the novel, the logic of commercial progress is thematized as a rapacious, even ravishing, force against which the umbrella maker Bourras (for instance) must defend his boutique "like a respectable girl defending her virtue" (260/*197–98*). Denise herself will become a woman precisely because she allows herself to be "borne away" by that force, to be raped (as it were) by the logic of history:

> It was here that she finally understood the power of the new forms of retailing and felt an enthusiasm for this force that was transforming Paris. Her ideas were maturing and a feminine grace had begun to emerge from the wild child who stepped off the train from Valognes. (295/*228*, 258/*196*)

Nowhere, however, is the specifically masochistic basis of Denise's reactive stoicism spelled out more clearly than in the crucial final paragraph of chapter 13:

> That night, Denise was once more unable to sleep. . . . She would have to watch right to the end the invincible working of life which requires death to engender its renewal. She no longer fought against it, but accepted this law of struggle, though her woman's soul filled with anguished compassion and sympathetic tenderness at the idea of suffering humanity. For years, she had been caught up herself in the cogs of the machine. Hadn't she bled? Hadn't she been beaten, driven out and insulted? . . . And the force that drove all before it took her in its turn, even though her arrival was meant to be a revenge. Mouret had invented this machine for crushing people . . . and she loved him despite it all for the greatness of what he was doing, she loved him more and more at each excess of his power, despite the flood of tears that swept over her when she witnessed the sacred suffering of the vanquished. (477/380)

If I may chart the novel's trajectory in a convenient (albeit schematic) fashion, the *Bonheur* begins with Denise's fascination at the sight of the headless mannequins in the window of Mouret's store and culminates in her full assumption of suffering here at the end of chapter 13 (more on chapter 14 in a moment). Or, to recast this trajectory in terms of that three-stage model proposed by Freud (in "A Child Is Being Beaten") to account for the development of the young girl's beating fantasies, the novel charts a regression from the consciously remembered, ostensibly sadistic fantasy of Freud's stage three—"My father is beating the child, he loves only me" [Mouret is beating the headless ladies,[16] he loves only me]—to the generally unconscious, masochistic scenario of stage two—"My father [Mouret] is beating me" (189–90). Zola's plot, in other words, teases out the masochistic fantasy underpinning an initial spectatorial conceit—Denise's fascination with the headless mannequins—that is sadistic in "form" only ("Child," 191). It thus confronts its reader with a vicissitude of the woman's "positive" Oedipus complex—namely, the fact that "the wish . . . to be beaten by the father stands very close to the other wish, to have a passive (feminine) sexual relation to him and is only a regressive distortion of it" ("Economic Problem," 169).

To readers sensitive to the question of psychological coherence, the final paragraph of chapter 13 cannot help but be puzzling. Several chapters previously, Denise had nearly given herself to Mouret upon his tearfully admitting to having suffered "like a child" in desire for her; she finds the courage to resist only when Mouret turns "brutal" (373/*294*). The novel appears to have a hard time deciding whether Denise loves Mouret for his weakness and corrigibility, or rather for his "pitiless" despotism (341/*267*).

I would explain this fundamental indecision in terms of the following paradox. I have argued that, as Zola's novel develops, Denise comes to stand for a "kinder, gentler" liberal democracy. Her gentle authority and reformist ambitions aspire to reconcile two essentially divergent senses of the term "liberalism": a respect for free market process and a generous concern for individual self-realization (see Williams, 176–79). But in order to encourage others "to take on the same burden of caring" (this is Laura Marks, speaking of the military wife), Denise must first, like the military wife, have sacrificed herself in masochistic fashion (59). In order to be the object of a generalized "masochistic identification," in other words, Denise must be reborn as a fetish, and this presupposes that (like Christ and his Hugoesque avatar) she has already fully assumed her own masochism: "Only she must suffer" (491/*391*).[17] Or, to borrow Mannoni's terms, Denise can occupy that "space of credulity" through which belief in a liberal overcoming of political despotism can be maintained only if she has submitted to the purported despotism of Octave Mouret. Her infantilizing in the novel's final pages is but a symptom of the way in which the novel has turned her into a repository of (essentially naïve) belief: "So, with the impetuosity of a child, she threw her arms around his neck, sobbing herself and stammering: 'But Monsieur Mouret, you [*vous*] are the one I love!'" (528/*421*).

As I read it, the *Bonheur*'s final infantilizing of Denise is not simply a gesture of male protest working in the interest of a tidy narrative resolution. For it suggests a more ambivalent gesture of active self-sacrifice, remarkably close to that analyzed by Sandor Ferenczi in his *Clinical Diary*, summarized here by Ruth Leys:

> The selfless or "kindness" reaction thus represented the capacity of the
> traumatized individual to masochistically submit to the violence of the other
> by mimetically incorporating the unpleasure situation, even as that act of
> imitation was at the cost of personal unity and autonomy. In the privacy of
> his Clinical Diary (though not in the published version of the "Confusion
> of Tongues"), Ferenczi gave the principle of mimetic identification an
> explicitly ethico-political-sexual meaning: the inspired and intelligent ability
> of the trauma victim to pacify the enemy by imitating or identifying with
> him represented a general, maternal principle of "appeasement" or "peace."
> The "wise" child, to whose coping mechanisms the traumatized adult

reverted, thus came to stand for a hypersensitive ability to selflessly yield to the selfish other as a means of saving the organism and the world. (174)

What this analysis suggests is that Denise's masochism not only functions as a specifically "feminine" means of parrying the traumatic violence suggested by a vision of headless mannequins and the aura of a dead wife. It should also be seen as having political and ethical repercussions that, while privileging feminine experience, ultimately transcend the "feminine" sphere.

Faith in the Republic

As a means of illustrating the "ethico-political-sexual meaning" of such an exemplary masochism, I would propose a brief reading of a film that offers some instructive points of convergence and divergence with Zola's *Bonheur,* Frank Capra's 1939 *Mr. Smith Goes to Washington.* Capra's film tells the story of Jefferson Smith (James Stewart), an idealistic young leader of boys who is appointed to the Senate by a local political machine. After coming to see the American democratic process as riddled with greed and corruption—and in the process winning the heart of Saunders, his hard-boiled secretary (Jean Arthur)—Smith mounts an epic filibuster that ends by bringing down the very machine that had appointed him, and with it Smith's supposed mentor, Senator Joseph Paine (Claude Rains). In Mannoni's terms, Capra's film charts the trajectory from infantile belief in the ideals and trappings of American democracy (Smith recites Lincoln and Washington by heart, loses his head on first spotting the Capitol dome, etc.) to disillusionment (seeing government of, by, and for the people as all a bunch of "hooey"), and finally to mystical, institutional faith (more on this in a moment). In an important sense, therefore, *Mr. Smith Goes to Washington* emblematizes that "fetishistic split" which Žižek has seen as "the very source of the strength of democracy": "*I know very well* (that the democratic form is just a form spoiled by stains of 'pathological' imbalance [the fact of corruption, manipulation, demagoguery]), *but just the same* (I act as if democracy were possible)" (*Looking Awry,* 168).

To this reading, the crucial moment in Capra's film is the filibuster Smith undertakes under the guidance, quite literally, of an increasingly smitten Saunders. For twenty-four hours Smith talks on, "bleary-eyed, voice gone," while official Washington hovers about "to be in on the kill." Diplomats from across the globe flock to the Senate chambers to witness what one radio commentator calls "democracy in action."

One is of course tempted to ask how a weary monologue, composed largely of readings from the Declaration of Independence, the Constitution, and Paul's letters to the Corinthians, might be said to constitute the very essence of democracy. The answer lies with Smith's audience, and particularly with the figure of the vice president (played by Harry Carey). The masochistic act that is Smith's filibuster serves to rekindle its audience's belief—the film in fact says "faith"—in a democratic order based on what Saunders had called "plain, direct, everyday common rightness." Page boys once again don their Boy Ranger buttons; senators listen, uncharacteristically, with rapt attention. Indeed, a rebirth of belief is precisely what drives a repentant Senator Paine to attempt suicide. The film then ends on a shot of the vice president smiling broadly and paternalistically at the weary but victorious Smith.

More than any of the film's other characters, the vice president functions as an embedded spectator—quick to recognize that Smith is "making a whole lot of sense" and quicker still to encourage his act of self-sacrifice. His closing smile thus stands in, ideologically, for our belief. We, the film's real spectators, know full well that democracy is an open invitation to demagoguery and corruption. It is precisely because we know this, however, that we can be invited to revisit our earlier (boyish?!) beliefs, now "sufficiently symbolized as to open onto faith" (Mannoni, 17). According to *Mr. Smith Goes to Washington*, it is an act of masochistic self-sacrifice that makes such a (re)birth into symbolic, institutionalized faith possible.

Of the many ways in which the linkage of democracy and masochism in *Mr. Smith* differs from that of the *Bonheur*, I would examine just two. I have argued that Denise's full assumption of her "own" masochism at the end of chapter 13 leads, in the following chapter, to a disappearance of her self through the constitution of that self as a fetish. In that space of power formerly reserved for the kingly body, Zola's novel places a womanly fetish figure who not only echoes the Republican Marianne but also, behind Marianne, the Virgin herself.

But in the radically homosocial world of *Mr. Smith*, where the rearing of "good boys" is made to stand for the very salvation of the American spirit, there can be no question of the male masochist himself becoming a fetish. Once again, the role of Republican fetish figure devolves upon an abstract femininity. In that moment at which Jefferson Smith is shown finally to have enthralled his fellow senators, he exhorts them to climb up onto the Capitol dome with "that lady that stands for liberty" and to "look at this country through her eyes." Smith can suffer for liberty, and in the process rekindle democratic faith. His status as a political neophyte, moreover, can assure that the locus of power here remains strictly open. Like Ronald Reagan in a more recent time, Smith functions as an "emblematic repository" of that typically American faith in what Joan Copjec has called "a precious, universal, 'innocent,' instance in which we can all [as Americans] recognize ourselves" (146). And yet Smith's particular moral gaze (which we as spectators are clearly asked to espouse) can in no way be reduced to the purely vacant gaze of the abstract—read "female"—Republican icon.

My second point concerns the localization of ideological value in time. When Žižek reformulates Mannoni's "Je sais bien, mais quand même . . ." to account for the puzzle that is democratic belief, he sharpens fetishistic logic to the point of pure, atemporal paradox.

> "Pure" democracy is not impossible because of some empirical inertia that prevents its full realization but which may be gradually abolished by democracy's further development; rather, democracy is possible only on the *basis* of its own impossibility; its limit, the irreducible "pathological" remainder [nationalism, for example], is its positive condition. (*Looking Awry*, 166)

With its unabashed chauvinism, *Mr. Smith* clearly exemplifies Žižek's point on the ineluctability for democracy of the "National Thing," conceived as "the way subjects of a given nation organize their collective enjoyment through national myths" (165). It also suggests, I have argued, that the institutional power of democracy depends upon a moment of radical disillusionment without which infantile, imaginary belief cannot be transformed into mature, symbolic faith.

But in no way does Capra's film believe that democracy is thus fundamentally unrealizable. By constantly juxtaposing Smith's image with those of Washington and Lincoln, the film's image track suggests that the full realization of democracy has already occurred—namely, in the early years of the American republic. The function of a "nobody" such as Jefferson Smith, whose very name signifies common greatness, is precisely to recapture this lost democratic spirit.

By contrast, and a bit more cannily, Zola's *Bonheur* looks to the future as the sole moment at which the promise of democracy (specifically, of liberal democracy) might be fully realized.[18] The futurity inherent in the figure of the increasingly maternal Denise may not rise to that level claimed by Lefebvre when he speaks of the symbolic woman of the Commune—that "beautiful and strong woman, in full bloom, with her opulent and often bared breast"—as a "confused and transposed image of historicity itself, of the birthing of man by woman, . . . as well as of the imminent birth of a new society, a new style of life" (130). Yet the novel does speak of Denise's push to better the working conditions of the Bonheur's employees, "with arguments that appealed to the very interests of the owners," as refining the capitalist mechanism in a way that could serve as "the seed for the vast trade unions of the twentieth century" (438/*348–49*).

Zola's writings on the subject of politics, as I noted in chapter 2, tend obsessively to rehearse a fundamental distinction between the real and the ideal, casting scorn on the follies and corruptions of real-life ministers and revolutionaries while keeping faith with a republican ideal based on "the profound virtues of the people" (Guedj, 124; Delas, 31; cf. Weinberg, 64; Girard, 526). Zola's contempt for what he called "the abominable scheming of the parties" in the early years of the Third Republic was matched only, in other words, by his belief in "the growing rumble of the coming democracy" ("Démocratie," 651). Colette Becker puts this point nicely when she writes:

> In [Zola] there were in effect two men: the sincere republican who yearned, not for revolution, but for an evolution of society toward justice and liberty, and the despiser of systems, of ideologies, and above all of politicians of all stripes. (265)

In the politicians of the Third Republic, as again in the clerks of Mouret's store, Zola found an overwhelming personal ambition, the effect of which was to mire the republic and the Bonheur in scenarios of pure repetition:

> In France today, the guide to being a perfect man of the State has but one rule of conduct: "Wear your colleagues out." . . . Since [Misters Ferry, Floquet, and Challemel-Lacour] are destined to chew one another up, they might as well begin there, swallowing one another in a couple of mouthfuls, so that the field is left empty [*pour que la place soit nette*]. With just a few chews, we would have our Republic. ("Parti," 449–51)

> Meanwhile Favier, whom Hutin treated with new condescension, was furtively observing him, cold and thin, with a bilious face, as though counting the mouthfuls in this stocky little fellow and waiting for his workmate to eat up Bouthemont before eating him up in his turn. (*Bonheur*, 357/*280*)

Denise Baudu becomes oddly exemplary for Zola because her fundamental lack allows her to avoid this repetitive trap, to stand for a pure sociopolitical futurity unsullied by the repetitive effect of personal ambitions.[19]

Reading Zola back through Žižek, it would appear that Zola's scorn for the self-interested mores of all players on the political stage of the young Third Republic (deputies, voters, and revolutionaries alike) was in fact a precondition of his abstract Republican faith. Above all, however, what allowed Zola to adhere to phenomena of whose real-life vices he was acutely aware (such as republicanism in general and universal suffrage in particular) was his profound faith in history's progressive "logic." As Daniel Delas has shown, Zola's journalistic diatribes against what he called in 1880 the "dirty scheming of a bunch of sly dogs who use universal suffrage to parcel out the country" in no way precluded him from speaking of universal suffrage as "the only absolutely logical tool of government" ("Suffrage," 633–634). It was the very same logic, in other words, that the *Bonheur* shows to have figuratively ravished Denise Baudu that would allow Zola to write that phrase I evoked in chapter 2: "I am theoretically for the Republic" (quoted in Delas, 34). Thus, Zola positioned himself politically by means of such self-consciously positivistic (and indeed androcentric) terms as "logic," "theory," and "science." It has been my hypothesis that this act of self-positioning was made possible only by a masochistic identification with embattled femininity, which it had in effect to disavow. The lesson of *Mr. Smith Goes to Washington*, which I would extend here to *Au Bonheur des dames*, is that even the most resolutely homosocial of discourses tends to depend upon a masochistic moment, a masochistic "kernel of enjoyment" (Lacan), which that discourse has ever so necessarily come to disavow.

7   *The Filmic Commune*

In the course of the preceding chapters, I have twice had occasion to reference a felicitous turn of phrase from Dominick LaCapra's analysis of post-traumatic acting out. In scenes marked by the compulsive return of a traumatic past, LaCapra writes, "the future is blocked or fatalistically caught up in a melancholic feedback loop" (*Writing,* 21). That sense of revolutionary futurity which one finds so strongly in Henri Lefebvre's reading of the Paris Commune, with its insistence on the self-constitution of the "people" in the festive experience of spontaneous and creative life, finds its limit, thus, in the persistence of a certain melancholic fixity.

In their own ways, however, each of the literary texts I have analyzed thus far engages in a complex negotiation with this melancholic foreclosure of futurity—a foreclosure traceable, I have argued, to the specific traumas of the Terrible Year. In *La Débâcle,* a melancholic confusion occasioned by the demise of the Napoleonic myth of national destiny triggers a no less mythic vision of collective rebirth, ambivalently voiced by Zola's melancholic protagonist, Maurice Levasseur. Victor Hugo's Commune–era writings explore a melancholy that the poet had long seen as inherent in the obscure spiraling of human history. But they point (again ambivalently) to a futurity made possible by the persistence of human sentiment, even in those quarters—in Cimourdain, as in Lantenac—where sentiment is apparently lacking. The reemergence of a "desire that makes one live" in Flaubert's *Tentation,* and the subsequent textualization of confused desire in his *Bouvard et Pécuchet,* serve as complex responses to Flaubert's mourning for the condition of the artist under the Second Empire. In Zola's *Au Bonheur des dames,* the specific confusions unleashed in and by the modern department store promote an essential futurity, progressively incarnated in the person of Denise Baudu, that effectively forestalls a fall back into melancholy.

To summarize my argument in these terms is to see a significant shift in confusion's role in the negotiation with post-traumatic melancholy.

Whereas confusion appears as a symptom of collective trauma and melancholic fixation in Zola's *Débâcle*, it is allied with a therapeutic futurity in our remaining texts—in Hugo (where it is linked to sentiment), as in Flaubert and Zola's *Bonheur* (where it is linked to desire).

My aim in this final chapter is to examine the afterlife of this complex articulation of confusion, melancholy, and futurity in what are arguably the two most notable films in a surprisingly thin body of cinematic work on the Paris Commune. In its implicit portrayal of the October Revolution of 1917 as both the return and the realization of Communard ideals, Grigory Kozintsev and Leonid Trauberg's remarkable *New Babylon* of 1929 practices a standard Soviet–era futurity. But it yokes that prolepsis to a historically controversial futurity of aesthetic form, in an attempt to parry (I will argue) an all-pervasive sense of melancholic loss.

When British filmmaker Peter Watkins looks back on the Commune from the vantage of the late twentieth and early twenty-first centuries, however, the grounds for melancholy (and the means of its overcoming) have shifted appreciably. The manifesto writings that Watkins produced in conjunction with his *La Commune (Paris, 1871)* may be melancholically fixated on the co-optation of that aesthetic promise implicit in *New Babylon* by the forces of global capitalism. Yet Watkins's film points to an overcoming of that melancholy through a process of democratic self-realization it finds inherent both in the Commune as historical event and in the very process of that event's filmic elaboration. With Watkins, the democratism that triggered Flaubert's grumpy melancholy and underwrote the commercial utopianism of Zola's *Bonheur* finds an exemplary realization in a conception of filmmaking as participatory process.

Aesthetic Futurity

Directed by Grigory Kozintsev and Leonid Trauberg, with a brilliant score by the young Shostakovich, the silent film *New Babylon* is a work of astonishing formal dynamism, a "once-in-a-lifetime synthesis of Eisenstein and Sennett, Lenin and Zola, Jacques Offenbach and Jelly Roll Morton [that] epitomizes the astonishing ferment of the Russian roaring '20's" (Hoberman). Widely regarded as both the culmination and the swan song of the avant-gardist Factory of the Eccentric Actor, or FEKS, the film premiered on March 18, 1929, at the height of Stalin's proletarianization campaign. After generating substantial critical debate, the film was banned, together with the FEKS, and the work of the collective "effectively erased from official Soviet history" (MacDonald, II).[1]

Set against the backdrop of the unfolding Commune, *New Babylon* tells the story of the benighted love between a Communard shopgirl, variously known as Louise or the Midinette[2] (Yelena Kouzmina), and a starving soldier of the Versaillais army by the name of Jean (Piotr Sobolevskii). To a remarkable degree, the film's plot hybridizes the two Zola novels I have analyzed in this study.[3] Far more so than Zola's *Bonheur*, where the references to revolutionary violence are consistently oblique, the film is a thoroughgoing meditation on the commonalties of capitalist commerce and revolutionary violence, in a context indelibly marked by personal loss.

Consider the resonances of that scene where we first meet Louise. Standing behind a counter of the Babylone Nouvelle department store, she hawks a piece of fabric to a crowd of frenzied shoppers, with the intertitular cry, "Going cheap!" Months later, having watched her lover unknowingly bayonet her father to death on a barricade of the *semaine sanglante*, Louise will knock Jean off the barricade, grab a piece of the same fabric, and (ironically) repeat her cry, "Going cheap!," as a painted mannequin from the Babylone Nouvelle burns at her side.

These Zolaesque resonances by no means exhaust the intertextual richness of Kozintsev and Trauberg's film. *New Babylon* consciously echoes late nineteenth-century French art (Degas's washerwomen, Renoir's portraits, Daumier's caricatures, Manet's vision of the Folies Bergères), though it does so in a way that breaks through the relative stasis of panoptic vision we saw in our reading of Zola's *La Débâcle* (Kozintsev, 9–10; Schmulevitch, 47). In Marx's "Civil War in France," moreover, Kozintsev and Trauberg found a specific style—the "anger and sarcasm of a revolutionary pamphlet"— remarkably close to that which they sought to realize in their film (8).

Yet *New Babylon*'s debt to Marx's "Civil War" is arguably more thematic than stylistic. The filmmakers' portrayal of bourgeois Paris as decadent spectacle consistently reads as a filmic gloss on the following lines from Marx:

> The Paris of M. Thiers was not the real Paris of the "vile multitude," but a phantom Paris, the Paris of the *franc-fileurs*, the Paris of the Boulevards, male and female—the rich, the capitalist, the gilded, the idle Paris, now thronging with its lackeys, its black-legs, its literary *bohême*, and its *cocottes* at Versailles, Saint-Denis, Rueil, and Saint-Germain; considering the civil war but an agreeable diversion, eyeing the battle going on through telescopes, counting the rounds of cannon, and swearing by their own honour, and that of their

prostitutes, that the performance was far better got up than it used to be at the Porte St. Martin. The men who fell were really dead; the cries of the wounded were cries in good earnest; and, besides, the whole thing was so intensely historical. ("Civil War," 83–84)

In accordance with these lines, *New Babylon* explicitly frames the events of the Commune with scenes depicting Versaillais repression as an elaborate piece of bourgeois theater. On March 18, while the Babylone Nouvelle's boss and a government deputy watch the rehearsal of a new operetta, the French army's regulars "try out their show" (as an intertitle puts it) in attempting to seize the cannons of the National Guard. When the soldiers refuse to "mow down the dogs"—that is, the women of Montmartre who had brought milk to the starving regulars so as to save Paris's guns—the boss pronounces the operetta with which these scenes are intercut "a flop." To this, the deputy responds, "Let *us* go to Versailles—there we'll try it out again."

The theme of repression as spectacle reappears in the final shot of the *semaine sanglante*. After picking himself up from his fall off the barricade, Jean turns in the direction of the camera. A shot/reverse shot sequence shows him gazing in puzzlement at a group of bourgeois, dressed in finery and madly applauding the barricades' fall from "the heights of Versailles." [4] With its bloody repression of the Paris Commune, the film suggests, the French bourgeoisie finally stages a successful production. [5]

In his portrait of the days leading up to the Bloody Week, Lissagaray speaks of the Commune as having entered "the period of immense lassitude," of a sense of "prostration" at both the Commune and the Ministry of War, and of General Dombrowski as suffering from a "bitter despair" (308/305, 312/309, 315/313). *La Débâcle* follows Lissagaray's lead in speaking of the Commune's leaders at this moment of general paralysis as "reduced to desperate measures" (876/475).

Ever faithful to the spirit of Lissagaray, on whom they appear to have modeled their Communard journalist, Kozintsev and Trauberg evoke this melancholy in a scene where the Commune's leaders learn that Paris has been surrounded and cut off by Thiers's forces. The incipient traumas to which this sequence clearly points are then realized in the scenes on the barricades, where we witness the mourning and despair of hitherto insouciant Communard fighters as their loved ones fall. In what is arguably the most poignant scene of the film, a member of the Commune (likely meant to suggest Jean-Baptiste Clément) sits down at a piano forming part of a besieged barricade to play Clément's 1866 ballad "Le Temps des cerises" (The Time of Cherries), over which Shostakovich gives us Tchaikovsky's haunting "Old French Song." [6] With the historical repression of the Paris Commune, Clément's ballad of lost loves took on a new and richer resonance as a ballad of lost dreams, thanks in large part to the evocation of trauma in the song's final stanza:

J'aimerai toujours le temps des cerises,
C'est de ce temps-là que je garde au coeur
Une plaie ouverte!
Et dame Fortune, en m'étant offerte
Ne saurait jamais calmer ma douleur . . .
J'aimerai toujours le temps des cerises
Et le souvenir que je garde au coeur!

I will always love the time of cherries,
Those times from which I hold in my heart
An open wound!
And the offerings of Lady Luck
Would never soothe my pain . . .
I will always love the time of cherries
And the memory I hold in my heart.

I alluded above to the extraordinarily mixed reception accorded *New Babylon* on its 1929 release. Although warmly praised in several quarters (both in the USSR and abroad) as an attempt to give the Commune an appropriately revolutionary filmic form, *New Babylon* struck many Soviet critics as scoffing at a heroic moment in European revolutionary history.[7] Looking back through a mass of old clippings in the mid-1960s, Kozintsev would recall a series of "passionate discussions, confused jabbering, public outcries—a tumult degenerating into scandal, brawl, and pitched battle," reminiscent not of an artistic debate but of a furious stadium brawl (5).

Given the acrimony of a debate that saw local newspapers create special rubrics for expressions of opinion "for and against *New Babylon*," Kozintsev and Trauberg's film can appear to twenty-first-century eyes as a surprisingly orthodox piece of Soviet filmmaking (quoted in Kozintsev, 6). The conflict between a virtuous, all-suffering working class and its decadent bourgeois oppressors is sharply drawn, and any historical details that might blur this melodramatic picture are simply omitted. The film's bourgeois figures are consistently parodic, given over to a hysterical frenzy of decadent behavior, whereas their working-class counterparts enjoy more sustained individuation in a series of far more developed scenes of popular life. Indeed, one would be hard pressed to find in *New Babylon* any trace of the specific historical complexities upon which so astute and radically pro–Communard an author as Lissagaray insists: for example, the multiple grounds for the Commune's failure, the various conflicts within and between the Commune's governing bodies, or the role of the petite bourgeoisie in the unfolding of the events.

Why, then, did the film run afoul of the Stalinist apparatchiks? Kozintsev and Trauberg's decision to make up their womanizing deputy to look like Lenin could not have helped. Nor did the film's aestheticism, and its relative failure to embed its characters' fate in a transparently meaningful sequence of historical events help endear the film to the crucial working-class audience (Kozintsev, 14). But the film's most egregious sin against an emerging Stalinist orthodoxy was doubtless what Marek Pytel has called its "humanist, pacifist sense," its implicit conviction that "innocence and vulnerability get hammered every time" (quoted in MacDonald, 11).

All extant prints of *New Babylon* build to a prophetic announcement of the Commune's return ("We shall come back, we, the Communards!") before closing on a shot of a rain-soaked wall, suggestive of the *mur des fédérés,* on which is scrawled "Vive la Commune."[8] Just prior to these concluding frames, however, we see Jean stumbling about, distraught, holding the shovel with which he has been ordered to dig the grave of the condemned Louise. The irony of Jean's task incites Louise to hysterical laughter, which she masters sufficiently to predict, "We shall meet again, Jean." In the doubleness of this ending, with its uneasy marriage of individual loss and collective rebirth, I find an ineluctable ambivalence—doubtless shaped by Stalin's proletarianization campaign and the Communist Party's increasing control over the Soviet film industry, but crucially mediated *by the film's form.*

In the three days prior to *New Babylon*'s 1929 release, Kozintsev and Trauberg cut 700 meters from what was originally a 2,900-meter film. Shostakovich hastily rearranged his score to account for these cuts, but that rearrangement is either lost or buried in a Russian archive (Pytel, 60). Any print of the film that attempts to synchronize the extant Shostakovich score to a film that runs nearly twenty minutes shorter thus involves a certain degree of speculation.

Fortunately, we have the testimony of both Shostakovich and Kozintsev on the precise effects they sought in the juxtaposing of film and score. In a December 1929 essay on his music for *New Babylon*, Shostakovich speaks of having "constructed a great deal on the principle of contrasts," as when he set a despairing Jean's barricade encounter with his lover Louise to "a giddy and 'obscene' waltz reflecting the Versaillais army victory over the Communards," or when he deployed the Marseillaise, firmly associated with Versailles, "in the most unexpected contexts (cancan, waltz, galop, etc.)" (quoted in Pytel, 26). Recalling the two filmmakers' initial conversations with the young composer, Kozintsev writes:

> We had the same ideas: not to illustrate the film's scenes, but to give them a new quality, a new dimension; to have the music cut against the grain of the action, so as to reveal its profound internal meaning . . . ; to make "La Marseillaise" blend into "La Belle Hélène"; to contrast the film's great tragic themes with the licentiousness of its galops and cancans. (14)

Let me cite two of the more uncontroversial instances of this principle of ironic contrast between the film's images and its musical score:

- At the end of the clearly traumatic barricade sequence, when Jean turns to face the group of applauding bourgeois, the actual shot of this audience is anticipated by the return of the "languid and worldly Versaillais waltz" from Offenbach's *La Belle Hélène* (Kozintsev, 14).
- Over the highly ambivalent final scenes discussed above, Shostakovich places a musical sequence—"a mutation of Offenbach's can-can, segueing into [a] burlesque circus march" that echoes the Marseillaise—which speaks *neither* to the experience of tragic loss *nor* to that of revolutionary rebirth (MacDonald, III).

Where Henri Lefebvre would come to see spontaneous popular festivity as the harbinger of a total revolutionary project, the makers of *New Babylon* locate festivity squarely on the side of a decadent bourgeoisie, except where the rhythms of that festivity bleed over into the tragic drama of a defeated working class, for plainly ironic effect.

On a visual level, *New Babylon* goes to great pains to keeps its bourgeois and proletarian worlds functionally separate, often through recourse to clumsy shot/reverse shot structures. Beginning with the onset of the Commune, as Myriam Tsikounas notes, we never see Jean and Louise together in the same frame (6). Indeed, when Louise momentarily puts her hand on Jean's shoulder during the fraternization scene from March 18, the matching of shot to reverse shot is so strikingly bad that viewers can be excused for wondering whether the hand is truly Louise's.

This separation breaks down, however, when the music of one world repeatedly bleeds into the other. The accelerating rhythm of the film's montage furthers this breakdown by effecting surprising parallelisms, as when the swaying of a joyful washerwoman at her work under the Commune mimics the swaying of an actress singing the Marseillaise, accompanied by the boss and the deputy (Schmulevitch, 46). The melodramatic contrasts so central to the film's diegesis, in other words, are regularly undercut through strategic, specifically formal cross contaminations. With this tacit undermining of its own melodramatic clarity, *New Babylon* formally suggests an ambivalent play of proximity and distance, doubling and difference. Witness, once again, that scene where Jean gazes back at the applauding bourgeoisie. After citing Georges Soria's account of how "lovers of strong emotions" would gather on the hills of Saint-Cloud, binoculars in hand, to watch the destruction wreaked by Versaillais shells, Barthélémy Amengual precisely captures the historical ambivalence of this scene:

> Strictly speaking, thus, there was no siege, no rupture or radical isolation between Paris and Versailles. Their "confusion," their false "dialogue," their proximity at a distance (the irrational shot/reverse shot of *New Babylon*) were realities. (62–63)

Of all the forms of confusion operative in Kozintsev and Trauberg's film, none is arguably more important that that which follows from the filmmakers' quest for a specifically dynamic, musical, and postnaturalist pictorialism. In a section from his memoirs devoted to *New Babylon*, Kozintsev speaks at length of the filmmakers' struggles to avoid the genteel decorum and visual stasis of "the detestable historical film" (9). After a series of futile attempts to "compel the filmstock to 'feel,'" he reports, the filmmakers hit upon a combination of techniques—including a dynamic juxtaposing of close-ups and long shots, the use of smoke in varying opacities, and the fitting of portrait lenses to create a self-consciously limited depth of field —whose combined effect was such that "human stories surge forth momentarily from the mass of a troubled and confused universe" (10). Here is Kozintsev responding to camerman Andre Moskvin's experiments to this effect, presumably for an early scene at the Bal Mabille:

> I saw in reality what I had only glimpsed in my boldest dreams. Painted in thick black and dazzling white, like birds of ill omen, stood men in evening dress, behind whom unfurled an orgy of painterly splashes, a magma of skirts, top hats, and ladies' headwear. A fantastic world, ghostly and feverish, stood

before me; it was living; it had become a reality. The non-existent world existed.

It was real life. But there was nothing naturalistic about it, nothing resembling a photographic copy. . . .

No, I saw something else. "Paris—delirium of the turbulent sea. The low notes of agitated waves . . ." (Mayakovsky). The black splashes were the bass notes, a confused crowd of endlessly changing contours—the waves. And the whole effect was one of maleficent delirium, as in that instant before catastrophe strikes. . . .

"The unique musical pressure" seemed to become visible.

From that moment on, I would abandon brushes and paint. I was in the process of discovering a type of dynamic painting that would supplant all my prior enthusiasms. (10)

The language with which Kozintsev here describes the extremely rapid cuts of frenetic bourgeois festivity at the Bal Mabille recalls the Impressionist *morcellement* we have seen repeatedly in Zola ("an orgy of painterly splashes, a magma of skirts, top hats, and ladies' headwear"). But Kozintsev rightly takes his distance from the painterly model. Even the comparison to music—Kozintsev earlier speaks of the film as a "visual symphony"—is ultimately inadequate (9). The "dynamic fresco" that is *New Babylon*—with its play of visual tonalities, its frenzy of interpenetrating figures and forms, and its consistent tracing of individual destinies against "the mass of a troubled and confused universe"—could only be cinematic (9–10). If futurity is precisely that which is foreclosed in melancholy, then it is surely the case that—on the far side of represented historical melancholies and contemporary melodramatic truths, including the truth of the Commune's return—*New Babylon* points to a specifically *aesthetic* futurity, whose actualization in the Soviet Union of 1929 and beyond was increasingly in doubt.

Melancholy in the Age of the Monoform

Whether we deem *New Babylon* truly innovative or derivative of earlier work by Griffith, Eisenstein, and others, Kozintsev and Trauberg's film plainly draws upon a variety of filmic techniques associated with the late 1910s and early 1920s as a revolutionary moment in the history of Western cinema—"techniques of rapid editing, montage, parallel action, cutting between scenes of different perspective (long shot, close shot), etc." (Watkins, "Crisis"). However much these techniques might point to an aesthetic futurity palliative to the deep sense of melancholy that pervades the film, this futurity remains ambivalent, if only on account of its debt to the frenzy of a decadent bourgeois festivity. In other words, to insist that the style of *New Babylon* was indeed revolutionary, as the vehemence of the Stalinist campaign against the film arguably confirms, is ultimately to miss Kozintsev and Trauberg's implicit acknowledgment of how determinative the hysteria surrounding the bourgeois "cash nexus" ultimately is to the formal ethos of their film.

I make this argument not to impugn the integrity of Kozintsev and Trauberg's effort (quite the contrary), but to raise the question of how the techniques of early cinema's most fabled pioneers might have contained within themselves their future co-optation by the forces of global capitalism. My touchstone in addressing this issue will be a series of manifesto writings produced by Peter Watkins in conjunction with *La Commune*.

Unlike his more richly nuanced film, Watkins's manifesto writings tend to rise and fall with the fate of a concept he developed some two decades prior—the Monoform. Defined as a "densely packed and rapidly edited barrage of images and sounds, the 'seamless,' yet fragmented modular structure [that] has become the staple of nearly all film and TV today," the Monoform is a mode of narrative that draws on the formal innovations of Kozintsev and Trauberg's generation, as listed above, but overlays these with "dense layers of music, speech and sound effects, abrupt sound cuts for shock effect, endless scenes saturated in music, repetitive and rhythmic dialogue patterns, [and a] constantly moving, tilting, jiggling, circling camera" ("Crisis"). Likening the Monoform to a rhythmic " 'grid' . . . clamped down over the living tissue of the story and the people involved in it—*and over our responses,*" Watkins sees its function as that of blurring "*the distinction between different themes and subjects, and between what might otherwise be entirely different emotional responses to them*" ("Crisis"). Of television news in the age of the Monoform, he writes, "There is no allowance for differentiation of information between a tragic airplane crash and someone who has painted their cucumbers pink" ("Crisis").

It would be easy (indeed, ridiculously so) to dismiss Watkins's reflections on the ideological effects of the Monoform—said to facilitate our collective withdrawal into a kind of "sanitized 'peace'; a privatized, self-centred space which replaces social action, collective energy, [and] critical discourse with consumption"—as the work of a modern-day Chicken Little ("Crisis"). As post-Foucauldians, we can certainly quarrel with Watkins's vision of the modern audiovisual media as a fully repressive system operated by a "small elite" of (unelected, contemptuous, and predominantly male) power brokers ("Crisis"). And there is surely more than a touch of political naïveté to Watkins's repeated calls to make "dramatic change in [the] mass media . . . *a Constitutional and Human Right*" ("Crisis"; cf. "Summary"). But simply to discount Watkins's writings would be to miss the real power in his analysis of the classist effects of a contemporary, media-driven youth culture given over to the blind worship of "violence, cynicism and speed"; in his critique of our modern media's failure to address the complexity and diversity of their various audiences and their concomitant support for the "drive towards globalization"; and in his account of an ambivalence endemic to those who work in mainstream media education—split as they are between an "open admiration of Popular Culture" and a "fascination" with radical discourse ("Crisis"). Indeed, few of us who teach literary and cultural studies in American universities today are immune from Watkins's critique of what he calls "pretend 'critical education' " ("Crisis").

In my introduction to this chapter, I suggested that one can—indeed, perhaps must—read Watkins's manifesto writings symptomatically. The sheer repetitiveness with which Watkins details the "key traumas" inflicted by our modern media, when read in conjunction with statements such as "we face an exceptionally bleak landscape today" or "we are now moving through a very bleak period in human history," clearly suggests a melancholic fixation on a lost world, "where ethics, morality, human collectivity, and commitment (except to opportunism) [were not yet] considered 'old fashioned' " ("Summary"; "Crisis").[9] Yet Watkins's analysis is by no means devoid of an inherent futurity. In the face of what he sees as modern TV's unconscionable abdication of its potentially democratic role, abetted by the co-optation of techniques that signified aesthetic futurity for Kozintsev, Trauberg, and others, Watkins advocates a reconceived futurity based on a "reflective, questioning, complex, participatory process possible within TV and the cinema" ("Crisis"). It is precisely this reconception of the modern audiovisual media as agents of participatory processes that is most clearly at stake in Watkins's *La Commune*, to which I now turn by way of a conclusion to this study.

(Re-)Living the Commune

Filmed over the course of thirteen days in July 1999, with a cast of 220 (most of whom had no prior acting experience), Watkins's film tracks the events of the Commune from March 17, 1871, through the mass executions of the *semaine sanglante*. Although major historical figures such as Thiers and Dombrowski appear from time to time, *La Commune* is principally structured as a chaotic string of reflections on the unfolding events by ordinary citizens, Communards and anti-Communards alike. Over the course of the film's five hours and forty-five minutes, we "see" many of the Commune's key moments, though typically with a significant indirection. In its closing sequence, for example, the film powerfully represents the summary executions of vanquished Communards through a slow pan of the faces of condemned men, women, and children as an officer in voice-over repeats the command to fire.

In an effort to counter the staccato rhythms he finds endemic to the Monoform, Watkins chooses to re-create life in Paris in the spring of 1871 through a series of "long, highly mobile uninterrupted takes" ("Commune"). An easily movable sound recording system and a uniformly lit set allow Watkins to keep his handheld camera constantly on the move—from speaker to speaker, group to group, room to room, or 'interior' to 'exterior'—in takes that can last ten minutes or more. One effect of this mobility is to convey with unparalleled precision the "fog of revolution"—"an impression of great disorder, of intense activity, a liberation of energies and statements which surge forward from all sides" (Les Inrockuptibles, quoted in Watkins, "Commune"). As Watkins acknowledges, this use of handheld cameras and what he elsewhere calls a "'you-are-there' style" are in fact staples of the Monoform; so, too, the film's tight cuts after significant action or dialogue, and its obvious borrowings from "the hit-and-rush tactics of contemporary TV" ("Crisis"; "Commune").

In what sense, then, might we see *La Commune* as giving its audience critical leverage on the Monoform as a standardized narrative mode? For Watkins, the French educational system's refusal to give the Commune more than a cursory glance is symptomatic of a more general "denial of history" traceable to the modern audiovisual media and their cult of ersatz popular culture ("Summary"). *La Commune*'s extensive use of intertitles, both to explain the complexity of historical events and to convey the travails of Parisian working-class life circa 1871, clearly cuts against this grain. Throughout the film, intertitles explore the rationale of Communard actions and decrees, the function of the Commune's administrative structures, the conflicts between various revolutionary powers, and the background and historical fate of individual characters. At the same time, they routinely compare the state of given social inequalities at the time of the Commune—

the concentration of wealth in the hands of the few, for example, or the fate of Algerians under French colonial rule—to the state of similar inequalities today.[10] In short, *La Commune* aims to put history back into play not only by appealing to the complexity of historical understanding, but also by rendering explicit an anachronism inherent in most good historical work, whatever the medium.

This last point takes us to what is clearly the most striking aspect of Watkins's film: its anachronistic insertion of television reporters into a nineteenth-century revolution. Throughout *La Commune*, reporters from Watkins's fictive Télévision Communale conduct live, on-the-scene interviews with participants in the events. Their colleagues at the Versaillais Télévision Nationale, by contrast, prove more adept in the mode of unctuous commentary. But both types clearly derive from what Watkins calls the press's "activist and interventionist role" on all sides of the historical Commune ("Commune").

La Commune's brilliant opening sequence lays this anachronism out precisely. Following a series of intertitles on the prehistory of the Paris Commune, a handheld camera takes us onto a sound stage, past a production crew with modern equipment. Two actors stand before us, in period dress. Gérard Watkins, who plays Communard reporter Gérard Bourlet, characterizes what we are about to see as "both a film on the Paris Commune and a film on the role of the mass media in society, both yesterday's and today's." In a way that arguably vitiates the filmmaker's position on the repressive agency of media elites, actress Aurélia Petit then speaks of her character, reporter Blanche Capellier, as embracing her profession to the point of failing to denounce "the power of the media . . . which she represents completely." From here, we embark on a tour of the film's sets, artfully designed to "hover," as Watkins puts it, "between reality and theatricality" ("Crisis"). In the course of this tour, Petit points to a table at which, during the previous day's filming, an officer of the Versaillais forces "condemned hundreds of Communards [from the 11th arrondissement] to an instantaneous death beneath the bullets of a firing squad." Shots of the now-empty set continue under Petit's line, "We ask you to imagine that we are henceforth on the 17th of March, 1871," and the beginnings of a voice-over by a fictional grandfather describing family life in a Parisian hovel in March 1871. The opening sequence of *La Commune*, in short, is a textbook example of what Watkins calls "bursting beyond the frame"—a back-and-forth movement between fiction and reality, history and contemporaneity, whose effect is to expose the hierarchical and manipulative practices of more conventional narrative modes.

One of the most fruitful avenues of reflection opened up by this, Watkins's filmic updating of Brecht's *Entfremdungseffekt,* turns on the question of how to develop what one character calls "a critical line of thought with respect to the media." At times, this critical thrust results in relatively straightforward, principled refusals. A crucial midfilm discussion between the two Télévision Communale reporters and a likewise "completely fictive" reporter for the *Père Duchêne* asks whether revolutionary journalists bear an obligation to critically analyze the movements they support. In this discussion, the TVC reporters warmly defend an interview style beholden to the Monoform—a pseudo-objective style that presents brief snippets of popular sentiment, constructed to suggest controversy, in a rhythm sufficiently jerky to hold viewers' attention. But with the re-creation several weeks later of a Committee of Public Safety, Gérard Watkins's character renounces a job that positions him as a spokesperson for Communard disinformation, and thus forces him to abdicate the very responsibility for critical reflection he had earlier declined. (Watkins's character reappears, in the role of guerrilla journalist, during the final days of the Commune.)

Significantly, however, some of the most perspicacious analyses of media abuses in *La Commune* come from the suave and obsequious talking heads of the Télévision Nationale. As TVN shows a series of "troubling" images of Versaillais repression, commentator François Foucard (played by François Foucard) bemoans this appeal to the base voyeurism of television viewers, predicting the development of a "flabby press that seeks to peddle its wares by appealing to the basest of instincts." In Peter Watkins's world, even the most unrepentant of Bonapartist bourgeois, turned apologue for Thiers's "serene, determined and generous . . . republic of order," can serve to articulate one of the radical filmmaker's most fundamental premises.

In his manifesto writings, Watkins argues for a "dynamic and experimental" approach to filmmaking—one that can serve as a model for a "truly democratic and participatory process" increasingly alien to our contemporary, media-driven democracies ("Commune"). Prior to the filming of *La Commune,* cast members were asked to do extensive research into the events, working together in groups—the Union des Femmes (Union of Women), soldiers of the National Guard, anti-Communard bourgeois—to "discuss the background of the people they were portraying," while considering "the links between the events of the Commune and society today"

("Commune"). Much of the film's second half is in fact devoted to conversations in which the actors explicitly reflect on the points of overlap and (less often) divergence between the Commune and their worlds. Thus members of the Union des Femmes discuss the plight of working women today through the analogous plight of Commune-era women. (Some ten minutes into this scene, we suddenly discover a row of men sitting in the back of the room, with their own views on the pleasures and tyrannies of work.) A subsequent scene in a cooperative workshop finds a group of male actors discussing not only the nature of cooperatives, but also the contemporary French media's complicity with the nation's moneyed classes, the castelike nature of modern France's political elite, the continuing fall in French voting rates, the globalist imposition of a single economic vision on peoples of the world, and so on.

In the absence of a style of rapid cutting intended to foster a formal simulacrum of narrative interest, these discussions—of which there are many more examples—can (and do) drag on. What gives *La Commune* its haunting power are those scenes where Watkins's practice of "bursting beyond the frame" serves to expose significant disjunctions between an actor and his character or *within us* as the film's viewers. Perhaps the most obvious instance of spectatorial disjunction occurs when a Communarde shouts these words into the camera:

> You know what pisses me off the most: you are busy filming this, and you others are busy watching this, and you don't give a damn. Whether this is a film or reality, you just sit there chattering away—*that's* what I'd like to rub out.

By suggesting here, as a reviewer from *Libération* put it, that "the Versaillais, they are us," this scene implicates *viewers and filmmakers alike* in what Watkins calls a "social schizophrenia" instituted and policed by "the spatial and psychological structure of the Monoform" (quoted in "Commune"; "Summary"). However open we might appear to be to seeing social problems "in terms of an open process inviting challenge, development, exploration [and] political action," our deep (if unarticulated) investment in the fragmentation, repetition, and closed narrative structures of the Monoform condemns us to "a DUAL EXISTENCE . . . not easily diagnosed or even discussed" ("Summary").

More powerful still are those moments in *La Commune* when actors are brought face to face with a disjunction between their actions in and out of character. Toward the film's end, for instance, we witness a sharp debate among some actors playing Communards as to whether they would fight if the Commune happened today. Those few who say they would *not,* cite the largely economic basis of contemporary power, the supposedly inevitable recuperation of revolutionary action, or their own romantic natures. Somewhat later, several women who play bourgeoises in the film express their disgust at the actions of their characters and the cruelty of the Versaillais reprisals. But perhaps the most striking instance of such a disjunction is that scene where an actress, playing the Communarde Margeurite Lachaise, calls for the execution of Captain Charles de Beaufort, despite what we then learn to be the actress's personal opposition to summary execution *and* her character's subsequent change of heart. One effect of this disjunction, I would argue, is to render all the more persuasive the actress's subsequent reflections on the place of sacrificial violence—toward the unemployed, the homeless, and illegal aliens—in a world of economic globalization.

Having spent a good deal of time in the *New Babylon* section of this chapter referring back to Zola, let me conclude this brief analysis of Watkins's *La Commune* with a comparison to Flaubert. In my readings of two of Flaubert's late works, *La Tentation de saint Antoine* and *Bouvard et Pécuchet,* I argued that Flaubert's melancholy in the wake of the Commune should be understood, first and foremost, as the effect of a rising democratism. By contrast, the melancholy of Peter Watkins' programmatic writings owes its origin to the *short-circuiting* of a democratic potential that Watkins sees as inherent in the modern mass media, television especially. However promising the textualization of desire may have appeared for Flaubert, moreover, the final lines of *Bouvard et Pécuchet* (where the clerks sit down at their double desk to resume their *Copie*) clearly suggest a failure to transcend melancholic repetition. Where Lefebvre's *Proclamation* points beyond such repetition by focusing on the lived experience of revolutionary passion (and the forms of confusion attendant thereto), Watkins's *La Commune* does so through a calculated doubling—a doubling of the Commune as historical event and of its filmic representation *as fully democratic processes of negotiation and testimony.* When members of the Union des Femmes, for example, discuss the difficulty of building democracy and leaving a space for others— both in the historical Commune *and* in its filmic elaboration—a gesture that might easily be seen as one of idealist naïveté has the signal virtue of parrying melancholy through a collective engagement in (and enactment of) "an experience filled with hope."

Notes

Introduction
The Commune and the Right to Confusion

1. The immediate context of this citation is a story from the childhood of André Gide illustrating what Lacan calls "the self's radical eccentricity with respect to itself," the fact that "at the most assented heart of my identity to myself, he [the other] pulls the strings" (*Écrits*, 524/*162–63*). It is precisely this radical heteronomy of the self, whereby the subject's actions return to him or her otherwise through the necessary mediation of the other, that guarantees the essential confusion of the human comedy.

2. Theodore Zeldin has argued that the historical claims for a Cartesian spirit supposedly inherent in the French nation are not only untenable in their own right (they are "legendary" in Auerbach's sense); they are doubly so in light of the "very chequered history" of French Cartesianism, which saw Descartes's authority variously evoked by the Jansenists in their struggle against the Jesuits, by the contributors to the *Encyclopédie* in their elaboration of a materialist philosophy, and by Victor Cousin in his campaign against precisely such materialism (*Intellect*, 223–24).

3. In suggesting that these phenomenal and cognitive modes of "confusion" predominate in the work I shall be analyzing here, I am by no means proposing that other senses of the word be ignored. One of the more useful strategies of a study that aims, as this does, to negotiate with the confusion inherent in unprocessed historical events is to explore how and why particular senses of a word such as "confusion" come to the fore in given conjunctures, and how these various senses inform one another in specific aesthetic and ideological contexts.

Two senses of "confusion" prove subordinate in late nineteenth-century French usage, for reasons worth noting. The first of these, which the *Petit Robert* dates back to the early twelfth century, understands "confusion" as the inner agitation that results from an awakening of shame, humiliation, or excessive modesty, often in tandem with a sense of regret. When Marianne avows feeling "giddy, speechless and ashamed [*confuse*]" in her first encounter with Valville, when Valmont tells Tourvel of the "shame [*confusion*]" aroused by his "unthinkable transgression" in having seduced her, they appeal to confusion in this sense (Marivaux, 73; Laclos, 325). Although not entirely absent from nineteenth-century fiction—witness Gilberte

Delaherche's confession of her adultery "with an abashed [*confus*], caressing gesture" in Zola's *La Débâcle* (612/214)—"confusion" as shame or modesty implies a self-reflexivity in the theater of the world largely foreign to Romantic and post–Romantic French culture.

If the first of these ancillary senses is very much in decline in French literature of the 1870s and beyond, the second is slowly emerging within a tradition of thought that would culminate in Kraepelin's theory of dementia praecox and Eugen Bleuler's conception of schizophrenia. The *Petit Robert* defines the phrase *confusion mentale* as "a pathological mental state, occasional or chronic, in which the patient demonstrates perceptual, mnemonic or intellectual disorders" ("Confusion," def. 2). Patients diagnosed as suffering from *confusion mentale* typically showed a loss of specific memories, spatial and temporal disorientation, delayed comprehension, diminished capacity for the association of ideas, and (in some accounts) an inability to integrate one's memories into a coherent personality. In its yoking of dementia to cognitive breakdown, *confusion mentale* thus functioned as a late avatar of the Lockean conception of madness, defined as an intellectual disorder or form of "mistaken reasoning" (Pick, 51). Of all the characters to be treated in the course of this study, Bouvard and Pécuchet are arguably the most mad, though it would be foolish to contest their mnemonic faculties or, perhaps especially, their associative skill.

Although of lesser interest here, *confusion* also figures in a series of established political and juridical phrases: *confusion des pouvoirs* (confusion of powers, "characteristic of a regime where the separation of powers is not in effect"); *confusion des peines* (concurrent sentences, following "the rule that sentences not be subject to cumulation"); *confusion des patrimoines* (confusion of heritages: a "merging of the assets and liabilities of the deceased with the assets and liabilities of his or her heir"); *confusion de part* ("the impossibility of determining paternity in the case of a child born more than six months after the mother's second marriage, but less than nine months after the death of the mother's first husband") ("Confusion," *Grand Dictionnaire*).

4. Some thirty years after its initial publication, Paul Lidsky's *Les Écrivains contre la Commune* remains the principal reference on such anti-Communard rhetoric, though important additions to (and qualifications of) Lidsky's findings can be found in the work of Susanna Barrows, Janet Beizer, Catherine Glazer, Jan Goldstein, Gay Gullickson, and Daniel Pick.

5. I exempt Hugo's work from this list because, as we shall see, its position on the Commune is more fundamentally ambivalent.

6. The phrase "Party of Order" referred initially to a confluence of Legitimist and Orleanist factions in the Legislative Assembly of the Second Republic (Marx, *Commune*, 307). But it persisted well into the era of the Commune in association with the government of Adolphe Thiers, as witness a passage from the London *Times* cited in chapter 1.

7. See, in the bibliography, the works of Janet Beizer, Charles Bernheimer, Catherine Glazer, Jan Goldstein, Jann Matlock, and Gladys Swain.

8. Freud would come to differentiate between the two conditions by arguing that the sense of guilt is "over-strongly conscious" in melancholia (as in obsessional neurosis), but unconscious in hysteria. "In melancholia the impression that the super-ego has obtained a hold on consciousness is even stronger [than in obsessional neurosis]. But here the ego ventures no objection; it admits its guilt and submits to the punishment" (*Ego,* 51).

9. By "desire as such," I mean not the impulse toward specific object(s) (*le désir de* or *un désir de*), but rather the hypostatizing of such impulsiveness as a constant, never fully satisfied aspect of human nature.

Chapter One
Why Confusion? Why the Commune?

1. Henri Lefebvre reports, for example, that the rise in workers' salaries in the final years of the empire was more than fully eclipsed by increases in the cost of living (75).

2. Behind Lefebvre's untranslatable phrase, several of the many slang meanings of *un jules* should be heard to resonate, including "a pimp," "a chamber pot," and (from the Second World War) "a German."

3. The irony of history would have it that March 18 was also the date of the funeral of Victor Hugo's oldest son, Charles (discussed in chapter 3).

4. Engels's pithy conclusion to his 1891 "Introduction to *The Civil War in France*"—"Look at the Paris Commune. That was the Dictatorship of the Proletariat"—when coupled with Lenin's elaboration of that idea in *The State and Revolution,* has led some to read the Commune as a forerunner of the October Revolution (34). But it is important not to minimize the differences. Despite well-known edicts suspending the sale of pawned objects and precluding landlords from evicting tenants, the Commune generally accepted the principle of private ownership. "Rather than an attack on property as such," Stewart Edwards writes of the uprising, "there was an attempt to shift some of the benefits of the industrial expansion of the previous period away from the large-scale financial and industrial capitalists back to the small entrepreneur and individual working man" (361). Perhaps the most stunning testimony that the Communards did not intend to overthrow the capitalist system is the fact that the Parisian stock exchange functioned almost without interruption. Indeed, as Lefebvre documents, share prices remained remarkably stable from late March to mid-May 1871 (301ff.).

5. Excessive deference to democratic principles would not be the only respect in which the leaders of the Commune have appeared, in hindsight, as overly timid. Many have argued that an immediate march on Versailles, before the army had had a chance to regroup, would have resulted in a resounding victory for the Parisian forces (though whether Bismarck would have allowed such a victory to stand is very much open to debate). Others have bemoaned the Commune's failure to seize the Bank of France, outside of whose gates Engels speaks of the Communards as "standing respectfully" in "holy awe" ("Introduction," 30).

6. On the "disordered multiplicity of action groups" in the period leading up to the Commune, see Lefebvre, 50 (also 153, 183).

7. I return to Lefort's conception of democracy, and its recent reinscription in the work of Slavoj Žižek, in my reading of Zola's *Au Bonheur des dames* in chapter 6.

8. The "Manifesto of the Central Committee of the 20 Arrondissements," published in *Le Cri du peuple* on March 27, contains the following two principles: "The principle of election applied to all civil servants or magistrates./The responsibility of representatives, and, consequently, their permanent revocability" (quoted in Lefebvre, 358).

In *La Proclamation de la Commune,* Henri Lefebvre clearly inflects Engels's reading in speaking of the "State that is withering away" as "more democratic than any other form of State" (391).

9. On the grounds for Lefebvre's break with the Situationists, see Trebitsch, "Moment," xxiii; and Ross, "Lefebvre," 78–80.

10. If the Paris Commune did indeed exemplify the "dictatorship of the proletariat," was Lenin's foregrounding of the Communist Party as agent of that dictatorship fundamentally deviant? Did the Commune in fact point toward a "withering away" of the state? How strong is the analogy between the Commune and the October Revolution? Etc., etc.

11. Lefebvre's interview with Kristin Ross gives March 28, 1871, as the date on which the women of Montmartre fraternized with the soldiers who had come to seize their cannon. I assume this is a typographical error.

12. Perhaps the most striking example of the Commune's self-defeating penchant for spectacle is the "monster concert" staged in the Tuileries gardens for the benefit of the Commune's widows and orphans, while Versaillais shells fell on the nearby Place de la Concorde (Lissagaray, 309/*306*).

13. Precisely how voluntary self-sacrifice might serve to constitute new political unities in an era of intense political turmoil is a question I shall return to in my readings of Victor Hugo's conception of the poet as martyr (chapter 3) and of the emblematic sufferings of Zola's Denise Baudu (chapter 6).

14. Speaking of the Situationists, Lefebvre notes in his interview with Kristin Ross: "Their idea . . . was that in the city one could create new situations by, for example, linking up parts of the city, neighborhoods that were separated spatially. And that was the first meaning of the *dérive*. It was done first in Amsterdam, using walkie-talkies" (73). Lefebvre died in 1991, shortly before the advent of the World Wide Web gave new meaning to the ideal of an electronically mediated metamorphosis of everyday life into a scene of endless festivity. Such a deferred realization, however, is entirely consonant with Lefebvre's emphasis on the future possibilities inherent in what may be presently impossible: "The past becomes the present, or becomes it once again, thanks to the realization of possibilities objectively bound up in the past" (*Proclamation,* 36).

15. Keith Reader rightly characterizes the English phrase "everyday life" as "a partially adequate English rendering of two French terms—*le quotidian*—which

stresses the monotony of the individual's daily existence—and *le vécu*, which stresses the existential quality of their response to it" (56).

For a moving (albeit frankly partisan) account of everyday life under the Paris Commune, see chapter 25 of Lissagaray's *Histoire*. Couched in the form of a fictive tour of Paris given to a "friend of the timid men of the timid provinces" just days before the Commune's fall, the segment concludes: "Such, my friend, is the Paris of the brigands. You have seen this Paris thinking, weeping, combating, working, enthusiastic, fraternal, severe toward vice" (294/*295*, 302/*302*).

16. The term "fused mass" is clearly a nod to Sartre's *Critique de la raison dialectique* (1960). On the French Communist Party's postwar attempt to portray Lefebvre as "the only Communist philosopher capable of stemming the influence of Sartre," see Trebitsch, "Preface," xi–xii.

17. Althusser's first major work, *Pour Marx*, appeared in the same year as *La Proclamation*, 1965.

18. "How, in the nineteenth century," Lefebvre asks, "could you excite crowds and spur the masses on with the concept of growth in the forces of production?" (127).

19. On the limits of revolutionary spontaneity, see Lefebvre's discussion of anarchist ideology (161–63).

20. With its insistence on the importance of symbolic action in the context of a spontaneous revolutionary festivity, *La Proclamation* clearly anticipated the events (and ideology) of May 1968. There are, of course, good reasons for this. As Lefebvre recalls, a key moment in the genesis of the *mouvement du 22 mars* took place in his seminar at Nanterre, with a discussion of how to protest the administration's blacklisting of disruptive students (in Ross, "Lefebvre," 82).

On the role of spontaneity in the May events, consider what Lefebvre says of the night of May 13 on the barricades: "And at about three in the morning—in complete bedlam, there was noise from all directions—a radio guy handed the microphone to Daniel Cohn-Bendit, who had the brilliant idea of simply saying, 'General strike, general strike, general strike.' And that was the decisive moment: it was then that there was action" (Ross, "Lefebvre," 82).

Ironically, though in a way entirely consistent with Lefebvre's understanding of historical "possibilities" (see note 14), *La Proclamation de la Commune* speaks of 1871 as involving a "spontaneous explosion that is not currently possible, but which is by no means absolutely precluded in a more distant future" (395).

21. I discuss the paradoxical effectiveness of a similarly naïve rhetoric of anticipation in my discussion of Hélène Cixous's manifesto writings in chapter 8 of my *Logics of Failed Revolt*.

22. This is obviously a more restrictive question than "Why did the Commune fail?" To pose this question as if in anticipation of a singular response is to fall into a "What if . . . ?" game endemic to so many accounts of the events, by participants and historians alike (see Lefebvre, 399 ff.). What if Blanqui had been available to lead the revolution on March 18? What if the Jules and their army had not been allowed to flee Paris on that day? What if the National Guard had immediately

marched on Versailles? What if the Commune had not been riddled by internal rivalries (between the Central Committee of the National Guard, the Commune, the Committee of Public Safety, and various neighborhood authorities)? What if a perception of the need for concerted political and military action had not come too little and too late? What if the Commune had seized the assets of the Bank of France? What if the Commune had used Parisian archives to help prove the case for revolution? What if the provinces had been reassured by the clear articulation of the federalist model, in accordance with the formula "To the Commune what is communal, to the Nation what is national" (quoted in Lissagaray 214/*201*)?

Clearly, the sheer proliferation of these questions testifies to the stunning artificiality (not to say bankruptcy) of the "What if . . . ?" game. One reason, I would argue, that Lissagaray's *Histoire* remains the single most compelling book on the Commune over a century after its publication lies in its complex and layered teasing out of the various determinants of the Commune's "failure"—including (but not limited to) those mentioned above. In Lissagaray's impassioned text, we have an eminently partisan account that also manages, to a remarkable degree, to engage in strong historiographical "thick description."

23. Jean-Marie Mayeur has noted a further source of confusion in that fact that during the *année terrible,* and well into the republic's early years, public opinion proved remarkably fluid. Thus, whereas the elections of February 1871 favored conservatives, the partial elections of the following July saw strong republican gains and those of 1874 a Bonapartist victory. In short, Mayeur concludes, the summer of 1871 opened a "confused period" (13). On the relative fluidity of party labels in the early years of the Third Republic, see Lejeune, 52.

24. I will have occasion in the following chapter to examine what Pick usefully calls the "double-bind" inherent in the late nineteenth-century rhetoric of degeneration—the fact that *dégénérescence* was seen both as the necessary product of a specific diseased state of the "social organism" and as "confined *within* a restricted number of bodies" (73).

25. The Commune's defenders were of course not loath to turn the tables on its bourgeois critics. Here is Lissagaray, on Versaillais violence toward Communard soldiers captured during the excursion of April 3: "The whole Parisian emigration, functionaries, elegants, women of the world and of the streets, all came with the rage of hyenas to strike the prisoners with fists, with canes and parasols, pushing off their kepis and cloaks, crying, 'Down with the assassins! To the guillotine!' " (189).

Chapter Two
The Time of Our Melancholy: Zola's Débâcle

1. Kristin Ross has shown how the popular perception that flawed maps helped seal the French army's defeat at the hands of the Prussians effectively fueled French "geography fever" in the following decade (*Emergence,* 93–94).

2. Henri Lefebvre echoes Zola's diagnosis here when he attributes the army's decline at the time of the Franco–Prussian War to the halfheartedness of hired

replacements, to the increasing bureaucratization of the officer corps, to the corrupting effects of colonial campaigns in Algeria and Mexico, and to a fantasmatic will to repeat the "imperial epic," concluding: "In practice, in 1870, the most unimaginable confusion reigns" (103).

3. As I argue in my reading of that novel in chapter 6, Zola's *Au Bonheur des dames* takes a markedly different approach to the void-in-the-space-of-power scenario in general, and to the question of feminine manipulation in particular.

4. When I speak of "disavowal" in this and subsequent chapters, I mean of course that mode of psychic defense which Freud termed *Verleugnung*, the essence of which Octave Mannoni has captured in the formula "Je sais bien, mais quand même. . . ." The fetishist, Mannoni argues, knows very well [*Je sais bien*] that the mother (and women in general) "don't have the phallus" (11). All the same [*mais quand même*], the fetishist maintains his belief in the existence of the maternal phallus through a substitute, which is the fetish itself. In this process of fetishistic disavowal Mannoni finds the origin of all those forms of belief, such as superstitions, which survive "the contradiction of experience" (12). The crucial point, for my purposes, is that the process of fetishistic displacement necessarily presupposes a prior avowal; " 'but all the same' only exists," as Mannoni puts it, "on account of 'I know very well' " (12–13). Thus, to cite Mannoni's example, the Hopi Indians' mystical, institutional belief in the godlike Katsina is made possible only by a repudiation—but not a repression—of naïve, infantile belief (16). Through an initiation process that shows young Hopi how profoundly they had been deceived—for the figures behind the terrible Katsina were in fact none other than their fathers and uncles—belief abandons its earlier, imaginary form and becomes "sufficiently symbolized as to open onto faith" (17). At the same time, Mannoni argues, the imaginary belief of children (and, to a lesser extent, of women) continues to play the role of a buttress shoring up adult (and particularly adult male) belief (18).

5. See the discussion of this tableau in Petrey, 88.

6. Zola here implicitly falls into the trap, which he had earlier denounced in an article on the National Assembly, of using the cabaret as "their supreme insult . . . the swear word with which they insult and condemn the people" (quoted in Barrows, 212).

7. Or to quote an instance from the novel: "Then Maurice understood. . . . We were unprepared, with second-rate artillery, less manpower than we had been given to believe, incompetent generals. . . . Even fate worked against us . . ." (453/72).

8. On the figure of the "bad worker" in anti–Communard literature, see Lidsky, 103–8.

9. Zola uses this phrase, in an article defending his novel from October 1892, by way of justifying his decision to show Napoléon III at Sedan with rouge on his cheeks (1455).

10. Communard fiction and historiography often acknowledge Communard melancholy, but typically link it to perceptions of the Commune's imminent demise. Here is Lissagaray, evoking the general mood on May 19: "On the terrace of the Tuileries, a dozen pickaxes beat a melancholy rhythm while digging a useless

trench. The Committee of Public Safety cannot, it reports, find men, yet it has one hundred thousand sedentary men and millions of francs at its disposal./We have entered the time of immense weariness" (308). I return to the question of Communard melancholy in my reading of *New Babylon* in chapter 7.

Chapter Three
Mourning Triumphant: Hugo's Terrible Year(s)

1. On the function of the neither/nor/but model in French theory of the 1960s and 1970s, see Starr, *Logics of Failed Revolt*, chap. 5 et passim.

2. Unless otherwise indicated, all parenthetical references in the remainder of this section, and in the section that follows, will be to *L'Année terrible*.

3. Yves Gohin usefully remarks that "the metaphors for Paris as the seat of progress in all its forms become, in Hugo, the figures and arms of a necessary mysticism. He needed a collective being (within history, outside the prophetic 'I') as a prop for his hopes, as the secular form of God's incarnation" (19).

4. We find traces of this conception in *Quatre-vingt-treize*'s labeling of the Vendée rebellion—which the novel explicitly associates with Hugo's Breton, largely royalist mother—as "a wound which is a glory" (232/152). Given all that has been made, by Hugo and others, of the poet's "forehead of genius," there would appear to be no small measure of self-reference in Hugo's report on the birth of Mirabeau: "When he came into the world, the superhuman size of his head put his mother's life in danger" (quoted in Robb, 195).

5. On the grounds for the incompletion of both "La Révolution" and "Le Verso de la page," see Brombert, 206.

6. Hugo had a long-standing habit of intervening in one conflict by drawing on materials from another. Discussing the poet's readings from *Les Châtiments* during the siege of Paris, Gohin remarks, "It is as the hero of another battle that Hugo intervenes in the present war" (9).

7. I return to vitalist biology in more detail in my reading of Flaubert's *La Tentation de saint Antoine* in the following chapter.

8. Unless otherwise noted, all parenthetical references in the remainder of this chapter will be to *Quatre-vingt-treize*.

9. In an important reading of the function of mourning in postwar Germany, Eric Santner reads mourning as a "ritual of de-auratization," such that the "self emerges out of the ruins of the primitive auratic symbiosis with the mother," provided that this process is "emphatically witnessed by the mother's gaze or that of some other significant person" (126). Following this argument, might we not read the massacre's sentimental evocation of this universalized protective maternity as an attempt expressly to counter the mourning implicit in the many signs of the destruction that is to come?

10. By thus reading the children as *agents* of a melancholy historicity brought to the fore by the events of the Terrible Year, but already evident in Hugo's drafts for

"Le Verso de la page," I am clearly not following Mehlman's reading of the massacre as proof that "the very subject or mode of existence of the volume is self-consumption"—that the book, in other words, "may be seen as destroying itself" (69).

11. To the extent that Cimourdain's suicide should be read as a failure, I find Ferguson's approach more fruitful when she argues that "*Quatrevingt-treize* places the legitimacy of the Third Republic in the rejection of Cimourdain's republic of the sword," such that Cimourdain's suicide "acts out the failure of his conception of relentless justice" (*Paris*, 170).

Chapter Four
Science and Confusion: Flaubert's Temptation

1. See also Seznec, "Monstres," 200; Gothot-Mersch, 34–35.

2. On the place of erudition in the seemingly oneiric *Temptation*, see the articles by Jean Seznec and, especially, Michel Foucault's " 'Fantastique,' " 9ff.

3. Unless otherwise specified, all references to Flaubert's correspondence will be to the as-yet incomplete Bruneau edition in the Bibliothèque de la Pléiade and will take the form *Corr.* 4:372. All of Flaubert's letters after 1875 will be quoted from the Conard edition and specified as such: *Corr.* (Conard) 8:335. The four volumes of the 1954 *Supplément* to that edition will be designated as S1, S2, S3, or S4. Where references to Flaubert's correspondence include page numbers in italics, these refer to the partial translation of Flaubert's letters by Francis Steegmuller.

4. All references in this chapter to *La Tentation de saint Antoine* refer to volume 1 of the Pléiade edition of Flaubert's works and will henceforth be given as numerals in parentheses within the body of my text. Italicized numerals following these refer to the Mrosovsky translation of this text.

5. In his 1848 essay on clerical liberalism, reprinted in *Questions contemporaines*, Renan writes: "From the moment in effect that one recognizes a given religious doctrine as absolutely and uniquely true, one can no longer admit that another doctrine has its share of truth. All absolute doctrines are essentially intolerant" (296).

6. In his characteristically rich "Flaubert et le syncrétisme religieux," Frank Paul Bowman captures the function and fate of religious symbols in Flaubert's text in these terms: "Rather than representing religion as freeing itself from the symbol to become philosophy, he reduces religion to the symbol, voids the symbol's ideological content through omission or occultation, and then proceeds to degrade and destroy the symbol, thanks in part to the play of resemblance and difference" (627).

7. It is customary to say that Hilarion is a composite of two allegorical figures from the earlier versions, Logic and Science, combining the former Logic's sophistic acumen with the former Science's aspect of a grizzled child. But neither Logic nor Science tries to show, as Hilarion does, that "the religious sentiment in itself is of the same stuff everywhere, corresponds to the same needs, responds to the same

fibers, dies by the same accidents, etc." Rather than serving to demonstrate the underlying unity of superstition, the march of the gods in the early versions simply *overwhelms* Antony; he is "lost in the whirlwind of all these gods who pass by" on their way to the abyss (Flaubert, *Oeuvres* [Masson], 1:517).

8. Unless otherwise specified, "Geoffroy Saint-Hilaire" here refers to Étienne Geoffroy Saint-Hilaire (1772–1844). I shall briefly discuss the work of Étienne's son, Isidore (1805–61), in connection with the problem of monstrosity.

9. The closest literary analogue to Hilarion's tactic of comparison and assimilation would be the syncretic gesture by which certain Romantic poets, particularly Hugo and Nerval, enacted the "unity of the various mythological conceptions" (Nerval, 656). In "Le Christ aux oliviers" (V, 1–4), Nerval assimilates Icarus, Phaeton, and Atys to the figure of Christ. Elsewhere he has Isis say, "Your prayers touched me . . . me, whose unique and all-powerful divinity the universe has worshiped in a thousand forms. Thus, they called me Cybele in Phrygia, Minerva in Athens, the Paphian Venus in Cyprus . . ." (657).

10. Of natural history in the classical age, Foucault writes: "By limiting and filtering the visible, structure enables it to be transcribed into language. It permits the visibility of the animal or plant to pass over in its entirety into the discourse that receives it" (*Mots,* 147/135).

11. I have in mind the battle scenes of *Salammbô* and, most particularly, the orgy of *L'Éducation sentimentale*—passages that all obstinately refuse Balzac's representational ideal in not aspiring to the status of a painting.

12. Flaubert's ideals of observation and description quickly placed him in opposition to a certain facile and tautological manipulation of the final cause. Here is the continuation of the first of my epigraphs above: "We lack science, above all. We flounder like savages in barbary. Philosophy as it is done and religion as it subsists are colored glasses that keep us from seeing clearly because 1) we have clear biases in advance, 2) we worry about 'why' before knowing 'how,' 3) man relates everything to himself. 'The sun is meant to light the earth.' We are still there" (*Corr.* 2:756). In other words, Diderot was right: "The how derives from beings, the why from our understanding." The "how" alone is scientific because it avoids the "why"'s trap of equating formal and final causes, of assuming that the actual state of a phenomenon is the result of a necessary progression toward that state as an end. Such an equation of formal and final causes lies at the heart of all biological theorizing in the Aristotelian tradition. When Geoffroy Saint-Hilaire *père* comes to criticize the doctrine of the preexistence of the monstrous germ, he does so by showing that such a doctrine simply postpones the explanation of monstrosity by burying the origins of the monstrous back in a prehistory of which the scientist in 1820 could know nothing.

13. Researchers of the eighteenth century had already treated such seeming aberrations "as substitutes for crucial experiments capable of deciding between two systems concerning the generation and development of plants and animals: preformation and epigenesis" (Canguilhem, 178). The honor of first suggesting that

monstrosities resulted from abnormalities of embryonic differentiation belongs to K.-F. Wolf for his 1772 tract, *De ortu monstrarum.*

14. See, for example, Flaubert's treatment of Apollo (134). With few exceptions, the gods of chapter 5 follow one another from east to west, from the Buddha's India through Persia and Chaldaea to Egypt and Rome, as if the story of humanity and its unending fund of superstition mimicked the path of the sun from the Levant to the Abendland. It is certainly ironic that Flaubert would have structured a chapter which ultimately shows that history is cyclical and that the destiny of all beliefs is dissolution or mutilation—"The gods must go down. . . . To each his turn; this is destiny!" (129/*189*)—on the model of a solar trope that, as Derrida shows in "La Mythologie blanche," has symbolized the West's philosophic access to the world of the Forms, the pure light of Christian revelation, reason as the sine qua non of clear and distinct ideas—in short, on the model of *the* privileged trope for Western philosophical and religious truth.

15. Critics have traced Antony's diabolic voyage into space to analogous voyages in the Gospel according to Matthew (4:8), in Byron's *Cain,* and in Goethe's *Faust.* Prototypes of that journey appear in three of Flaubert's juvenilia: *Agonies, La Danse des morts,* and *Smarh* (see Bem, 112).

16. *Ethics* I, 28 (in Benedict de Spinoza, *Reader,* 103–4). See also Spinoza's celebrated worm-in-the-bloodstream example (*Oeuvres,* 1179–80).

17. Spinoza tries to avoid the paradox by *proving* the necessary existence of God as pure essence. As finite beings, we cannot know God in his entirety because to know God would be to become God. We can approach such knowledge only through what Spinoza calls *scientia intuitiva.* Yet we know that God must exist because we can perceive the essence of the one substance that is alternatively God and the world. However, once God is proven by Spinoza's version of Descartes's Ontological Argument, it becomes possible to say that "each idea of each body, or of each singular thing which actually exists, necessarily involves an eternal and infinite essence of God" (*Ethics,* II, 45; in *Reader,* 144).

18. Flaubert, *Bouvard* (Cento), 34. If one remembers that only in the final version of the *Temptation* does Flaubert have the Devil speak as a Copernican or a Newtonian—in other words, only in the 1874 text might the discourse of Science have appeared self-evident to the nineteenth-century reader—it is all the more tempting to think that the Flaubert of 1874 might be trying to catch his reader in the assumption that science is necessarily all that remains, all that could remain, once "superstitions" have fallen into the abyss. It is difficult at the end of the pseudo-historic march *not* to read the arrival of a Science "without hate, fear, pity, love or God" as anything but the dawn of a new era. We can all the more expect Flaubert to have counted on this reaction to the extent that he himself had said of history and a project of natural history based on observation: "It is through these that we will discover new worlds" (*Corr.,* 3:353).

19. Bowman writes: "The jumbling of religious content effected by syncretism is only a special case of a more general jumbling symbolized by the melon prized by

Bernardin de Saint-Pierre and Fourier: 'As he had grown different species side by side, the sweet melons were mixed up with the watermelons, large Portuguese with Grand Mogul, and with the proximity of the tomatoes completing the anarchy, the result had been abominable hybrids tasting like pumpkins'. . . . Thus Flaubert undermines religious syncretism as an aspect of a more general and serious endeavor, his questioning of the romantic notion of a harmony between self, words, world and transcendence, for which he substitutes a vision of ironic chaos" (635–36).

20. When the discourse of Science founders against that same principle of noncontradiction which had earlier assured its hegemony, however, it proves that there is no vantage point outside of stupidity from which stupidity itself might be mastered. Or, as Flaubert famously put it: "Stupidity is not on one side and Wit on the other. It's like Vice and Virtue; only the cunning can distinguish them" (*Corr.*, 2:585–86). Commenting on this letter, Christopher Prendergast has written: "The discourse of Wisdom, which assumes its own serene detachment from bêtise, is by virtue of that assumption, exceedingly stupid, displaying the complacent idiocy of a presumed innocence" ("Quotation," 268). In comporting himself as a master of knowledge, the Devil is no less innocent, no less idiotic than Antony had been when he responded to Hilarion by repeating the Nicene Creed. In both cases, innocence functions as a sign of desire, hence of a certain virtue. Ultimately, the *Temptation's* agonistic relation between scientist and saint proves to be a relation between two innocents, whose common virtue can be said to lie in their unending desire for their respective ideals.

21. Compare the following passage from Flaubert's *Carnets de lecture*: "The artist not only bears all of humanity within himself, he reproduces its history in the creation of his work: first, confusion [or murkiness, *du trouble*] . . . all is mixed up (the barbarian era); then analysis, . . . the disposing of parts (the scientific era); finally, he comes back to the initial synthesis, now opened up in its execution" (*Oeuvres* [Club], 8:261).

As I noted in my Introduction to this study, Renan's *L'Avenir de la science* outlines a dialectical evolution of the "human spirit" that runs along much the same lines. For Renan, just as the human spirit has known three ages, so does the human mind go through three successive stages in coming to know a complex object—"1) a general and confused view of the whole; 2) a distinct and analytical view of the parts; 3) a synthetic recomposition of the whole with the knowledge one possesses of the parts" (968/*282*).

For the purposes of this study, however, I find Geoffroy's account especially useful. For while it presents an analogous dialectic of confusion, differentiation, and synthesis, it also—in quintessentially Flaubertian style—thematizes ideas as furniture. See, in this regard, furniture as it defines our impressions of Emma and Mme. Arnoux, and especially Flaubert's "Sustained comparison of a good head and a good house . . ." (*Oeuvres* [Club], 8:273).

22. In his journal entry for October 18, 1871, Goncourt writes: "Flaubert confides to me that the Saint's defeat is due to the *cell*, the scientific cell. What is curious is that my astonishment astonishes him" (*Journal*, 2:468).

23. See, for example, Seznec, "Monstres," 221; and Mitroi, 129.

24. On the ways in which Flaubert's use of simile in the *Temptation*'s final scene serves to reinforce our sense of the work as a specifically *literary* vision, see Olds, 177 et passim.

25. Against Theodor Reik, who argues that the *Temptation*'s final scene is "overdetermined by the wish . . . to see that which is secret, hidden, sexual," I concur with Carlo Testa that this pulverization of Antony's self effectively "foregrounds the specifically liberating aspect of the mystical vision of *life bypassing sexuality*. . . . What the observing eye 'adores' here is the all-comforting certitude of the general principle of non-sexual reproduction" (Reik, "Flaubert," 149; Testa, 138).

26. "Since he is not defined by possession, Gustave will define himself by desire—that is to say, he will define himself sumptuously and universally as that which he does not have" (Sartre, *Idiot*, 1:1079).

27. In a recent article, Gisèle Séginger accounts for a change in Flaubert's approach to science in these terms: "In the 1870's, Flaubert's attitude with respect to the sciences and their history changed markedly. Whereas in the correspondence of the 1850's he valorized scientific objectivity and opposed science (in the singular) to moral prejudices, to religious or political beliefs, in the 1870's he saw the sciences as bringing the imaginary into relief, just as beliefs do. . . . From this point on, he will be interested . . . in manners of seeing, in *scientific gazes*, in science as imaginary practice" ("Fiction," 132).

On the extent to which the final *Tentation* contains within itself *Bouvard et Pécuchet* as its "minuscule and unbounded double" (Foucault), see Gothot-Mersch, "Introduction," 31ff.; and Foucault "'Fantastique,'" 26–30.

28. On the *Temptation* as a form of diversion, see also the letters of March 31, 1871 (to Sand: "I am going to try to return to my poor *Saint Anthony* and forget France" [*Corr.*, 4:300]); of May 3, 1871 (this chapter's second epigraph [*Corr.*, 4:318]); and of October 6, 1871 (to Edma Roger des Genettes: "To forget it all, I have thrown myself furiously into *Saint Anthony* and have come to enjoy a *terrifying exaltation*" [*Corr.*, 4:383]).

29. Flaubert's melancholy circa 1870 could easily be deduced from the evidence of the third *Temptation* alone. Antony's bitterness and world-weariness, the fatigue inspired in him by "the same monotonous actions, the long-drawn-out days, the ugliness of the world, the stupidity of the sun," permeate the 1874 text and lead him to a project of suicide through pantheistic absorption that Flaubert's text will ultimately refuse him (152/*217*). Echoes of modern French revolutionism in general, and of the Paris Commune in particular, are likewise easy to find: in Antony's remark that the first Council of Nicaea (like the Commune) "had such disgraceful members"; in the presence of crowds taking their revenge on statues, furniture, and books, "a thousand fragilities of whose function they are ignorant, and which, for that reason, exasperate them"; in the revolutionary resonances of Atys's self-castration (33/*69*, 41/*78*, 121/*180*).

30. Sartre: "But to the extent that he helped to prepare it, he cannot vomit up this 'era of *boorishness*' without vomiting himself along with it. Hysterical somatization through vomiting has the function of expressing this *unspeakable* circle: men are killing him, he internalizes the events of September 4th in the form of a hysterical belief in stomach cancer; the Republic is not only an external transformation of the environment, it is *himself as other*" (3:496/5:460).

31. In his journal entry for March 19, 1871, Goncourt complains of "a feeling of fatigue at being French" (*Journal*, 2:396). Some months later, after the Commune's demise, Sand admits to Flaubert that her faith in human perfectibility through experience and reason has been profoundly shaken by "this infamous Commune": "And now I wake from a dream to find a generation divided between idiocy and delirium tremens"; elsewhere, Sand pronounces herself "infected with the sickness of my people and my nation" (in Flaubert, *Corr.*, 4:335/*178*, 4:374/*179*). As for Gautier, Flaubert reports that, in the months leading up to his death in October 1872, Gautier said on repeated occasions, "I am dying of the Commune" (*Corr.*, 4:598).

32. The death of the Latins, in the context of a vitalist dialectic whereby "today's victors are the vanquished of tomorrow," is a constant theme of Renan's 1871 work, *La Réforme intellectuelle et morale* (331). Attributing this theme to "German naturalists," Renan turns its logic against his German interlocutors, asking in a letter to David Friedrich Strauss: "How can you believe that the Slavs will not do to you what you are doing to others?" (434, 456).

33. Françoise Gaillard rightly argues that Sartre's recourse to the Oedipal scenario in *L'Idiot* is every bit as tautological, "since it proceeds from a simple identification of the particular with a preconceived general concept," as the Marxist methodology Sartre explicitly challenges, the inevitable outcome of which can be reduced to the phrase "the bourgeoisie is always the bourgeoisie" ("Imaginaire" 15, 11).

Of Prussian demands in the wake of Sedan, Sartre writes: "They correspond precisely to the typical behavior of the scientist. What is experimentation if not a systematic, cold, deliberate, and passionless procedure? And what about the systematic, cold, deliberate, and rigorous practice of civil, political, and military engineers, specialists in the applied sciences?" (3:598/5:557). On the category of "technician of practical knowledge," see Sartre's *Plaidoyer*.

34. Glossing a letter in which Flaubert states that "there are no longer any races," Eugenio Donato writes: "For Flaubert, the end of history means a general collapsing of all differences—racial, social, political—into mediocrity, mediocrity understood literally as the property of being in the middle, that is to say, of not sustaining any differential space or opposition" (44). As an instance of the sort of contradiction that one finds everywhere in Flaubert's letters, and that necessitates a form of thick description, I would argue that Donato's claim both is and is not the case—is, because Flaubert conceived of mounting egalitarianism, democratization, and bourgeoisification as fundamentally entropic; is not, inasmuch as the cycle of rise and collapse is fated to continue. ("And so on.")

Chapter Five
The Party of Movement: Flaubert's Bouvard et Pécuchet

1. The French indefinite pronoun *on* poses serious problems of translation. Depending on the context, it can variously be rendered as "one," "they," "people," "we," or as an active placeholder for a passive construction. Flaubert's conception of the *on* as an "enormous collective fool" clearly privileges the third-person active senses of this word. In order to make my opening argument easier to follow, however, I have opted to simply leave *on* untranslated.

2. The sense of a bric-a-brac world might also be viewed as a product of the "historical tendency," inasmuch as that tendency promoted a heteroclite vision of the present state of any culture or institution. At one point in *L'Éducation sentimentale*, for example, Deslauriers speaks of "this beautiful and widely admired social order" as "made up of Louis XIV scraps and Voltairean ruins, covered with a Napoleonic whitewash and shards from the English constitution" (177). For Flaubert, as for Deslauriers, the heteroclite phenomenon functions as a ribald affront to the seriousness of whatever social or natural order denies it. Yet Flaubert's position is ultimately more subtle. Because he who laughs is also part of the social and natural order he derides on the evidence of that phenomenon, and because he finds that order to have suddenly taken on an aspect of nihilistic disorder, the vision of the heteroclite phenomenon also sets him on the track of a pure order or ideality beyond the heteroclite world. Inevitably, as my reading of the *Temptation* has suggested, this ideality is founded on mystifications that are subject to discovery at any moment. It is therefore permanently threatened by that relapse into inauthentic experience which we associate with Romantic irony.

3. Flaubert, in other words, was an early proponent of what I have called (in an eponymous study of French theory after May 1968) the "logics of failed revolt." The most obvious point of crossover between my argument here and that of *Logics* involves what I am here calling "antiagonism," but which Barthes (a key figure for *Logics*) called "neither-norism" (*ninisme*). In his 1957 *Mythologies*, Barthes defines "neither-norism" as "that mythological figure which consists in weighing two contrary terms against one another, so as ultimately to reject them both" (241). In seeing neither-norism as "a figure of bourgeois myth," which finds its origin in "a modern form of liberalism," Barthes is likely, as so often in the early work, to be thinking of Flaubert.

4. On style in the *Dictionnaire*, see Jean-Jacques Thomas's "Poétique de la 'bêtise.'"

5. The ease with which Bouvard and Pécuchet guess the dénouements of the novels they read suggests that they live in a time when plots are no longer perceived as natural, but are either seen as obsessively partial and repetitive or easily seen through. If the "plotting" of the hostile *on* with which I began this chapter underlies what is the closest approximation in *Bouvard et Pécuchet* to a unified plot, its value in maintaining the reader's interest is nonetheless limited. Flaubert's novel has not one plot so much as a series of partial plots. Composed of a sequence of conflictual

situations that most often lead only to the threshold of another, contingently related situation, the novel lacks the overall dramatic movement so often conveyed by less unlikely forms of plotting. The challenge of writing *Bouvard et Pécuchet* was thus that of imparting movement to an essentially repetitive story, one that makes only a perfunctory gesture toward the traditional plot, and of imparting that movement through the force of style alone. "It must walk, run and flash like lightning, or I'll die trying, and I don't plan to do so" (*Corr.*, 2:525). The project of giving movement and life to a fundamentally inert subject was thus doubly a project against death—against the author's own death and against the death of the fictional matter. It is only such a project against death which, if successful, would merit that most serious appellation, "the *pinnacle of Art*" (*Corr.*, 4:878).

6. Sartre rightly argues that Flaubert foresaw, in another context, "the advertising techniques that, a century later in our 'consumer societies,' persuade consumers that each of us will be 'more and more ourselves' if we all buy the same products" (*Idiot, 3:624/5:582*).

7. See Foucault, "Author." Like Flaubert, Foucault tends to interpret the transgression of open revolt as the manifestation of a will to power or domination. This is why, as John Rajchman has argued, Foucault ultimately eschewed the ethic of transgression he saw to be characteristic of modernism proper in favor of "an ethic of constant disengagement from constituted forms of experience, of freeing oneself for the invention of new forms of life" (37).

8. With the false naïveté of an ambitious and jealous nature, du Camp goes on to ask: "Revenge for what? He became famous overnight; . . . he had many devoted men friends and enviable set of women friends." Du Camp eventually concedes (how could he not?) that Flaubert sought revenge against "human stupidity" (quoted in Flaubert, *Oeuvres* [Masson], 1:35).

When Bouvard and Pécuchet decide they are "capable of writing," Pécuchet imagines writing a book as an act of vengeance; Bouvard chooses for his subject an old writing master ("Nothing could be funnier than this character" [218/*142–143*]). After a week, they merge these two books into one. The book they would have written, had they gotten any further than this, would of course have been uncannily like *Bouvard et Pécuchet*.

9. To paraphrase Tomashevsky, the reader agreed to read innocently so as to catch the signs that the author gives, confident that these signs or motifs would eventually be made to coalesce into themes (90 et passim).

10. Claude Mouchard makes a similar point relative to Flaubert's appropriation of technological discourse: "The reader who would like to truly 'understand' what the text of the novel is talking about would have to go back to the manuals Flaubert mentions. But the risk is that one would enter into an infinite play of cross-references that is one of the temptations of technological discourse, despite its pretensions to an immediate and efficacious clarity. This drift in the direction of a knowledge always subject to further elucidation would make reading the novel even more impossible than does the immediate obscurity of the citations" (67).

11. My reading of the *Temptation* in the preceding chapter falls squarely into the latter camp, whose undisputed standard-bearer is Jean Seznec for his decades of research into the bookish sources of that work.

12. Within limits that remain to be delineated, the best of these readings do use particular passages as ways into discussion of the problematics of the book as a whole. See, among other examples: Gaillard, "Inénarrable" and "Réel"; Duchet, "Écriture"; and Mouchard, "Terre."

13. For the purposes of this study, I take the following passage from Renan's 1869 essay "La Monarchie constitutionenelle de France" ("Constitutional Monarchy in France"), reprinted in his *Réforme intellectuelle et morale*, as a snapshot (necessarily one-dimensional) of French liberal thinking of the period: "The liberal program is at the same time a truly conservative program. A limited and controlled constitutional monarchy; decentralization, diminution of the government, strong organization of the commune, the district and the department; individual activity given a wide range of action in the domains of art, spirit, science, industry and colonization; a decidedly pacifist foreign policy that abandons all claims to territorial aggrandizement within Europe; the development of strong primary education and fostering of a higher education capable of giving a solid philosophical grounding to the mores of the educated class; formation of an upper chamber resulting from varied modes of election and effecting not only a simple numeric representation of citizens but also a representation of diverse interests, duties, specializations and aptitudes; governmental neutrality on social questions; freedom of association; gradual separation of Church and State . . . : all this is what we dream of when we seek out [a social program grounded in] what is possible" (513–514).

14. "It is further of note that when Freud introduces the term 'agency'—literally 'instance,' understood in a sense, as Strachey notes, 'similar to that in which the word occurs in the phrase "a Court of the First Instance" '—he introduces it by analogy with tribunals or authorities which judge what may or may not pass" (Laplanche and Pontalis, 16).

15. It is, of course, entirely typical of Flaubert's novel that Bouvard and Pécuchet elsewhere dream of holding a specifically institutional power: "They wrote to the king to ask for the establishment in the Calvados of a nursing institute of which whey would be professors" (130/79).

16. "It will be recalled that the borrower, when he was questioned, replied first that he had not borrowed a kettle at all, second that it already had a hole in it when he borrowed it, and third that he had given it back undamaged and without a hole" (Freud, *Jokes,* 205).

17. I read Bouvard and Pécuchet's refusal of death—"the greatest problem of all, the one that contains all the others" (322/*219*)—as a refusal of just that sort of totalizing discourse for which they elsewhere so obviously yearn.

18. Schehr's point is slightly different: "Though the concept of the text has contributed so enormously to this liberation of our individual and collective endeavors, thereby inspiring in many a false sense of freedom from canon, meaning, practice, and history, it does not mean that textuality is itself free" (4).

19. *Bouvard et Pécuchet* couches this injunction in a typically comic mode when Bouvard and Pécuchet respond to their neighbors' fear that their educational principles favor a "leveling down and immorality" by advocating, among other measures, a rigorous gradation of intellectual capacities: "arrange the French in a hierarchy where you must periodically take an examination to keep your rank" (404/*280*).

Having done much with Flaubert's distaste for Renan's prewar Germanophilia, Sartre goes on to argue that "if the mandarins—like Renan—came to power and followed his advice (no more lies, no more foolish beliefs, truth, science), they too would begin by banishing him from their city, as Plato banished the poets" (*Idiot*, 3:611/*5:570*).

Chapter Six
Democracy and Masochism: Zola's Bonheur

1. "Madame Marty also said she was dead from exhaustion, but took no less profound a pleasure [*n'en jouissait pas moins profondément*] in this tiredness, the slow death of her strength amidst this inexhaustible display of merchandise" (327/*255*).

2. "Then, woman was dressed again, the white wave of this cascade of linen slipped behind the quivering mystery of skirts, the chemise stiffened by the dressmaker's finger, the cold bloomers keeping the folds from their box, all this dead percale and dead muslin, scattered across the counters, thrown aside, and piled up, was about to come alive with the life of the flesh, warm and redolent with the smell of love, a white cloud sanctified, bathed in night, the slightest flutter of which, to reveal the pink glimpse of a knee in the depths of this whiteness, would devastate the world. Then there was another room, baby clothes . . . (502/*400*).

3. With Denise Baudu, we are in fact a long way from the decadent hermaphroditism of a Thérèse Raquin.

4. In *The Desire to Desire*, Mary Ann Doane has shown how a "doubling of female types" characteristic of women's pictures of the 1940s reflects an analogous split between the woman's role as worker (parodically exemplified by Norman Rockwell's "Rosie the Riveter") and as guardian of the domestic sphere (29). In support of her contention that the woman's "split subjectivity" is ultimately "subsumed under the category of beauty," Doane cites an ad for Tangee lipstick, two sentences of which I cannot resist reproducing here: "It's a reflection of the free democratic way of life that you have succeeded in keeping your femininity—even though you are doing man's work!/If a symbol were needed of this fine, independent spirit—of this courage and strength—I would choose a lipstick" (quoted at 29).

5. On Zola's decision to give his novel "a happy end," see Henri Mitterand's notes to the Pléïade edition of the novel, especially 3:1681–1682. Given the infantilizing of Denise in the novel's final pages (discussed below), I think there is good reason to prefer Zola's original account of Denise as "happy or rather *unhappy* at the end" (3:1681).

6. If the *Bonheur* were a novel by Flaubert, the task of proving this investment would have been made appreciably easier by the novelist's tendency to dwell on his affective investments with specific characters in his correspondence. But there is nothing of the sort in Zola's letters, such that the argument for libidinal investment must be made solely on evidence internal to the novel, as I do in the following pages.

7. On the risks inherent in the practice of symptomatic reading, see chapter 4 of Starr, *Logics of Failed Revolt*.

8. See also Žižek *Sublime Object,* 147; Mouffe, 11; and Copjec, 153–54. I explore some of the implications of this commonplace in the final chapter of *Logics.*

9. Democracy appears throughout this essay as the necessary outcome of a life force into which "everything enters . . . , even unsavory and destructive elements" (651). Thus, not only does the rhetoric of Zola's "La Démocratie" significantly parallel that of the 1883 *Bonheur* (analyzed below), but that rhetoric also suggests the necessity of that practice of symptomatic reading I shall engage in here: "If our time is still an unsettled one, the signs are ever clearer with each passing day. What we all hear is the growing rumble of the coming democracy" (651). What Zola's essay does not address, however, is that specific conjunction of capitalism and democracy captured in the formula "liberal democracy," a conjunction that I shall argue is "contained by default" (*portée en creux*) by Zola's text (see Althusser and Balibar, 1:23).

10. On the function of symbolic mobility in the cult of the Virgin, upon which the republican cult of Marianne is plainly grafted, see Kristeva, 305–306 et passim. On the Third Republic as paradoxical political regime, see chapter 1 of this volume.

11. Denise in fact anticipates that "depoliticized and eroticized" Marianne whom Debora Silverman has shown to have predominated in turn-of-the-century France: "Marianne 1900 bounds through the skies, a childlike figure fused at her side. United with nature, maternal, and sexual: this triad of qualities was . . . a particularly compelling combination in the French fin de siècle" (144–45).

12. Later in her study, Gullickson finds this exclusionary logic in the myth of the *pétroleuse*: "Just as Marianne could represent the republic in which she had no political identity, the pétroleuse could represent the Commune that excluded individual women from its ruling bodies and even, for the most part, from the ranks of its defenders" (224).

13. I am reminded, in this connection, of what Zola wrote in his notebook upon rejecting the idea of having Mme. Hédouin give Denise to Mouret on her deathbed: "That would present the advantage of leaving a single man at the head of this multitude of women [*peuple de femmes*]" (*Rougon-Macquart,* 3:682).

14. Peter Watkins's *La Commune,* discussed in the following chapter, contains a poignant scene in which the wife of a National Guardsman, surrounded by her children, expresses her fears that her husband has been killed by Versaillais forces. (He has been, or will soon be.) Agnès Noiret never in fact utters an *all the same* clause, deeming the Commune worthy of the most grievous sacrifices. But as

viewers we are so inured to this rhetoric—both from television and from Watkins's film—that it is hard not to hear it nonetheless.

15. Kaja Silverman has noted the instability of Freud's tripartite division of masochism into "erotogenic," "feminine," and "moral" types: "No sooner are these distinctions enumerated than they begin to erode. . . . The tripartite division thus gives way rather quickly to one of those dualisms of which Freud is so fond, with both feminine and moral masochism 'bleeding' into each other at the point where each abuts into erotogenic masochism" (188). Cf. Reik, *Masochism,* 277ff.

16. By contrast, Freud notes that the children being beaten "are almost invariably boys, in the phantasies of boys just as much as in those of girls" ("Child," 191).

17. Emily Apter discusses the case of male masochists who "become" the fetish, and details the ways in which this mechanism is mediated by the figure of Christ, in her *Feminizing the Fetish,* 132–33.

18. Judith Butler makes a strong case for a necessary futurity inherent in a concept of democracy (in this case, radical democracy) in her "Arguing with the Real" (*Bodies,* 187–222). On the futurity of Zola's vision, see note 9.

19. Inasmuch as Denise avoids that trap of personal ambition and bourgeoisification into which Zola's male revolutionaries typically fall, she might be seen as one of the few true revolutionaries in Zola's work (see Guedj, 134–35).

Chapter Seven
The Filmic Commune

1. Throughout this section, quotations from Ian MacDonald refer to three postings MacDonald made to a Shostakovich discussion list in December 1999. The roman numerals in my parenthetical references denote the number of the posting.

2. The name Louise appears only in the film's shooting script; the film itself refers to this character simply as a *midinette.* As the *Petit Robert* reminds us, the colloquial expression *une midinette* denotes a young woman of provincial extraction employed in the Parisian garment and fashion industries and, by extension, a naïve and sentimental young girl.

3. In a 1978 article on the genesis of *New Babylon,* Trauberg speaks of the scripts's initial debt to "the Zolian epic," citing these two novels and Zola's *L'Argent.* He goes on to note, however, that "later we began to have doubts about the style and so rectified the original screenplay" (8). I return to the question of this rectification at the end of this section.

4. In a 1978 letter to Myriam Tsikournas, Trauberg evokes this scene as an "illustration" of the phrase, which he attributes to Marx: "The bourgeois of Versailles who applaud the fall of the barricades" (8). My guess is that Trauberg is here conflating two passages in Marx's "Civil War"—the long passage cited above and this: "The first batch of Parisian prisoners brought into Versailles was subjected to revolting atrocities, . . . while Mesdames Thiers and Favre, in the midst of their

ladies of honour (?), applauded, from the balcony, the outrages of the Versailles mob" (65).

5. Historians of the Second Empire have long noted how the regime used elaborate public spectacles—international expositions, the opening of the Suez Canal, wars in Italy and Mexico, and the like—to entertain and pacify the French public.

6. In the film, this figure appears to be killed by a Versaillais shell. Although he fought on one of the last barricades, the historical Clément managed to flee to Belgium, then England, returning to France with the general amnesty of 1880 (Noël, 134).

7. On the Commune's specific exemplarity in Soviet ideology, see Pytel, 12.

8. Marek Pytel has uncovered an alternate ending in the film's original shooting script. Instead of prophesying the Commune's return, this version ends with a vision of Jean "hunched, wet, insignificant and destroyed," while a sergeant pats him "paternally" on the shoulder, saying: "Don't worry, son. You'll get used to it" (58). In this form, as Pytel astutely notes, *New Babylon* is no longer "an exhortation for revenge," but "an incitement to mutiny and an exercise in sedition" (58).

9. "Thirty years (or more) of Hollywood role models; of closed narrative structures; of ultra-rapid language forms which (deliberately) allow no time for reflection. Thirty years of propagating consumerism and competitiveness (along with the 'virtues' of silence, passivity, and non-criticism); of TV 'experts' who act as our social surrogates; of soap-opera characters who become our idols. The destruction of history and its complex lessons; a distancing from foreign cultures and the suffering in seemingly far-away corners of the planet. All of these, and many other traumas, have severely affected our ability to reflect, resist, collectivise; even recognise what is happening" (Watkins, "Summary").

10. If Watkins's film is by no means blind to the Paris Commune's place in the long line of modern European revolutions (from 1789 to 1917 and even 1968), its most consistent point of comparison is with the contemporaneous colonization of Algeria. Witness the film's long succession of testimonials on the massacres, confiscations of land, and repression of indigenous cultures inflicted by the French colonizer; its intertitles on the post-Commune transfer of French soliders to Algeria to crush insurrection there and on the belated amnesty (1895) for the Algerian insurrectionists; and Watkins's decision to juxtapose "Le Temps des cerises" with Akli Yahiatène's impassioned, haunting song of Algerian exile, "Ya El Menfi," as the film's credits roll.

Bibliography

Agulhon, Maurice. *Marianne au combat: L'Imagerie et la symbolique républicaines de 1789 à 1880.* Paris: Flammarion, 1979. Translated by Janet Lloyd as *Marianne into Battle: Republican Imagery and Symbolism in France, 1789–1880.* Cambridge: Cambridge University Press, 1981.

Althusser, Louis, and Étienne Balibar. *Lire "Le Capital."* 2nd ed. 4 vols. Paris: Maspero, 1975.

Amengual, Barthélémy. "À l'Assaut du ciel." *Positif* 131 (1971): 60–64.

Apter, Emily. *Feminizing the Fetish: Psychoanalysis and Narrative Obsession in Turn-of-the-Century France.* Ithaca, NY: Cornell University Press, 1991.

Apter, Emily, and William Pietz, eds. *Fetishism as Cultural Discourse.* Ithaca, NY: Cornell University Press, 1993.

Arvon, Henri. *L'Anarchisme.* Paris: Presses Universitaires de France, 1951.

Auerbach, Eric. *Mimesis: The Representation of Reality in Western Literature.* Translated by Willard R. Trask. Princeton, NJ: Princeton University Press, 1953.

Balzac, Honoré de. "Avant-propos." In his *Oeuvres complètes.* Edited by Pierre-Georges Castex. 1:7–20. Paris: Gallimard (Pléïade), 1976.

Barnes, Hazel. *Sartre & Flaubert.* Chicago: University of Chicago Press, 1981.

Barnouw, Jeffrey. "The Cognitive Value of Confusion and Obscurity in the German Enlightenment: Leibniz, Baumgarten, and Herder." *Studies in Eighteenth-Century Culture* 24 (1995): 29–50.

Barrows, Susanna. "After the Commune: Alcoholism, Temperance, and Literature in the Early Third Republic." In *Consciousness and Class Experience in Nineteenth-Century Europe,* 205–218. Edited by John M. Merriman. New York: Holmes & Meier, 1979.

Barthes, Roland. *Mythologies.* Paris: Éditions du Seuil, 1957.

———. *S/Z.* Paris: Éditions du Seuil, 1970. Translated by Richard Miller as *S/Z.* New York: Noonday, 1974.

Baudoin, Charles. *Psychanalyse de Victor Hugo.* Paris: Armand Colin, 1972.

Becker, Colette. "Les Rougon-Macquart." In *Manuel d'histoire littéraire de la France,* 5:257–68. Edited by Claude Duchet. Paris: Éditions Sociales, 1977.

Beizer, Janet. *Ventriloquized Bodies: Narratives of Hysteria in Nineteenth-Century France.* Ithaca, NY: Cornell University Press, 1994.

Bell, David. *Models of Power: Politics and Economics in Zola's Rougon-Macquart.* Lincoln: University of Nebraska Press, 1988.

Bellet, Roger. "Logique et incarnation révolutionnaires dans le journal *Le Père Duchêne.*" In *Les Écrivains français devant la guerre de 1870 et devant la Commune,* 113–120. Edited by Madeleine Fargeaud and Claude Pichois. Paris: Colin, 1972.

Bem, Jeanne. *Désir et savoir dans l'oeuvre de Flaubert: Étude de la Tentation de saint Antoine.* Neuchâtel: La Baconnière, 1979.

Benjamin, Walter. *Illuminations.* Translated by Harry Zohn. Edited by Hannah Arendt. New York: Schocken Books, 1969.

Bernheimer, Charles. " 'Être la Matière!': Origin and Difference in Flaubert's *La Tentation de saint Antoine.*" *Novel* 10, no. 1 (Fall 1976): 65–78.

Bernheimer, Charles. *Figures of Ill Repute: Representing Prostitution in Nineteenth-Century France.* Cambridge, MA: Harvard University Press, 1989.

Bersani, Leo. *A Future for Astyanax.* Boston: Little, Brown, 1976.

La Bible: Nouveau testament. Edited and translated by Jean Grosjean and Michel Léturmy. Paris: Gallimard (Pléïade), 1971.

Biermann, Karlheinrich. "Patriotisme idéaliste, socialisme humanitaire et l'épopée noire de l'histoire: 'L'Année terrible' (1872)." In *Lectures de Victor Hugo: Colloque franco-allemand de Heidelberg,* 33–41. Edited by Mireille Calle-Gruber and Arnold Rothe. Paris: Nizet, 1986.

Blau, Herbert. "Comedy Since the Absurd." *Modern Drama* 25 (1982): 545–66.

Blumenfeld-Kosinski, Renate. "La Structure dynamique de *La Tentation de saint Antoine* de Flaubert: Une Mémoire féconde." *Romanic Review* 74, no. 1 (1983): 46–53.

Bodley, John Edward Courtenay. "France: History, 1870–1910." In *Encyclopaedia Britannica.* 11th ed. Vol. 10, 873–894. New York: Encyclopaedia Brittanica, 1910.

Bourdieu, Pierre. *Esquisse d'une théorie de la pratique, précédé de trois études d'ethnologie kabyle.* Geneva: Droz, 1972.

Bowman, Frank Paul. "Flaubert et le syncrétisme religieux." *Revue d'histoire littéraire de la France* 81, no. 4–5 (1981): 621–636.

Brombert, Victor. *Victor Hugo and the Visionary Novel.* Cambridge, MA: Harvard University Press, 1984.

Burke, Kenneth. *The Philosophy of Literary Form: Studies in Symbolic Action.* Baton Rouge: Louisiana State University Press, 1967.

Butler, Judith. *Bodies That Matter: On the Discursive Limits of "Sex."* New York: Routledge, 1993.

———. *The Psychic Life of Power.* Stanford, CA: Stanford University Press, 1997.

Butor, Michel. "La Forme de *la Tentation.*" *L'Esprit créateur* 10, no. 1 (Spring 1970): 3–12.

Cahn, Théophile. *La Vie et l'oeuvre d'Étienne Geoffroy Saint-Hilaire.* Paris: Presses Universitaires de France, 1962.

Canguilhem, Georges. *La Connaissance de la vie.* Paris: Vrin, 1971.

Capra, Frank, dir. *Mister Smith Goes to Washington.* 1939.

Cardin, Dominique. "Le Principe des métamorphoses: Essai sur la dernière version de *La Tentation de saint Antoine* de Flaubert." *Dalhousie French Studies* 28 (1994): 99–109.

Caruth, Cathy. *Unclaimed Experience: Trauma, Narrative, and History.* Baltimore: Johns Hopkins University Press, 1996.

Caruth, Cathy, ed. *Trauma: Explorations in Memory.* Baltimore: Johns Hopkins University Press, 1995.

Chambers, Ross. *Mélancolie et opposition: Les Débuts du modernisme en France.* Paris: Librairie José Corti, 1987.

Christianson, Rupert. *Paris Babylon: The Story of the Paris Commune.* London: Penguin Books, 1994.

Clark, Priscilla Parkhurst. *Literary France: The Making of a Culture.* Berkeley: University of California Press, 1987.

La Commune (Paris 1871). Directed by Peter Watkins. Starring Gérard Watkins and Aurélia Petit. Dorianne Films, 2000. Videodisc.

Coombes, John E. "State, Self and History in Victor Hugo's *L'Année Terrible.*" *Studies in Romanticism* 32, no.3 (Fall 1993): 367–78.

Copjec, Joan. *Read My Desire: Lacan Against the Historicists.* Cambridge, MA: MIT Press, 1994.

Corbin, Alain. "Le XIXe Siècle ou la nécessité de l'assemblage." In *L'Invention du XIXe siécle,* 153–159. Edited by Alain Corbin et al. Paris: Klincksieck and Presses de la Sorbonne Nouvelle, 1999.

Culler, Jonathan. *Flaubert: The Uses of Uncertainty.* Ithaca, NY: Cornell University Press, 1974.

Daudet, Alphonse. *Contes du lundi.* Edited by Louis Forrestier. Paris: Livre de Poche (Classiques), 1983.

Debray-Genette, Raymonde. "Flaubert: Science et écriture." *Littérature* 15 (Oct. 1974): 41–51.

———, ed. *Flaubert à l'oeuvre.* Paris: Flammarion, 1980.

Delas, Daniel. "Zola et la démocratie parlementaire." *Europe* no. 468–69 (1968): 27–36.

Denby, David. "Civil War, Revolution and Justic in Victor Hugo's *Quatrevingt-treize.*" *Romance Studies* 30 (Autumn 1997): 7–17.

Derrida, Jacques. *De la Grammatologie.* Paris: Minuit, 1967.

———. "La Mythologie blanche." In his *Marges de la philosophie,* 247–324. Paris: Minuit, 1972.

———. *Positions.* Paris: Minuit, 1972.

———. *Spectres de Marx: L'État de la dette, le travail du deuil et la nouvelle Internationale.* Paris: Galilée, 1993.

Descombes, Vincent. *L'Inconscient malgré lui.* Paris: Minuit, 1977.

Deutsch, Helene. "The Significance of Masochism in the Mental Life of Women." *International Journal of Psycho-analysis* 11 (1930): 48–60.

Doane, Mary Ann. *The Desire to Desire: The Woman's Film of the 1940s.* Bloomington: Indiana University Press, 1987.

Donato, Eugenio. *The Script of Decadence: Essays on the Fictions of Flaubert and the Poetics of Romanticism.* New York: Oxford University Press, 1993.

Duchet, Claude. "Écriture et désécriture de l'histoire dans *Bouvard et Pécuchet*." In *Flaubert à l'oeuvre*, 103–133. Edited by Raymonde Debray-Genette. Paris: Flammarion, 1980.

Edwards, Stewart. *The Paris Commune, 1871*. Chicago: Quadrangle Books, 1971.

Engels, Frederick. "Introduction to 'The Civil War in France.'" In *Karl Marx and Frederick Engels: On the Paris Commune*, 21–34. Moscow: Progress Publishers, 1971.

Fargeaud, Madeleine, and Claude Pichois, eds. *Les Écrivains français devant la guerre de 1870 et devant la Commune*. Paris: Colin, 1972.

Ferguson, Priscilla Parkhurst. *Paris as Revolution: Writing the Nineteenth-Century City*. Berkeley: University of California Press, 1994.

———. "*Quatrevingt-treize*: Turning the Terror to Account." In *Unfinished Revolutions: Legacies of Upheaval in Modern French Culture*, 65–80. Edited by Robert T. Denommé and Roland H. Simon. University Park: Pennsylvania State University Press, 1998.

Flaubert, Gustave. *Bouvard et Péchuchet: Édition critique, précédée des scénarios inédits*. Edited by Alberto Cento. Paris: Nizet, 1964.

———. *Bouvard et Pécuchet*. Edited by Claudine Gothot-Mersch. Paris: Gallimard (Folio), 1979. Translated by T. W. Earp and G. W. Stonier as *Bouvard and Pécuchet*. New York: New Directions, 1954.

———. *Correspondance*. 9 vols. Edited by Louis Conard. Paris: Conard, 1926.

———. *Correspondance*. 4 vols. Edited by Jean Bruneau. Paris: Gallimard (Pléiade), 1973–1988. Partially translated and edited by Francis Steegmuller as *The Letters of Gustave Flaubert*. 2 vols. Cambridge, MA: Harvard University Press, 1980–1982.

———. *L'Éducation sentimentale*. Paris: Garnier (Classiques), 1964.

———. *Oeuvres*. Edited by Albert Thibaudet and René Dumesnil. Paris: Gallimard (Pléiade), 1951.

———. *Oeuvres complètes*. 2 vols. Edited by Bernard Masson. Paris: Seuil, 1964.

———. *Oeuvres complètes*. 16 vols. Paris: Club de l'Honnête Homme, 1972.

———. *Supplément*. 4 vols. Edited by Jean Pommier, René Dumesnil, and Claude Digeon. Paris: Conard, 1954.

———. *La Tentation de saint Antoine*. In *Oeuvres*, 25–164. Translated by Kitty Mrosovsky as *The Temptation of Saint Anthony*. London: Penguin, 1980.

Flourens, Gustave. "De l'Unité de la composition et du débat entre Cuvier et Geoffroy Saint-Hilaire." *Journal des savants* (Nov. 1864): 712–724.

Foucault, Michel. "Un 'Fantastique' de bibliothèque." *Cahiers Renaud-Barrault* (Mar. 1967): 7–31.

Foucault, Michel. *Les Mots et les choses*. Paris: Gallimard, 1966. Translated as *The Order of Things: An Archaeology of the Human Sciences*. New York: Random House, 1970.

Foucault, Michel. "What Is an Author?" In *Textual Strategies*, 141–160. Edited by Josué Harari. Ithaca, NY: Cornell University Press, 1979.

Frappier-Mazur, Lucienne. "La Guerre et l'idée de la nation: Autour de *La Débâcle* d'Émile Zola." *Excavatio* 9 (1997): 141–48.

Frappier-Mazur, Lucienne. "Guerre, nationalisme et différence sexuelle dans *La Débâcle* d'Émile Zola." In *Masculin/féminin: Le XIXe Siècle à l'épreuve du genre,* 167–81. Edited by Chantal Bertrand-Jennings. Toronto: Centre d'Études du XIXe Siècle Joseph Sablé, 1999.

Freud, Sigmund. "A Child Is Being Beaten: A Contribution to the Study of the Origin of Sexual Perversions." Translated by James Strachey. In *The Complete Psychological Works of Sigmund Freud.* Vol. 17, 177–204. London: Hogarth.

———. *The Complete Psychological Works of Sigmund Freud.* Translated by James Strachey. 24 vols. London: Hogarth.

———. "The Economic Problem of Masochism." Translated by James Strachey. In *The Complete Psychological Works of Sigmund Freud.* Vol. 19, 157–70. London: Hogarth.

———. "Fetishism." Translated by James Strachey. In *The Complete Psychological Works of Sigmund Freud.* Vol. 21, 152–57. London: Hogarth.

———. *Inhibitions, Symptoms and Anxiety.* Edited and translated by James Strachey. In *The Complete Psychological Works of Sigmund Freud.* Vol. 20, 87–174. London: Hogarth, 1959.

———. *Introductory Lectures on Psycho-Analysis.* Edited and translated by James Strachey. In *The Complete Psychological Works of Sigmund Freud.* Vols. 15 and 16. London: Hogarth, 1959.

———. *Letters of Sigmund Freud.* Translated by Tania Stern and James Stern. Edited by Ernst L. Freud. New York: Basic Books, 1960.

———. *New Introductory Lectures on Psycho-Analysis.* Edited and translated by James Strachey. In *The Complete Psychological Works of Sigmund Freud.* Vols. 21 and 22. London: Hogarth, 1959.

———. "Remembering, Repeating and Working Through (Further Recommendations on the Technique of Psychoanalysis II)." Translated by James Strachey. In *The Complete Psychological Works of Sigmund Freud.* Vol. 12, 145–56. London: Hogarth.

Gaillard, Françoise. "Imaginaire du social ou social de l'imaginaire: De deux points de vue en matière d'analyse socio-historique." In *Opérativité des méthodes sociocritiques,* 7–26. Edited by Ralph Heyndels and Edmond Cros. Montpellier: C.E.R.S., 1984.

———. "Une Inénarrable Histoire." In *Flaubert et le comble de l'art: Nouvelles Recherches sur Bouvard et Pécuchet,* 75–87. Edited by Pierre Cogny. Paris: Editions C.D.U./SEDES, 1981.

———. "Le Réel comme représentation." *Études de lettres* 2 (1982): 77–89.

Gaudant, Mireille, and Jean Gaudant. *Les Théories classiques de l'évolution.* Paris: Dunod, 1971.

Geertz, Clifford. *The Interpretation of Cultures.* New York: Basic Books, 1973.

Geoffroy Saint-Hilaire, Étienne. "De l'Application de la théorie des analogues à l'organisation des poissons." *Gazette médicale* 1 (1830).

————. *Fragment sur la nature, ou Quelques Idées générales sur les existences du monde physique considérées d'ensemble et dans l'unité.* Paris, 1929.

Girard, Marcel. "Positions politiques d'Émile Zola jusqu'à l'affaire Dreyfus." *Revue française de science politique* 5 (1955): 503–28.

Glazer, Catherine. "De la Commune comme maladie mentale." In *Les Discours du cliché*, 63–70. Edited by Ruth Amossy and Elisheva Rosen. Paris: C.D.U.-S.E.D.E.S., 1982.

Godwin, William. *Enquiry Concerning Political Justice.* Edited by K. Codell Carter. Oxford: Clarendon Press, 1971.

Gohin, Yves. "Préface." In *L'Année terrible*, 7–20. Edited by Yves Gohin. Paris: Gallimard, 1985.

Goldstein, Jan. "The Hysteria Diagnosis and the Politics of Anticlericalism in Late Nineteenth-Century France." *Journal of Modern History* 54 (June 1982): 209–39.

————. "'Moral Contagion': A Professional Ideology of Medicine and Psychiatry in Eighteenth- and Nineteenth-Century France." In *Professions and the French State: 1700–1900*, 181–222. Edited by Gerald L. Geison. Philadelphia: University of Pennsylvania Press, 1984.

Goncourt, Edmond de, and Jules de Goncourt. *Journal.* Edited by Robert Ricatte. Paris: Robert Laffont (Bouquins), 1989.

————. *Journal des Goncourt, Mémoires de la vie littéraire.* Paris: Charpentier, 1911.

Gothot-Mersch, Claudine. "Introduction." In *La Tentation de saint Antoine*, 7–45. Edited by Claudine Gothot-Mersch. Paris: Gallimard (Folio), 1983.

Grand Dictionnaire universel du XIXe siècle. Edited by Pierre Larousse. 17 vols. Paris: Administration du Grand Dictionnaire Universel, 1866–1890.

Grant, Richard. "Edmond de Goncourt and the Paris Commune." *Massachusetts Review* 12 (1971): 521–27.

Guedj, Aimé. "Les Révolutionnaires de Zola." *Cahiers naturalistes* 36 (1968): 123–37.

Guerlac, Suzanne. *The Impersonal Sublime: Hugo, Baudelaire, Lautréamont.* Stanford, CA: Stanford University Press, 1990.

Gullickson, Gay L. *Unruly Women of Paris: Images of the Commune.* Ithaca, NY: Cornell University Press, 1996.

Halévy, Daniel. *La Fin des notables.* Vol. 1 of *La Fin des notables.* Paris: Grasset (Pluriel), 1995.

————. *La République des ducs.* Vol. 2 of *La Fin des notables.* Paris: Grasset (Pluriel), 1995.

Hoberman, J. "When Communism Was in Flower." *Village Voice*, Oct. 4, 1983, 66.

Howells, Christina. "Flaubert's Blind Spot: The Fetishization of Subjectivity. Some Notes on the Constitution of Gustave in Sartre's *L'Idiot de la famille*." In *Situating Sartre in Twentieth-Century Thought and Culture*, 29–38. Edited by Jean-François Fourny and Charles D. Minahen. New York: St. Martin's Press, 1998.

Hugo, Victor. "Actes et paroles, 1870–1871–1872 (extraits)." In *L'Année terrible, avec des extraits de Actes et paroles, 1870–1871–1872*, 229–66. Edited by Yves Gohin. Paris: Gallimard (Poésie), 1985.

————. *L'Année terrible, avec des extraits de Actes et paroles, 1870–1871–1872*. Edited by Yves Gohin. Paris: Gallimard (Poésie), 1985.

————. "Carnets de la guerre et de la Commune." In *Voyages,* 1035–1210. Edited by Jean-Claude Nabet, Guy Rosa, Caroline Raineri, and Carine Trévisan. Paris: Robert Laffont (Bouquins), 1977.

————. *Les Misérables*. Edited by Maurice Allem. Paris: Gallimard (Pléiade), 1951.

————. *Préface de Cromwell*. [1827]. Edited by Michel Cambien. Paris: Larousse, 1971.

————. *Quatrevingt-treize*. Edited by Yves Gohin. Paris: Gallimard (Folio Classique), 1979. Translated by Lowell Bair as *Ninety-three*. New York: Bantam, 1962.

Humphries, Jefferson. "Bouvard et Pécuchet and the Fable of Stable Irony." *French Forum* 10, no. 2 (1985): 145–62.

Huyssen, Andreas. "Mapping the Postmodern." *New German Critique* 33 (1984): 5–52.

Jacob, François. *La Logique du vivant: Une Histoire de l'hérédité*. Paris: Gallimard, 1970.

James, Henry. *Henry James: Literary Criticism*. New York: Library of America, 1984.

Jarry, Alfred. *Oeuvres complètes*. 3 vols. Edited by Michel Arrivé. Paris: Gallimard (Pléiade), 1972–1988.

Kenner, Hugh. *Flaubert, Joyce and Beckett: The Stoic Comedians*. Berkeley: University of California Press, 1962.

Klein, Melanie. *The Selected Melanie Klein*. Edited by Juliet Mitchell. New York: Free Press, 1986.

Kozintsev, Grigori. "La Fin des années vingt." *Cahiers du cinéma* 230 (1971): 5–14.

Kristeva, Julia. *Histoires d'amour*. Paris: Denoël, 1983.

Lacan, Jacques. *Écrits*. Paris: Seuil, 1966. Translated by Bruce Fink, with Héloïse Fink and Russell Grigg, as *Écrits: A Selection*. New York: Norton, 2002.

LaCapra, Dominick. *Writing History, Writing Trauma*. Baltimore: Johns Hopkins University Press, 2001.

Laclos, Choderlos de. *Les Liaisons dangereuses*. Edited by Yves Le Hir. Paris: Garnier (Classiques), 1961.

Laplanche, Jean, and J.-B. Pontalis. *The Language of Psycho-analysis*. Translated by Donald Nicholson-Smith. New York: Norton, 1973.

Lefebvre, Henri. *La Proclamation de la Commune*. Paris: Gallimard, 1965.

Lefort, Claude. *L'Invention démocratique: Les Limites de la domination totalitaire*. Paris: Fayard, 1981.

Lejeune, Dominique. *La France des débuts de la IIIe République: 1870–1896*. Paris: Armand Colin, 1994.

Leys, Ruth. *Trauma: A Genealogy*. Chicago: University of Chicago Press, 2000.

Lidsky, Paul. *Les Écrivains contre la Commune*. Paris: La Découverte, 1999.

Lissagaray, Prosper-Olivier. *Histoire de la Commune de 1871*. [1876]. Paris: La Découverte, 2000. Translated by Eleanor Marx Aveling as *History of the Commune of 1871*. 2nd ed. New York: International, 1898.

Lukács, Georg. *The Historical Novel.* Translated by Hannah Mitchell and Stanley Mitchell. Lincoln: University of Nebraska Press, 1983.

Luoni, Flavio. "Saint Antoine et les deux voies vers la matière." *La Revue des lettres modernes: Histoire des idées et des littératures* (1994): 135–53.

MacDonald, Ian. "New Babylon I." Online posting. Dec. 4, 1999. DSCH-List. http://www.siue.edu/~aho/musov/dschl/nbab1.html.

———. "New Babylon II." Online posting. Dec. 6, 1999. DSCH-List. http://www.siue.edu/~aho/musov/dschl/nbab2.html.

———. "New Babylon III." Online posting. Dec. 14, 1999. DSCH-List. http://www.siue.edu/~aho/musov/dschl/nbab3.html.

Macpherson, C. B. *The Life and Times of Liberal Democracy.* Oxford: Oxford University Press, 1977.

Mannoni, Octave. "Je sais bien, mais quand même. . . ." In *Clefs pour l'imaginaire, ou l'autre scène.* Paris: Seuil, 1977.

Marivaux, Pierre. *La Vie de Marianne, ou les aventures de Madame la comtesse de ★★★.* Edited by Frédéric Deloffre. Paris: Garnier (Classiques), 1963.

Marks, Laura. "Tie a Yellow Ribbon Around Me: Masochism, Militarism and the Gulf War on TV." *Camera Obscura* 27 (1991): 55–75.

Marx, Karl. "The Civil War in France: Address of the General Council of the International Working Men's Association." In *On the Paris Commune.* By Karl Marx and Fredrick Engels. Moscow: Progress Publishers, 1971.

———. *The Class Struggles in France, 1848–1850.* New York: International Publishers, 1964.

———. "The Eighteenth Brumaire of Louis Bonaparte." In *The Marx-Engels Reader.* Edited by Robert C. Tucker. Second Edition. New York: Norton, 1978.

Marx, Karl, and Frederick Engels. *On the Paris Commune.* Moscow: Progress Publishers, 1971.

Matlock, Jann. *Scenes of Seduction: Prostitution, Hysteria, and Reading Difference in Nineteenth-Century France.* New York: Columbia University Press, 1994.

Mayeur, Jean-Marie. *Les Débuts de la Troisième République, 1871–1898.* Nouvelle histoire de la France contemporaine 10. Paris: Éditions du Seuil, 1973.

Mehlman, Jeffrey. *Revolution and Repetition: Marx/Hugo/Balzac.* Berkeley: University of California Press, 1977.

Mitroi, Anca. "*La Tentation de saint Antoine* ou 'ceci n'est pas un monster.'" *French Literature Series* 22 (1995): 125–37.

Mitterand, Henri. "La Débâcle: Étude." Edited by Henri Mitterand. In *Les Rougon-Macquart: Histoire naturelle et sociale d'une famille sous le Second Empire,* 5:1353–1560. Paris: Gallimard (Pléïade), 1967.

Moreau, Pierre-François. *Les Racines du libéralisme: Une anthologie.* Paris: Éditions du Seuil, 1978.

Mouchard, Claude. "Terre, technologie, roman: À propos du deuxième chapitre de *Bouvard et Pécuchet.*" *Littérature* 15 (1974): 65–74.

Mouchard, Claude, and Jacques Neefs. "Vers le Second Volume: Bouvard et Pécuchet." In *Flaubert à l'oeuvre,* 169–217. Edited by Raymonde Debray-Genette. Paris: Flammarion, 1980.

Mouffe, Chantal. *The Return of the Political*. London: Verso, 1993.

Neefs, Jacques. "L'Exposition littéraire des religions (*La Tentation de saint Antoine*, 1874)." *Revue d'histoire littéraire de la France* 81, no. 4–5 (July–Dec. 1981): 637–47.

Nerval, Gérard de. *Oeuvres*. Edited by Henri Lemaitre. Paris: Garnier, 1966.

New Bablyon [*Novyi Vavilon*]. Directed by.Grigorii Kozintsev and Leonid Trauberg. Starring Elena Kuzmina and Pyotr Sobelevsky. [1929]. Eccentric Press, 1999. Videocassette.

Noël, Bernard. *Dictionnaire de la Commune*. Paris: Mémoire du Livre, 2000.

Nunley, Charles. "(En)gendering Terror: Women and Violence in *Quatrevingt-treize*." In *The Play of Terror in Nineteenth-Century France*, 35–44. Edited by John T. Booker and Allan H. Pasco. Cranbury, NJ: Associated University Presses, 1997.

Olds, Marshall. "Hallucination and Point of View in *La Tentation de Saint Antoine*." *Nineteenth-Century French Studies* 17, no. 1 (Fall 1988): 170–85.

Orr, Mary. "Stasis and Ecstasy: *La Tentation de Saint Antoine* or the Texte Boulversant." *Forum for Modern Language Studies* 34, no. 4 (Oct. 1998): 335–44.

Outram, Dorinda. *The Body and the French Revolution: Sex, Class and Political Culture*. New Haven, CT: Yale University Press, 1989.

Le Petit Robert. Edited by Paul Robert. Paris: Le Robert, 1986.

Petrey, Sandy. *History in the Text: "Quatrevingt-Treize" and the French Revolution*. Amsterdam: John Benjamins, 1980.

———. "La République de *La Débâcle*." *Les Cahiers naturalistes* 54 (1980): 87–95.

Pick, Daniel. *Faces of Degeneration: A European Disorder, c. 1848–c. 1918*. Cambridge: Cambridge University Press, 1989.

Plessis, Alain. *De la Fête impériale au mur des fédérés, 1852–1871*. Nouvelle histoire de la France contemporaine 9. Paris: Éditions du Seuil, 1979.

Polan, Dana. "A Vertigo of Displacement: An Introduction to the Sartrean Spectacle of *L'Idiot de la famille*." *Dalhousie Review* 64, no. 2 (Summer 1984): 354–75.

Porter, Laurence M. "Projection as Ego Defense in Flaubert's *Tentation de saint Antoine*." In *Critical Essays on Gustave Flaubert*, 150–164. Edited by Laurence M. Porter. Boston: G. K. Hall, 1986.

———. *Victor Hugo*. New York: Twayne, 1999.

Prendergast, Christopher. "Flaubert: Quotation, Stupidity, and the Cretan Liar Paradox." *French Studies* 35 (1981): 261–77.

Pytel, Marek. *New Babylon: Trauberg, Kozintsev, Shostakovich*. London: Eccentric Press, 1999.

Rajchman, John. *Michel Foucault: The Freedom of Philosophy*. New York: Columbia University Press, 1985.

Reader, Keith A. *Intellectuals and the Left in France Since 1968*. New York: St. Martin's Press, 1987.

Reik, Theodor. "Flaubert and His *Temptation of Saint Anthony*." In *Critical Essays on Gustave Flaubert*, 145–150. Edited by Laurence M. Porter. [1912]. Boston: G. K. Hall, 1986.

————. *Masochism in Modern Man.* Translated by Margaret H. Beigel and Gertrud M. Kurth. New York: Farrar, & Rinehart, 1941.

————. *L'Avenir de la science.* Vol. 3 of *Oeuvres complètes de Ernest Renan.* Edited by Henriette Psichari. Paris: Calmann-Lévy, n.d. [1890]. Translated as *The Future of Science.* Boston: Roberts Brothers, 1891.

Renan, Ernest. *Questions contemporaines.* Vol. 1 of *Oeuvres complètes de Ernest Renan.* Edited by Henriette Psichari. Paris: Calmann-Lévy, n.d. [1868].

————. *La Réforme intellectuelle et morale.* Vol. 2 of *Oeuvres complètes de Ernest Renan.* Edited by Henriette Psichari. Paris: Calmann-Lévy, n.d. [1871].

Robb, Graham. *Victor Hugo: A Biography.* New York: Norton, 1997.

Rosa, Guy. "Politique du désastre: Victor Hugo durant 'L'Année terrible.'" *Europe* 671 (Mar. 1985): 170–88.

————. "*Quatrevingt-treize* ou la Critique du roman historique." *Revue d'histoire littéraire de la France* 75, no. 2–3 (March–June 1975): 328–43.

Ross, Kristin. *The Emergence of Social Space: Rimbaud and the Paris Commune.* Minneapolis: University of Minnesota Press, 1988.

————. "Lefebvre on the Situationists: An Interview." *October* 79 (Winter 1997): 69–83.

Roth, Michael. "Hysterical Remembering." *Modernism/Modernity* 3, no. 2 (1996): 1–30.

Sachs, Murray. "Reasons of the Heart: George Sand, Flaubert, and the Commune." In *The World of George Sand,* 145–52. Edited by Jeanne Fuchs, Natalie Datlof, and David A. Powell. New York: Greenwood, 1991.

Saint-Amand, Pierre. "Hot Terror: *Quatrevingt-treize.*" *SubStance* 27, no. 2 (1998): 61–72.

Santner, Eric L. *Stranded Objects: Mourning, Memory, and Film in Postwar Germany.* Ithaca, NY: Cornell University Press, 1990.

Sartre, Jean-Paul. *L'Idiot de la famille.* Paris: Gallimard, 1971–1972. Translated by Carol Cosman as *The Family Idiot: Gustave Flaubert.* 5 vols. Chicago: University of Chicago Press, 1981–93.

Schehr, Lawrence. *Rendering French Realism.* Stanford, CA: Stanford University Press, 1997.

Schivelbusch, Wolfgang. *The Railway Journey: The Industrialization of Time and Space in the 19th Century.* Berkeley: University of California Press, 1986.

Schlegel, Friedrich. *Friedrich Schlegel's Lucinde and the Fragments.* Translated by Peter Firchow. Minneapolis: University of Minnesota Press, 1971.

Schmulevitch, Eric. "La Nouvelle Bablyone." *Positif* 194 (1977): 44–49.

Schor, Naomi. *Breaking the Chain: Women, Theory, and French Realist Fiction.* New York: Columbia University Press, 1985.

————. "Devant le Château: Femmes, marchandises et modernité dans *Au Bonheur des dames.*" In *Mimesis et semiosis: Littérature et représentation,* 179–86. Edited by Philippe Hamon and Jean-Pierre Leduc-Adine. Paris: Nathan, 1992.

Schwartz, Vanessa R. *Spectacular Realities: Early Mass Culture in Fin-de-Siècle Paris.* Berkley: University of California Press, 1998.

Séginger, Gisèle. "L'Artiste, le saint: Les Tentations de Saint-Antoine." *Romantisme* 55 (1987): 79–90.

———. "Fiction et transgression épistémologique: Le Mythe de l'origine dans *La Tentation de saint Antoine* de Flaubert." *Romanic Review* 88 (1997): 131–44.

Serman, William. *La Commune de Paris, 1871.* Paris: Fayard, 1986.

Seznec, Jean. "Saint Antoine et les monstres: Essai sur les sources et la signification du fantastique de Flaubert." *PMLA* 58 (Mar. 1943): 195–222.

———. "Science et religion chez Flaubert d'après les sources de *La Tentation de saint Antoine.*" *Romanic Review* 33 (1942): 360–65.

Shostakovich, Dmitri. *The New Babylon, Five Days—Five Nights.* Conducted by James Judd. Performed by the Berlin Symphony Orchestra. Capriccio, 1990.

Silverman, Debora. "The 'New Woman,' Feminism, and the Decorative Arts in Fin-de-Siècle France." In *Eroticism and the Body Politic.* Edited by Lynn Hunt. Baltimore: Johns Hopkins University Press, 1991.

Silverman, Kaja. *Male Subjectivity at the Margins.* New York: Routledge, 1992.

Sonnenfeld, Albert. "La Tentation de Flaubert." *Cahiers de l'Association Internationale des Études Françaises* 23 (May 1971): 311–26.

Spinoza, Baruch de. *Oeuvres complètes.* Edited by Madeleine Francès, Roland Caillois, and Robert Misrahi. Paris: Gallimard (Pléiade), 1954.

———. *A Spinoza Reader: The Ethics and Other Works.* Edited and translated by Edwin Curley. Princeton, NJ: Princeton University Press, 1994.

Spivak, Gayatri Chakravorty, and Michael Ryan. "Anarchism Revisited: A New Philosophy." *Diacritics* 8, no. 2 (Summer 1978): 66–79.

Starr, Peter. *Logics of Failed Revolt: French Theory After May '68.* Stanford, CA: Stanford University Press, 1995.

Stendhal [Henri Beyle]. *Le Rouge et le noir: Chronique du XIXe siècle.* Paris: Garnier (Classiques), 1973.

Stivale, Charles J. "Le Plissement and la fêlure: The Paris Commune in Vallès's *L'Insurgé* and Zola's *La Débâcle.*" In *Modernity and Revolution in Late Nineteenth-Century France,* 143–154. Edited by Barbara T. Cooper and Mary Donaldson-Evans. Newark: University of Delaware Press, 1992.

Strickland, Geoffrey. "Maupassant, Zola, Jules Vallès and the Paris Commune of 1871." *Journal of European Studies* 13 (1983): 298–307.

Swain, Gladys. "L'Âme, la femme, le sexe et le corps: Les métamorphoses de l'hystérie à la fin du XIXe siècle." *Le Débat* 24 (1983): 107–27.

Testa, Carlo. "Representing the Unrepresentable: The Desexualization of Desire in Flaubert's 'Etre la matière!.'" *Nineteenth-Century French Studies* 20, nos. 1–2 (Fall–Winter 1991–1992): 137–44.

Thomas, Jean-Jacques. "Poétique de la 'Bêtise': Le Dictionnaire des idées reçues." In *Flaubert et le comble de l'art: Nouvelles recherches sur Bouvard et Pécuchet.* Edited by Pierre Cogny. Paris: Éditions C.D.U./SEDES, 1981.

Thorel-Cailleteau. "À propos de *La Débâcle.*" *Les Cahiers naturalistes* 67 (1993): 57–62.

Thorlby, Anthony. *Gustave Flaubert and the Art of Realism.* London: Bowes and Bowes, 1956.

Tomashevsky, Boris. "Thematics." In *Russian Formalist Criticism: Four Essays,* 61–95. Translated by Lee T. Lemon and Marion J. Reis. Lincoln: University of Nebraska Press, 1965.

Trauberg, Léonid. "Comment Est Né *La Nouvelle Babylone.*" *L'Avant-scène du cinéma* 217 (1978): 8.

Trebitsch, Michel. "Preface." In *Critique of Everyday Life,* 1:ix–xxviii. By Henri Lefebvre. Translated by John Moore. London: Verso, 1991.

———. "Preface: The Moment of Radical Critique." In Henri Lefebvre, *Critique of Everyday Life,* ix–xxix. Translated by John Moore. London: Verso, 2002

Trilling, Lionel. *The Liberal Imagination: Essays on Literature and Society.* New York: Scribner's, 1950.

Tsikounas, Myriam. "Une Démonstration politique exemplaire." *L'Avant-scène du cinéma* 217 (1978): 6–7.

Vallès, Jules. *L'Insurgé.* Edited by Marie-Claire Bancquart. Paris: Gallimard (Folio), 1975.

Watkins, Peter. "La Commune de Paris." *Peter Watkins: Filmmaker and Media-Critic.* 2000. http://www.peterwatkins.lt/varyk.htm.

———. "The Crisis in the M.A.V.M." *Peter Watkins: Filmmaker and Media-Critic.* 2000. http://www.peterwatkins.lt/varyk.htm.

———. "Summary of the Web-Site." *Peter Watkins: Filmmaker and Media-Critic.* 2000. http://www.peterwatkins.lt/varyk.htm.

Weinberg, Henry. "Ironie et idéologie: Zola à la naissance de la Troisième République." *Cahiers naturalistes* 42 (1971): 61–70.

Williams, Raymond. *Keywords: A Vocabulary of Culture and Society.* Rev and enl. ed. New York: Oxford University Press, 1983.

Williams, Roger L. *The World of Napoleon III: 1851–1870.* New York: Free Press, 1965.

Wiraith, Paul. "France: History to 1870." In *Encyclopaedia Britannica,* 10:801–73. 11th ed. New York: Encyclopaedia Britannica, 1910.

———. *Anxiety & Hypocrisy.* Vol. 5 of *France 1848–1945.* Oxford: Oxford University Press, 1981.

———. *Intellect & Pride,* Vol. 3 of *France 1848–1945.* Oxford: Oxford University Press, 1980.

Zeldin, Theodore. *Politics & Anger.* Vol. 2 of *France 1848–1945.* Oxford: Oxford University Press, 1982.

Žižek, Slavoj. *For They Know Not What They Do: Enjoyment as a Political Factor.* London: Verso, 1991.

———. *Looking Awry: An Introduction to Jacques Lacan Through Popular Culture.* Cambridge, MA: MIT Press, 1991.

———. *The Sublime Object of Ideology.* London: Verso, 1989.

Zola, Émile. *Au Bonheur des dames.* Paris: Gallimard (Folio), 1980. Translated and edited by Robin Buss as *Au Bonheur des Dames (The Ladies' Delight).* London: Penguin, 2001.

————. *La Débâcle.* Edited by Henri Mitterand. In *Les Rougon-Macquart: Histoire naturelle et sociale d'une famille sous le Second Empire* 5:399–912. Paris: Gallimard (Pléïade), 1967. Translated by Leonard Tancock as *The Debacle.* London: Penguin, 1973.

————. "La Démocratie." In Zola's *Oeuvres complètes,* 14:650–55. Edited by Henri Mitterand. Paris: Cercle du Livre Précieux, 1966–1969.

————. *Germinal.* Paris: Garnier (Classiques), 1979.

————. *Jacques Damour, suivi de Le Capitaine Burle.* Edited by Jacques Noiray. Paris: Livre de Poche, 2001.

————. *Oeuvres complètes,* 15 vols. Edited by Henri Mitterand. Paris: Cercle du Livre Précieux, 1966–69.

————. "Le Parti de l'indignation." In Zola's *Oeuvres complètes,* 14:447–52. Edited by Henri Mitterand. Paris: Cercle du Livre Précieux, 1966–69.

————. *Les Rougon-Macquart: Histoire naturelle et sociale d'une famille sous le Second Empire.* 5 vols. Edited by Henri Mitterand. Paris: Gallimard (Pléïade), 1960–67.

————. "Le Suffrage universel." In his *Oeuvres complètes,* 14:632–37. Edited by Henri Mitterand. Vol. 14, 632–637. Paris: Cercle du Livre Précieux, 1966–69.

————. "La Vertu de la République." In his *Oeuvres complètes,* 14:711–16. Edited by Henri Mitterand. Vol. 14, 711–716. Paris: Cercle du Livre Précieux, 1966–69.

Index